PRACTICAL

.p:!ng

BASW

Editorial Advisory Board:
Robert Adams, Terry Bamford, Charles Barker, Lena Dominelli,
Malcolm Payne, Michael Preston-Shoot, Daphne Statham and
Jane Tunstill

Social work is at an important stage in its development. All
professions must be responsive to changing social and economic
conditions if they are to meet the needs of those they serve. This
series focuses on sound practice and the specific contribution which
social workers can make to the well-being of our society in the
1990s.

The British Association of Social Workers has always been conscious of its role in setting guidelines for practice and in seeking to
raise professional standards. The conception of the Practical Social
Work series arose from a survey of BASW members to discover
where they, the practitioners in social work, felt there was the most
need for new literature. The response was overwhelming and
enthusiastic, and the result is a carefully planned, coherent series of
books. The emphasis is firmly on practice, set in a theoretical
framework. The books will inform, stimulate and promote discussion, thus adding to the further development of skills and high
professional standards. All the authors are practitioners and teachers of social work, representing a wide variety of experience.

JO CAMPLING

A list of published titles in this series follows overleaf

PRACTICAL SOCIAL WORK

Robert Adams *Self-Help, Social Work and Empowerment*

David Anderson *Social Work and Mental Handicap*

James G. Barber *Beyond Casework*

Peter Beresford and Suzy Croft *Citizen Involvement: A Practical Guide for Change*

Suzy Braye and Michael Preston-Shoot *Practising Social Work Law*

Robert Brown, Stanley Bute and Peter Ford *Social Workers at Risk*

Alan Butler and Colin Pritchard *Social Work and Mental Illness*

Crescy Cannan, Lynne Berry and Karen Lyons *Social Work and Europe*

Roger Clough *Residential Work*

David M. Cooper and David Ball *Social Work and Child Abuse*

Veronica Coulshed *Management in Social Work*

Veronica Coulshed *Social Work Practice: An introduction (2nd edn)*

Paul Daniel and John Wheeler *Social Work and Local Politics*

Peter R. Day *Sociology in Social Work Practice*

Lena Dominelli *Anti-Racist Social Work: A Challenge for White Practitioners and Educators*

Celia Doyle *Working with Abused Children*

Angela Everitt, Pauline Hardiker, Jane Littlewood and Audrey Mullender *Applied Research for Better Practice*

Kathy Ford and Alan Jones *Student Supervision*

David Francis and Paul Henderson *Working with Rural Communities*

Michael D. A. Freeman *Children, their Families and the Law*

Alison Froggatt *Family Work with Elderly People*

Danya Glaser and Stephen Frosh *Child Sexual Abuse*

Bryan Glastonbury *Computers in Social Work*

Gill Gorell Barnes *Working with Families*

Cordelia Grimwood and Ruth Popplestone *Women, Management and Care*

Jalna Hanmer and Daphne Statham *Women and Social Work: Towards a Woman-Centred Practice*

Tony Jeffs and Mark Smith (eds) *Youth Work*

Michael Kerfoot and Alan Butler *Problems of Childhood and Adolescence*

Joyce Lishman *Communication in Social Work*

Mary Marshall *Social Work with Old People (2nd edn)*

Paula Nicolson and Rowan Bayne *Applied Psychology for Social Workers (2nd edn)*

Kieran O'Hagan *Crisis Intervention in Social Services*

Michael Oliver *Social Work with Disabled People*

Joan Orme and Bryan Glastonbury *Care Management: Tasks and Workloads*

Malcolm Payne *Social Care in the Community*

Malcolm Payne *Working in Teams*

John Pitts *Working with Young Offenders*

Michael Preston-Shoot *Effective Groupwork*

Carole R. Smith *Adoption and Fostering: Why and How*

Carole R. Smith *Social Work with the Dying and Bereaved*

Carole R. Smith, Marty T. Lane and Terry Walsh *Child Care and the Courts*

Gill Stewart and John Stewart *Social Work and Housing*

Christine Stones *Focus on Families*

Neil Thompson *Anti-Discriminatory Practice*

Neil Thompson with Michael Murphy and Steve Stradling *Dealing with Stress*

Derek Tilbury *Working with Mental Illness*

Alan Twelvetrees *Community Work (2nd edn)*

Hilary Walker and Bill Beaumount (eds) *Working with Offenders*

Children, their Families and the Law

Working with the Children Act

Michael D. A. Freeman

MACMILLAN

First published 1992 by
THE MACMILLAN PRESS LTD
Houndmills, Basingstoke, Hampshire RG21 2XS
and London
Companies and representatives
throughout the world

ISBN 0–333–54590–7 hardcover
ISBN 0–333–54591–5 paperback

A catalogue record for this book is available
from the British Library.

Printed in Hong Kong

Reprinted 1994

To my own children, Hilary and Jeremy, no longer
children in terms of the Act but always mine

Contents

Table of Cases

Preface

To offer a book on the Children Act 1989 with it already in operation requires a justification. I have written commentaries on previous legislation, including the 1975 Children Act, within weeks of their passage through Parliament. But the 1989 Act, in many ways such a new beginning, required and deserved reflection and critical appraisal. By publishing now I am able to offer the only book to cover not just the Act but also the large number of Regulations, the new Rules and the very comprehensive Department of Health Guidance, as well as the new edition of *Working Together*. Furthermore, by waiting, an integrated treatment has become possible.

This book puts the Act into a historical context and relates the new concepts, principles and institutions to the sociological research from which they have emerged. The book also contains a fuller treatment of existing case law than the commentaries published earlier. But this is a book about social work and how social workers can use the Act as a resource, and not just a commentary on a complex piece of legislation. Not surprisingly, therefore, part III of the Act on the family support and children in need is the central and the lengthiest chapter, with the principle of partnership given its appropriate emphasis. There is also a very full explication of care, the new minimum conditions and the effects and the most detailed discussion of accommodation and ways of retaining it where there is opposition to so doing.

The book is, it is hoped, constructive and practical. It offers guidance and it is not afraid to criticise. The Act was greeted with euphoria and, as yet, there has been all too little critique of it. By relating the Act to its history and ideology, I hope to be offering a book of value to the student of social administration, social policy and law. But it is primarily a guide to practice under the Act, drawing attention to problems, to pitfalls and to possible solutions.

Although, in a series entitled Practical Social Work, I have no doubt that the book will be of value to lawyers as well, both those in private practice and in legal centres as well as to local authority lawyers and those who work for voluntary organisations. This is one of the reasons for including a large number of legal references. But, with the primary audience being the social work profession and allied helping professions, the intention has been to make the book as jargon-free as is compatible with accurate and insightful presentation.

I hope I have brought to this book my experience as a children's rights campaigner as well as my expertise as a lecturer and trainer within the legal and social work profession. Many of the ideas in this book have been tested in the many lectures I have given on the Children Act to audiences of social workers, solicitors, the police and educationalists up and down the country and, indeed, as far away as New Zealand, where I lectured on comparisons between our new law and theirs, generally regarded as even more radical. Naturally, I have learnt a lot from comments made and questions asked and am grateful to those who assisted in this way.

It is normal to send out the manuscript of a book to interested colleagues and other professionals. I would have liked to do so, but the financial constraints at University College London, where I teach, no longer make this possible. They also meant that I was teaching fifteen hours a week whilst writing the book. Perhaps 'academic abuse' is about to be discovered!

I am grateful to all those who have assisted with the preparation of this book, including those who have given permission to quote them. My wife's support was invaluable: her work with children going back to the days when there were child care officers and now her work with the mentally handicapped provided me with insights which gave the book additional value. The manuscript could not have been produced without the patience and care of Edith Ray and to her I offer my sincerest gratitude.

The book was completed on Christmas Eve 1991 (it would not be diplomatic to say when it was started!) The law is stated as at that date, though it has been possible to include a few later references.

MICHAEL D. A. FREEMAN

1

Reforming Children's Law: History and Ideology

The Children Act is 'the most comprehensive and far-reaching reform of child law in living memory'. It provides a new legal framework, but it does more than that. It rewrites the language of child care law and practice. It represents a change in attitude towards children and their families. The Act is about 'parental responsibility', which is for life; about 'support for children and families' where those 'in need' require assistance to carry out this responsibility; and about 'partnership', in many senses the key concept, although it does not appear in the Act itself. It requires, as the *Cleveland* report (1988) did, that 'the child is a person and not an object of concern'. The Act is a product of many sources, including reports of inquiries into a series of abuse scandals in the late 1980s (London Borough of Brent (1985), London Borough of Greenwich (1987), London Borough of Lambeth (1987), Cleveland (1988)). But of these it is the influence of the *Cleveland* report which is most profound. Social workers had been criticised in the earlier reports for not using statutory coercive powers firmly enough (Parton (1986), Stevenson (1986), Freeman (1990)). The *Cleveland* report criticised them for an over-reliance upon compulsory measures and for paying too little attention to parents by adopting a perspective which placed 'a strong focus on the needs of the child in isolation from the family' (*Cleveland* report, para. 4.57).

Genesis

The Children Act is a new beginning. A understanding of how far back its genesis should be traced may only become clearer as the

1

framework and the principles of the Act are put into practice. On one level the Act goes back as far as the Colwell tragedy (DHSS, 1974) which signified child care is a battle ground and spelt the beginnings of its politicisation (Parton, 1985). The 1975 Act, though dubbed a 'children's charter', was a victory for those who espoused permanency policies. It should have led to an increased emphasis on planning and to better decision-making, focusing on the need of the child. But often it did not do so. The 1980s were characterised by precipitate over-reliance on coercive measures, in particular the place of safety order (Packman, 1986; Millham *et al.*, 1986; cf. Dingwall *et al.*, 1983). There may have been more attention given to removing children than deciding what should then be done. Such children were often cut off from their families through a series of cumulative steps (the denial of access, the assumption of parental rights, freeing for adoption). There was a feeling that decision-making was often little more than crisis management. Perhaps, not surprisingly, there were often frequent placement changes and breakdowns. (Berridge and Cleaver, 1987). Ironically, the Darting-ton study (Millham *et al.*, 1986) echoed the findings of Rowe and Lambert's *Children Who Wait* (1973) (a seminal influence on the 1975 Act) that children, with no meaningful links with their families and no satisfactory substitute homes, were drifting into care.

It was at this point that the Blom-Cooper reports into the Beckford and Carlile cases were published (London Borough of Brent, 1985; London Borough of Greenwich, 1987). Looked at now, from the perspective of the early 1990s, they appear as a hiccup. Statements like 'We are strongly of the view that social work can . . . be defined *only* in terms of the functions required of it by their employment agency operating within a statutory framework' and 'We are conscious that social workers do not always take readily, or kindly, to legal intervention in the practice of social work' (London Borough of Brent, 1985, p. 12 and 152) may have struck a chord at the time, but now appear to have missed the point. Social workers were criticised for not being sufficiently interven-tionist and for not using legal powers swiftly or decisively enough. These criticisms may have been wide of the mark but their impact was soon seen in Cleveland where public perception was of an over-zealous use of legal powers by social workers, doctors and other welfare professionals.

If social workers could be criticised for not acting swiftly enough and for acting too swiftly, some sense had to be injected into this confusion and contradiction. In reality, as is now clear, the contradiction was in part one between findings in a few 'hard cases' where something had gone badly wrong and research studies which were documenting the failures of a child care system, itself influenced by those very findings in the child death enquiries. Social work had become 'confrontational, antagonistic and defensive', whereas what was required was a 'more collaborative and inclusive spirit' (Packman and Jordan, 1991, p. 320).

This is the background to the Children Act 1989 but this would not have come about without initiatives from Parliament, central government and the Law Commission. The process started in 1984 with the House of Commons Social Services report *Children in Care*. This concluded that there was a need for a thorough review of legislation and practice in the area of child care (House of Commons, 1984). The impetus for reform was carried forward in the inter-departmental consultative document *Review of Child Care Law* (DHSS, 1985). The Government's response was a White Paper, *The Law on Child Care and Family Services*, published in January 1987 (DHSS, 1987). Independently of the initiative of the Social Services Committee, the Law Commission had decided to review the legal position of children when there were private disputes (usually between parents) about their care or custody. Its report on *Guardianship and Custody* (Law Commission, 1988) and its Working paper on *Wards of Court* (Law Commission, 1987) have had a profound influence on the making of the Children Act.

Consensus and ideology

That the Children Act is based largely on consensus is in no small measure due to those institutions which attempted to reconcile the conflicts that existed and make sense of the research findings. Stating there was consensus is easy: explaining why is more difficult.

It has been suggested (Fox Harding, 1991(b): see also 1991(a)) that the Act is a product of a number of value positions: (i) laissez-faire and patriarchy; (ii) state paternalism and child protection; (iii) defence of the birth family and parents' rights and (iv) children's rights and child liberation. That each of these positions can be detected in provisions in the Act is true. The presumption of non-intervention (s.1(5)), keeping compulsory intervention to a minimum, both in public and private matters, is the clearest example of laissez-faire. It is the keynote to an understanding of the whole Act.

But the Act not only strengthens the position of parents (by getting the state off their backs), it also strengthens the powers of local authorities to intervene. For example, the 'trigger' for care includes for the first time prognosis by social workers that the child is 'likely' to suffer 'significant harm' (s.31(2)). The new child assessment order (s.43), allowing removal of a child for investigative purposes, where there is suspicion but no hard evidence, is a further example. There are also clear instances of the pro-birth family perspective. An official guide to the Act tells us that the Act 'rests on the belief that children are generally best looked after within the family with both parents playing a full part and without resort to legal proceedings' (Lord Chancellor's Department, 1990). Thus, there is a new emphasis on the provision of services to children and families 'in need' (part III), and a greater emphasis on 'contact' between children and their families when circumstances dictate that they are separated (Thoburn, 1991). 'Parental responsibility', a key concept in the Act, is never lost by parents, even when it may seem they have behaved without it. The fourth value position (children's rights) is also not neglected. The child may initiate court actions: for example, s/he may challenge an emergency protection order (s.45(8)), seek contact when in care (s.34(2)), ask for a care order to be discharged (s.39(1)), seek the court's leave to obtain a s.8 order making decisions where s/he is to live or with whom have contact (s.10(2),(8)). It is usually a precondition that the child has sufficient understanding to make the application but this is not always so (see s.34(2)). There is also greater recognition of the child's wishes and feelings (s.1(3)) and more extensive use of separate representation of children by guardians ad litem (s.41). Some observers (e.g. Hodgson, 1990) say the Act has 'empowered' the child. To a large extent this is so, but, as with so much else in the Act, the position is not maintained consistently, for example in relation to divorce where the position of the child is weakened. Which of these value positions is dominant is contentious. For Fox Harding it is paternalism and the defence of birth parents' rights, and laissez-faire is not a 'dominant motif' (1991(b), p. 185). I, on the other hand, see the non-interventionist strand in the Act as the dominant one (Freeman, 1992). The presence of such different ideologies suggests the conflicts of the 1980s have not truly been resolved, that divisions were papered over and that, not far below the surface, conflict remains.

It tends to be forgotten that legislation is a political act with political consequences, using political language and political symbols (Edelman, 1977). In the debating of the Children Act words like 'compromise' and 'balance' were used. Thus, we are told in the official Guide to the Act that it 'strikes a new balance between the autonomy of the family and the protection of children'. But Acts do not 'strike' balances: they establish frameworks within which decisions (themselves political and taken moreover within political constraints) are made. If a balance is struck (and where) thus depends on those whose day-to-day decisions are the Act in practice – social workers, lawyers, courts. It also depends, crucially, on the availability of resources, on the acquisition of skills, on the existence of enough trained personnel.

Consensus can be constructed by co-opting potential opposition. If images can be projected with which those from a different value position can identify, legislation can result with which all can approve. If this amounts to 'reconciling the irreconcilable' (Freeman, 1991), the consensus may be fragile and precarious. This could well be the case with the Children Act of 1989.

The image projected was that of the family. For the 'right' the family is a 'haven in a heartless world' (Lasch, 1977), a quintessentially private space. It is the place where 'Victorian values' reign, a place of private security and closeness. It is also gender-ordered. The family is, in this view (Mount, 1982), the last defence of the individual against a tyrannical and interfering social and political system. Whether this is myth or mystification, nostalgia or delusion, in the minds of the Right the family functions according to prescription. So, parents behave with parental responsibility, disagreements between them are resolved amicably. If outside intervention is necessary, it is on conciliation, rather than the courts, that attention should focus. The philosophy at the root of this was articulated well by Goldstein, Freud and Solnit in their influential *Before the Best Interests of the Child*, when they wrote that a policy of minimum coercive intervention by the state accorded with their 'firm belief as citizens in individual freedom and human dignity' (1979, p. 12). But *whose* 'freedom' and *what* 'dignity' does such a philosophy uphold?

The new Act can be seen as a product of this thinking of the Right about the family, but, conveniently, it has been able to co-opt ideas from the Left as well. The target for most coercive intervention into the family has long been the working class. Children in care are concentrated in areas of high social deprivation (Bebington and Miles, 1989). It is the working class family which, in these terms, has suffered from intrusive and welfarist social work intervention. An Act which not only reduces coercive intervention and rids the statute book of such class-imbued concepts as being of 'such habits or mode of life as to be unfit to have care of [a] child' (a ground for assuming parental rights), but also emphasises support, as the Children Act does, especially in part III, can be expected to win plaudits from the Left. There is enough in the Act for those who wish to see the problems of social work clients in materialistic, rather than individualistic, terms. As far as the Left is concerned this is an Act which tells the local state to work with, not against, families ('partnership') and to provide support (day care, family centres, financial support) so as to obviate the need to intervene into the lives of families. If resources are not available, so that it becomes necessary to prioritise resource distribution, in effect to cut down on the broad category of children 'in need' (Barber, 1990) the Left may come to see the Act as one which carries out the agenda of the Right but neglects the needs of the families for which they stand. In a very real sense this is an Act which privatises the family (of course, 'it says nothing about privatization' – see Packman and Jordan, 1991, p.315): it is an Act which bears the 'hallmarks of Thatcherism' (*cf* Packman and Jordan, 1991, p.315).

Introductory comment on the Act

The Act is both comprehensive and integrated. It brings together the public and private law relating to children. The concept of adoption and the law of child support remain relatively untouched: otherwise there are radical changes throughout child law.

It sweeps much away and creates much that is new. Concepts like custody, care and control and access have gone. There is no more 'voluntary care', resolutions to assume parental rights or custodianship. The place of safety order has been abolished. The use of wardship by local authorities has been restricted (s.100). There are to be no more criminal care orders (s.90; Harris, 1991). Children should no longer be able to be committed to care for school refusal. On divorce the 'satisfaction hearing' has gone and the ability of the court to scrutinise arrangements for the child has been reduced.

The Act has a new philosophy: partnership, a presumption of non-intervention (s.1(5)). It has new principles: the child's welfare is paramount; the frowning on delay; and the insistence that an order should not be made unless it is 'better' for the child. It has new concepts, of which the most fundamental is the replacement of parental rights and duties by 'parental responsibility' (s.2). There are new orders: the s.8 private orders; the new family assistance order (s.16); the education supervision order (s.36), the new weapon for tackling school refusal; the emergency protection order (s.44) replacing the place of safety order and the new child assessment order (s.43). There are now orders pending appeals, an innovation of importance that will smooth the transition between care and home. There are, for the first time, interim supervision orders (s.38). There are new restrictions: on wardship (s.100), on the upgrading of a supervision order to a care order, which will now require proof afresh of the minimum conditions.

There is a new emphasis on the family. Children 'in need' is defined by legislation for the first time (s.17(10),(11)). There is a greater recognition of the child as a participant in the decision-making processes affecting him or her, with a concomitant move away from seeing the child as an object of intervention or just as a 'social problem'. The *Gillick* decision (1986) has left its mark. The status of the unmarried father is enhanced (the ways he can acquire parental responsibility have been enhanced (s.4). The position of grandparents and of relatives is strengthened. The Act takes greater cognisance of the culturally pluralistic society that we now are (see s.22(5). The status of the guardian ad litem is also strengthened (s.42) and children will be so represented more regularly than has been the case in the past.

The Act integrates and it breaks down barriers. The distinction between the private law of children (disputes between parents being the clearest example) and the public (or welfare) law relating to them becomes a false dichotomy. On an application for a care order, it will now be possible for the court to make a 'private law' order, such as a residence order directing that children should live with grandparents. Care orders can be made in any 'family proceedings' and these are defined very broadly (s.8(3),(4)). So, for example, if a wife applies for an order to oust her husband from the matrimonial home because of his violence (under the Matrimonial Homes Act 1983), the court could ask the local authority to investigate with a view to bringing an application for care (s.37). The 'most valuable features of wardship' (Law Commission, 1988, para. 4.20) are integrated into the statutory jurisdiction, so that all tiers of the courts can, for example, make a prohibited steps order forbidding a child to be moved from a school.

The ambit of the Act is wider than has been conventional, embracing children in categories previously excluded from children's legislation: children with disabilities, children in long-stay hospitals, the mentally handicapped and even children in independent boarding schools. Local authorities are given new responsibilities for the welfare of such children. There is a new court structure. There is, as yet, no Family Court. Instead, what has been designed is concurrent jurisdiction between the three tiers of magistrates (or family proceedings) courts, county courts and the High Court. There are 'start' and 'transfer' rules, which should ensure that cases find their right level. Most public law cases will start, and finish, in the family proceedings courts. More effort has been directed to training the magistrates and the judges than ever before. The courts are to be pro-active, a feature of the Act being not just the directions that all courts can make, but also the novel timetabling provisions (see s.11 and s.32). There is, too, a new 'open-door' policy of access to the courts. The Rules have been designed to ensure, whenever possible, that the courts adopt a non-adversarial stance.

References

Barber, S. (1990) 'Heading Off Trouble', *Community Care*, 840, 23.
Bebbington, A. and Miles, J. (1989) 'The Background of Children Who Enter Local Authority Care', *British Journal of Social Work*, 19, 349.
Berridge, D. and Cleaver, H. (1987) *Foster Home Breakdown*, Oxford, Blackwell.
Brent, London Borough of (1985), *A Child in Trust*, London Borough of Brent.
Cleveland (1988), *Report of Inquiry into Child Abuse in Cleveland*, Cm.412, London, HMSO.
Dingwall, R. *et al.* (1983) *The Protection of Children*, Oxford, Blackwell.
DHSS (1974) *Report of Committee of Inquiry into the Care and Supervision Provided in Relation to Maria Colwell*, London, HMSO.
DHSS (1985) *Review of Child Care Law*, London, HMSO.
DHSS (1987) *The Law on Child Care and Family Services* London, HMSO, Cm.62.
Edelman, M. (1977) *Political Language: Words that Succeed and Policies that Fail*, New York, Academic Press, 1977.
Fox Harding, L. (1991a), *Perspectives in Child Care Policy*, London, Longman.
Fox Harding, L. (1991b), 'The Children Act 1989 in Context: Four Perspectives in Child Care Law and Policy', *Journal of Social Welfare and Family Law*, 179–93, 285–302.

Freeman, M. D. A. (1990), 'The Politics of Child Care' in M.D.A. Freeman (ed), *Critical Issues in Welfare Law*, London, Stevens, 103–22.

Freeman, M. D. A. (1991) 'Reconciling the Irreconcilable', *Social Work Today*, 23(7) 17–19 (10 October).

Freeman, M. D. A. (1992) 'In the Child's Best Interests? Reading the Children Act Critically', *Current Legal Problems*.

Gillick (1986) *Gillick* v. *West Norfolk and Wisbech Area Health Authority*, [1986] AC 112.

Goldstein, J. *et al.* (1979) *Before the Best Interests of the Child*, New York, Free Press.

Greenwich, London Borough of (1987) *A Child in Mind*, London Borough of Greenwich.

Harris, R. (1991) 'The Life and Death of The Care Order (Criminal)', *British Journal of Social Work* 21, 1–17.

House of Commons (1984) *Children in Care*, London, HMSO.

Lambeth, London Borough of (1987) *Whose Child?*, LB of Lambeth.

Lasch, C. (1977) *Haven in a Heartless World – The Family Besieged*, New York, Basic Books.

Law Commission (1987) *Wards of Court*, London, HMSO.

Law Commission (1988) *Guardianship and Custody*, London, HMSO.

Mount, F. (1982) *The Subversive Family*, London, Jonathan Cape.

Packman, J. *et al.* (1986), *Who Needs Care?* Oxford, Blackwell.

Packman, J. and Jordan, B. (1991) 'The Children Act: Looking Forward, Looking Back', *British Journal of Social Work*, 21, 315–27.

Parton, N. (1985) *The Politics of Child Abuse*, London, Macmillan.

Parton, N. (1986) 'The Beckford Report: A Critical Appraisal', *British Journal of Social Work*, 16, 511–30.

Rowe, J. and Lambert, L. (1973), *Children Who Wait*, London, Association of British Adoption Agencies.

Stevenson, O. (1986) 'Guest Editorial on Beckford Inquiry', *British Journal of Social Work*, 16, 499–510.

Thoburn, J. (1991) 'The Children Act 1989: Balancing Child Welfare with the Concept of Partnership with Parents', *Journal of Social Welfare and Family Law*, 331–44.

2

Principles, Parents and Partnership

Overarching the whole Act is a set of principles. These are partly to be found in section 1 under the heading 'Welfare of the Child'. But, equally important, are the principles underlying parental responsibility and the concept of partnership with parents which permeates many provisions in the Act and has been constantly stressed in official guidance (Department of Health, 1990). The principles, the concept of parental responsibility and the philosophy of partnership must be grasped before the details of the Act can be mastered.

The principles

There are *four* principles contained in section 1.

(*a*) The *first* (s.1(1)) states:

'When a court determines any question with respect to
(a) the upbringing of a child; or
(b) the administration of a child's property or the application of any income arising from it, the child's welfare shall be the court's paramount consideration.'

This applies to care proceedings and emergency protection proceedings as it does to disputes between parents (*Guidance and Regulations*, vol. 1, para. 1.7).

It will be remembered that the criterion used to be (see the Guardianship of Minors Act 1971 s.1) 'first and paramount'. The

10

Law Commission, wisely I believe, would have formulated the new test as 'the welfare of the child shall be the court's only concern' (Law Commission, 1988, para. 3.14). The Act retains the legal 'state of the art' expression 'paramount'. The courts (and it should be noted that this injunction applies only to the courts)[1] have in recent years begun to interpret 'first and paramount' to mean 'only', so that in the majority of cases little difference should be detected. But, even recently, the courts have invoked the rights of unimpeachable parents[2] and have failed to suppress their own moral abhorrence of lesbianism[3] and of certain religious or quasi-religious groups, such as scientologists.[4] With the test now formulated in terms of the paramountcy of the child's welfare, such considerations should be extraneous. 'Paramount', one leading judge has explained,[5] means the child's welfare 'determines the course to be followed'.

Of course, welfare or the child's best interests is an indeterminate notion (Mnookin, 1975; Elster, 1987). If, for example, there is a dispute between estranged parents about a child's living arrangements the judge has to compare expected utilities. He needs information. He needs predictive ability, to be able to assess the probability of various outcomes and evaluate the advantages and disadvantages of each. And, he needs some source for the values to inform his choice. All three of these requirements pose considerble problems (Freeman, 1983).

Information may be garnered from a number of sources: the parties, the child, the reports of welfare officers, medical and psychiatric reports, where relevant. The Act emphasises the importance of welfare reports (s.7) and stresses that the wishes and feelings of the child, considered in the light of age and understanding, are significant considerations (s.1(3)).

But, even with relatively copious information, prediction of the probable results of alternative outcomes is hazardous. 'Present-day knowledge about human behavior provides no basis for the kind of individualized predictions required'. (Mnookin, 1975). The experiences, the events, the changes that the child will encounter are imponderables. The difficulty of making accurate predictions is attested to by the well-known Berkeley group study of 166 infants born in 1929. The aim was to observe the emotional, mental and physical growth of 'normal' adults (MacFarlane, 1964). Arlene Skolnick, summarising the research, noted that the most surprising finding was 'the difficulty of predicting what thirty-year-old adults would be like even after the most sophisticated data had been gathered on them as children' (1973, p.378). Judges have to make decisions with nothing like such data.

Furthermore, since 'welfare' is not a value-neutral concept, decisions will often emphasise one aspect of welfare over another. Thus, in one recent decision[6] a disciplinarian father was preferred to an easy-going mother; in another[7] a Jehovah's Witness mother was denied custody because the children would not celebrate Christmas; in a famous American case[8] the judge prioritised 'stability and security over freedom of conduct and thought with an opportunity to develop individual talents'. There is also the question of whether we are looking to what is best for the child now, next year, when he is ten or eighteen or, for that matter, thirty. A court recently said[9] that short-term interests should prevail over long-term needs because it was always possible to vary an arrangement. But others may be less confident that this can be achieved successfully.

The sub-section states that the principle applies to 'any question'. This is not strictly true. In adoption the child's welfare remains only the 'first consideration' (Adoption Act 1976 s.6) and even this principle does not apply to every decision: in particular, it does not apply to the decision to dispense with a parent's agreement on the ground that she is withholding it unreasonably[10] (Bevan, 1984). In divorce matters the child's welfare is not considered at all, though it is the 'first consideration' when financial provision and property adjustment are the issue[11] (Matrimonial Causes Act 1973, s.25 (1)). In cases where one parent is trying to oust the other, the child's welfare is merely one consideration.[12] It is possible that this limitation will not survive the Act, but we will not know until we see how the courts respond to the argument that this is a question relating to the upbringing of a child and should be governed by the paramountcy principle. But, even in wardship, where the 'golden thread' is that the child's welfare comes 'first, last and all the time',[13] the courts have found questions relating to children which are not governed by the paramountcy rules.[14]

(b) The *second* principle exhorts us to remember that any delay in determining questions about the upbringing of a child in court is likely to prejudice the welfare of the child (s.1(2)). The *Guidance* explains (vol.1, para.1.8) that delay is generally harmful to children 'not only because of the uncertainty it creates for them but also because of the harm it does to the relationship between the parents and their capacity to co-operate with one another in the future'.

Courts have often stressed that delay is to be avoided,[15] but this is the first time that Parliament has said so. Four points should be noted. First, this provision applies to all proceedings in which questions relating to a child's upbringing arise. Adoption and freeing applications are included and so are proceedings brought in the juvenile (youth) courts. Secondly, it is not said that delay is necessarily prejudicial (it is a 'general principle' that delay is 'likely' to prejudice welfare). Of course, there are cases where delay may be beneficial to the child: for example, holding up a decision to see whether a child can adjust to a particular environment or waiting for a welfare report which assists a better decision. The delay injunction should not be looked at rigidly. Thirdly, the principle must be looked at in the context of welfare reports. The Act favours these (see s.7) but inevitably they cause some delay. This may affect the choice of reporter in some instances, but it should not rule out the ordering of welfare reports where they are likely to be of value. A balance has to be struck. Fourthly, the implications of s.1(2) should be examined. To give effect to the principle, the Act and the Regulations under it give the control of the progress of a case to the court, rather than the parties. The court will be required to draw up a timetable (see sections 11, 32) and take appropriate measures to reduce delay to a minimum.

(*c*) *Thirdly*, the Act contains a novel checklist to which courts considering a contested s.8 order or any order under part IV (care, supervision etc.) (see s.1(4)) but not, for example, emergency protection orders or a parental responsibility order, are to have regard (s.1(3)). The novelty lies not so much in the matters specified, as in the fact that there is a checklist. It is Parliament's indication of its perception of the content of a child's welfare. It should assist the courts to operate the welfare principle. It should assist in the preparation of relevant evidence. It should focus the attention of all sides on the relevant issues. It may go some way towards cutting out delay and avoiding prolonged hearings. It may help achieve some consistency across the country. Although the appellate courts are reluctant to overturn a decision of a trial judge[16] (s/he has heard and seen the parties), where the checklist is ignored or the importance of any of the factors underestimated, an appeal may well be sustained.

The checklist numerates a number of factors. There is no indication of weight or of how the factors are to be viewed. What is offered is flexible guidance. To a large extent the checklist reflects existing practice. For example, the likely effect on the child of any change in his circumstances (s.1(3)(c) has been constantly stressed by the courts[17] (Eekelaar and Clive, 1977). It is the law's recognition of the psychological insight of attachment (Bowlby, 1971, Rutter, 1981).

It is, I believe, significant that the 'ascertainable wishes and feelings of the child' considered in the light of age and understanding are placed first. Clearly, the older the child, the more persuasive his or her views will be. The word 'ascertainable' indicates that, wherever possible, an attempt should be made to ascertain a child's opinions.[18] Social workers acting as welfare officers or guardians ad litem should make the child's wishes known to the court (see Family Proceedings Courts (Children Act 1989) Rules 1991 r.11(4)(b)). Reports ought to explain how the child's views were ascertained. It should be remembered that a child can express wishes or feelings through non-verbal communication. It should also be stressed that to understand a child's communication it needs to be set 'in the context of his or her daily living situation, past experiences and racial and cultural background' (Thurgood, 1990, p.52). Children may 'shy back from full awareness of their feelings, especially when conflicts of loyalty come into question' (A. Freud, 1965).

It is important that those interviewing children to ascertain wishes and feelings should remember:

(*i*)   to be aware of his or her own biases;

(*ii*)   to minimise closed or leading questions;

(*iii*)   to remain as objective and impartial as possible;

(*iv*)   to establish a good relationship;

(*v*)   to ask initially open-ended, non-leading questions;

(*vi*)   to be alert to the cognitive and moral developments level of the child;

(*vii*)   to minimise cues given to a child about what s/he is supposed to say;

(*viii*)   to remain calm and not show irritation when the child's response is not what is or what was expected or desired (Freeman, 1990, pp. 34–6).

The courts have frowned on the use of inappropriate methods to interview a child[19] (Douglas and Wilmore, 1987). Further, a child's actions must not be misinterpreted.

Some account of the remainder of the factors on the checklist will now be given.

The next factor is the child's physical, emotional and educational needs (a good account is Kellmer-Pringle, 1980, see also Black, 1990). Needs should be objectively assessed, though in the eyes of one judge[20] to talk of needs was simply a way of expressing an adult's preference in an apparently child-centred way. The assessment of emotional needs is often likely to be the most difficult and possibly subjective. The courts may rely on welfare reports and the reports of psychiatrists, but psychiatric reports should not be sought where the child does not have psychiatric problems.[21] Though any principle that young children should normally be with their mother has now been eclipsed,[22] it is a matter that might well be considered under 'needs'. Thus, where the father intended to use a child-minder, the court favoured the mother who, it was thought, was better capable of fulfilling the child's emotional needs.[23] Keeping siblings together is not specifically mentioned (but see s.23(7)), but this could be seen as an emotional need.

The likely effect of any change in circumstances is another factor on the checklist. As indicated, this is a clear reflection of existing practice. Thus, for example, where children are in care the courts have justified refusing access orders to parents because, so it was said, it would be too disruptive to the child to re-introduce the parent.[24] It seems that this is in conflict with the research evidence and certainly with the intentions of the new Act.[25] It may not be a difficult view to overturn. This factor should be looked at in conjunction with the warning that delay is 'likely to prejudice the welfare of the child' (s.1(2)), for emphasising the status quo may encourage delay or prevarication by one party.[26] This should not be tolerated.

The fourth factor in the checklist is the child's age, sex, background and any characteristic which the court considers relevant. Age and sex are not likely to be used as they were formerly when the courts developed principles that young children needed their mothers and older boys were better with their fathers.[27] But both matters remain relevant. There is however no evidence to suggest that a child's well being is affected by the gender of the parent with whom s/he is living (Chambers, 1984–5). 'Background' includes religion, racial origin and cultural and linguistic background. These four factors must be considered by local authorities when making decisions about children they are looking after (see s.22(5)(c) and below), but s.1 makes them matters for consideration in the wider context. Race is, and is likely to remain, a contentious issue: the courts have said they will not prioritise it over other aspects of a child's welfare.[28] There is some evidence that black children reared in white families experience confusion about their identity.[29] This justified moving a child of mixed race from a white foster mother where he had lived for 18 months from birth to a black family[30] – a decision which provoked considerable controversy.[31] Local authorities which adopt policies about the placement of black children may be susceptible to judicial review if it is considered that they are 'fettering their discretion'.[32] They should also consider the compatibility of such a policy, or an individualised application of it, with the paramountcy principle in s.1(1). 'Background' includes culture in its broadest sense. It would extend to a matter such as a child's vegetarianism.

But there is a major issue of policy involved, which will be considered in greater depth in the chapter on care: to what extent should we take account of the cultural practices of minority groups? Should we tolerate practices we find abhorrent? (Poulter, 1986). Parliament has now[33] ruled that female circumcision is unlawful. How is our knowledge that this may take place to influence a decision about where a child is to live? The courts have decided[34] that a child's culture is to be discounted where the care being offered is unacceptably poor. But in that case, which concerned a mother from Vietnam, the court was convinced that the mother's disciplinary measures were unacceptable also in the rural Chinese culture from which she came. Supposing they had been the norm there: would the courts then subject a child to behaviour which we believe might result in 'significant harm'? It is a difficult question to resolve, not least because 'significant harm' itself needs to be situated within culture (see also below).

As far as religion is concerned, the courts do not pass judgment on religious beliefs,[35] but are understandly concerned about the social and emotional effects of particular religions.[36] Where the concern, however, is that a Jehovah's Witness parent might not consent to a child's blood transfusion, this could be tackled by making a specific issue order (s.8).

The court is also to have regard to any harm which the child has suffered or is at risk of suffering. It should be noted that the reference is to 'harm', not 'significant harm'. One area where this factor may be highly significant is the contact dispute where there is an allegation of sexual abuse. All cases will turn on their own facts but 'the principle is clearly established that cases of sexual abuse which show a danger of the repetition of that conduct if access is afforded to a parent, or indeed which show continuing or recent disturbance, may warrant. . . . a total withdrawal of access'.[37] Social workers have been warned that when they come to court to assist it 'to find what is best for a child they should include everything and conceal nothing in their evidence'.[38] Though stated in this context, this is of general application.

The next factor in the checklist is 'how capable each of his parents, and any other person in relation to whom the court considers the question to be relevant, is of meeting his needs'. The courts have stressed that parents can learn, but children should not have to wait.[39] They favour two-parent families[40] and have deprecated a rota of child-minders.[41] This factor may also be of relevance when the effect of a contact order on the parent caring for the child is considered: if it can be shown that it will undermine her ability to care an order may be refused, though such a decision will not be taken lightly.[42]

Finally, the range of powers available to the court under the Children Act is to be considered. It should be noted:

(i)   the courts have the power to make orders other than those applied for (s.10(1), 31(5)). A s.8 order can be granted to anyone without application (s.10(1)(b))

(ii) there are important restrictions in the Act: for example, a child cannot be committed to care in wardship proceedings (s.100(2)) and residence and contact orders cannot be made in favour of local authorities (s.9(2)).

(iii) courts should not make orders unless 'doing so would be better for the child than making no order at all' (s.1(5), discussed below).

(iv) the powers available include the power to make a family assistance order (s.16, discussed below).

(v)   one power available to the courts is the power to prevent further applications (see s.91(14)).

(d) The fourth principle in s.1 is, arguably, the key to an understanding of the whole Act. This is the presumption of non-intervention or the minimal intervention principle. Section 1(5) states:

'Where a court is considering whether or not to make one or more orders under this Act with respect to a child, it shall not make the order or any of the orders unless it considers that doing so would be better for the child than making no order at all'.

This creates a presumption against court action, and has clear implications throughout the Act. It applies to private law and public law orders. It will affect the work of solicitors, both their fact-gathering and their relations with clients (who will need to be weaned away from beliefs that courts exist to make orders). It will affect the work of social workers and lawyers working for local authorities. For example, the knowledge that care is no panacea will mean that courts will need to be convinced that a care order will be beneficial to a child's well-being. The court will need to know why the order is being sought and what it is hoped will be achieved by it. The evidence which social workers present on care applications must take account of this.

The impact of the minimal intervention principle may be noticed first in the private law area, particularly in divorce. The number of post-divorce orders about children will decline considerably. The work of conciliators and counsellors will increase as those denied court resolutions seek the informal justice of agreements and settlements (Bottomley and Roche 1988). The significance of the principle will be felt even more forcibly in the public law area. It applies to care orders, supervision orders, education supervision orders (s.36), contact orders (s.34), interim orders (s.38) and orders pending appeals (s.40), as well as to emergency protection orders (s.44) and child assessment orders (s.43). So, for example, even if the local authority successfully sustains the minimum conditions for a care order (in s.31(2)), no order will be made unless it can also satisfy the court that the making of an order would be better for the child than making no order. The court (in most cases lay magistrates sitting as a Family Proceedings Court) will be asked to predict and to balance: to assess the child's future, to compare utilities and to undertake a balancing exercise. Local authorities may expect to be confronted by a new breed of 'Rumpoles' with briefcases bulging with newspaper cuttings about foster care breakdown, sexual abuse in children's homes, forcible feeding, drugging, 'pin-down' (Levy and Kahan, 1991) and other failures and foibles of the public care system (Utting, 1991), hectoring magistrates into not making orders. It is too early to say how magistrates will react and what the attitude of the appeal courts will be. If a trend of refusing care orders develops, there may be a glut of applications for leave to seek the inherent jurisdiction[43] of the High Court (s.100(3)). If the High Court reacts sympathetically, it could undermine one of the main objectives of the legislation. The critical equation of order or no order will not be easy to solve. It is all too easy to underestimate the effect that preparation of a case to surmount the minimal intervention hurdle will have on social work resources. It is also easy to gloss over the impact that the principle will have on children. They may well be the losers (Freeman, 1992).

Parental responsibility

The concept of parental responsibility is so basic to the Act that the first question that any professional confronted by a case concerning children will need to answer is: 'Who has parental responsibility for this child?'

The shift from parental rights and duties to parental responsibility, with parents as trustees for their children, is to be welcomed. It contains three messages. First, that responsibility is more important than rights. The courts have anyway stressed that parental rights were only justified in so far as they enabled a parent to perform his or her duties towards the child.[44]

Secondly, that it is parents, and not therefore children, who are the decision-makers. The *Gillick* decision[45] limited the power of parents to make decisions for their mature children. But, despite assurances of the Lord Chancellor to the contrary,[46] the Act appears to have overturned this principle. In all the euphoria about the empowerment of children under the Act, this has hardly been noticed. And yet the shift can already be detected. In a case reported in the very week the Children Act came into operation (but decided in July 1991), the Court of Appeal decided that if a 'Gillick-competent' child declines to consent to medication (in this case anti-psychotic drugs) 'consent can be given by someone else who has parental rights or responsibilities'[47] (that is by a parent or by a court exercising its wardship or statutory jurisdiction).

Thirdly, the emphasis on parental responsibility conveys the all-important message that it is parents, and not the state, that have responsibility for children. The consequences of this need to be spelt out. Parents have responsibility in a normative sense even when in fact they act with complete disregard for that responsibility. So wedded is the Act (and the Government) to the ideology that individual parents must have responsibility that, short of adoption, there is no way that a parent with parental responsibility can divest him or herself of it (Eekelaar, 1991; Freeman, 1992). Even where the child is in care under a care order, the parents retain parental responsibility. As we shall see, the local authority is also vested with it (s.33(3)) and can control the way in which parents can exercise their parental responsibility, but, nevertheless, parents retain their parental responsibility – albeit, perhaps, only in a symbolic or ideological sense.

The definition (or non-definition) of parental responsibility is found in s.3(1) of the Act. It means 'all the rights, duties, powers, responsibilities and authority which by law a parent of a child has in relation to the child and his property'. These rights etc. are not listed: they are to be found in the existing law,[48] as this is interpreted to meet changing conditions. It is, I believe, rather unfortunate that the definition should start with 'rights' and not with 'responsibilities' but too much significance should not be attached to this.

Mothers[49] always have parental responsibility. Only the fathers of legitimate children automatically have parental responsibility,[50] but other fathers can acquire it in a number of ways (discussed below). More than one person may have parental responsibility at the same time (s.2(5)): a common example is the divorced parent with whom the child is not living (or even for that matter having contact). In reality, of course, this is a provision which improves the status of fathers (Freeman, 1992; Roche, 1991). Parental responsibility is not lost when the child is accommodated by the local authority (s.20) or when another person or the local authority (see s.33) acquires it (s.2(6)) (but see Tunnard, 1991). Each person who has parental responsibility may take action alone to meet it (s.2(7), but cannot do anything incompatible with any order under the Act (s.2(8)). So, a divorced father with parental responsibility cannot insist that the child lives with him when there is a residence order in favour of the mother in existence. A parent with parental responsibility cannot insist that her child lives with her when the court has made a care order in favour of the local authority (s.33(1)). Parental responsibility cannot be surrendered (s.2(9)), though arrangements can be made for others to meet it (s.2(11)). However, this does not remove the primary responsibility. A further illustration of the significance of parental responsibility is that a person with parental responsibility may apply for a s.8 order without the leave of the court.

As already indicated, the unmarried father does not have parental responsibility. He can acquire it in five different ways:

(*i*)   by applying to the court for a parental responsibility order (s.4(1)(a));

(*ii*) by making an agreement with the mother in the 'prescribed form' under s.4(1)(b). An informal agreement may be interpreted as a delegation of responsibility under s.2(9). It should be stressed that the result of a formal agreement will be that mother and father share responsibility for the child;

(*iii*) by obtaining a residence order (see s.12(1));

(*iv*) by being appointed as the child's guardian by the court (s.5(1));

(*v*) by being appointed as the child's guardian by the mother or another guardian, but this will only take effect after the mother's death.

The fact that a child is in the care of a local authority is no impediment to the making of an order under s.4[51] nor does the order, if granted, confer enforceable parental authority.

A parental responsibility order is governed by the paramountcy principle (s.1(1)) and the presumption of 'no order' (s.1(5)). The checklist in s.1(3) is not relevant (s.1(4)), but the court would nevertheless consider some of the factors in the list worthy of consideration (in particular, the child's wishes and feelings). It has been said[52] that the father's 'character and history' are relevant. The essence of the question is: can the natural father show that he is a father to the child, not in the biological sense (though if there is a dispute as to paternity this will have to be proved as well), but in the sense that he has established or is likely to establish such a real family tie with the child that he should now be accorded the corresponding legal tie? It will be easier, one judge said, to ask: 'has he behaved, or will he behave, with parental responsibility for the child?'.[53] In another case it was said that the matters to be taken into account are the degree of commitment shown by the father to the child, the degree of attachment between them, as well as the father's reasons for applying for the order.[54]

Two important consequences attach to the father's acquisition of parental responsibility, as far as the local authority is concerned. First, if the child is accommodated by the local authority (under s.20), the father can now remove the child (s.20(8) and see below for further discussion of this problem). Secondly, if the child is in care he, as well as the local authority, has parental responsibility. The implications of this have already been referred to. The local authority may, however, apply for the order or a parental responsibility agreement to be brought to an end (s.4(3)). In deciding whether to end a s.4 order or agreement, the court must regard the child's welfare as its paramount consideration and be satisfied that discharging the order is better than making no order at all. (s.1(1) and s.1(5)). It is probable that the court is more likely to end an agreement (perhaps where the mother was subjected to undue pressure) than an order, unless the circumstances have substantially changed. It should be stressed that, as a parent, the father can apply for contact (s.34), whether or not he has obtained parental responsibility.

Partnership

It may be that the principle of partnership was to be found in earlier legislation but, if so, it was lost from practice. It was in the *Review of Child Care Law* (DHSS 1985) that the word in the current context was first used. Even where the child cannot remain at home, the *Review* argued, the emphasis should be on maintaining family links 'to care for the child in partnership with rather than in opposition to his parents, and to work towards his return to them' (para. 2.8). This was picked up by Fisher *et al.* (1986), p. 125):

> 'In our view, this philosophy of partnership with clients, in which the primary caring role of the family is reasserted but effectively *supplemented* by public services, must be reintroduced into national policy and practice. The "good society" must, in our view, treat those in need of child care services as fellow citizens rather than as "inadequate" parents or children.'

The word 'partnership' as such is not in the Act but it is clear that many of the provisions are informed by the view of the 'good society' just described. Indeed, the Lord Chancellor (Hansard HL vol. 502, col. 491) said that 'partnership with parents based on agreement should so far as possible be the guiding principle for the provision of services'. The Department of Health's guide to the *Principles and Practice* (1990, p. 8) states:

> '*The development of a working partnership with parents is usually the most effective route to providing supplementary or substitute care for their children.* Measures which antagonise, alienate, undermine or marginalise parents are counter-productive. For example, taking compulsory measures over children can all too easily have this effect though such action may be necessary in order to provide protection.'

And so, for example, it advocates (*idem*) that if young people cannot remain home, placement with relatives or friends should be explored before other forms of placement are considered. It points to research showing that placement with relatives is 'usually more successful' than one outside the 'family circle'. It goes on to point out (*idem*) that:

> '*if young people have to live apart from their family of origin, both they and their parents should be given adequate information and helped to consider alternatives and contribute to the making of an informed choice about the most appropriate form of care.*'

There is evidence that parents can be more actively involved in the decision-making process about their children even when they, for one reason or another, cannot be involved in day-to-day care. The Honeylands project (Brimblecombe and Russell, 1987) shows that parents can be part of the evaluation of a programme. Work in Oxfordshire has demonstrated that parents can organise respite care. The acknowledgement that the parents in interaction with the social services can be experts and may sometimes know more about their children's needs than, for example, paediatricians is not easy for professionals to swallow. But most parents whose lives do not come under social services' surveillance certainly believe this. How many social workers would feel happy if a case conference were convened on their child, and they were told they could not be present or could not participate?

If the partnership philosophy underlying the Act is to become more than rhetoric, there should be fewer cases where the local authority needs to make a decision against the *wishes* of parents or a child. Fewer children should be separated from parents and fewer who are should cease to have meaningful contact with their parents and wider family. Thoburn (1991, pp. 334–6) has pointed to four consequences:

(i) there should be fewer occasions when it is necessary to make a decision that a child cannot go home. She makes this statement 'hesitantly' because of evidence of a relationship (Farmer and Parker, 1991) between breakdown and re-abuse (but compare Trent, 1989 where a similar proportion in a smaller sample experienced breakdown in their homes as in substitute families);

(ii) because of the injunction to avoid compulsion, there will be more children permanently in accommodation with parents holding full parental responsibility. Parental rights cannot be assumed. In such cases complex and careful negotiations with the parents (and child if s/he is old enough) about appropriate placements will become necessary;

(*iii*) 'shared care will become a long-term option for more children' (ibid., p. 335). There will be, in other words, 'supplementary' rather than 'substitute' parents (or carers). Putting partnership into practice in this situation may be especially difficult (see Millham *et al.*, 1986);

(*iv*) more children who cannot go home will be in touch with their parents and wider family. The presumption of reasonable contact (s.34; Sch. 2, para. 15), with contact as a 'right of the child', means that policies to promote contact even where the child is permanently placed have to be introduced. There is evidence (Fratter *et al.*, 1991) that permanent substitute placements are less likely to break down where contact with parents and and/or siblings is retained.

Examples of partnership in the Act are too numerous to list but I would draw attention to the following:

Sch. 2, para. 1(1): take reasonable steps to identify extent of children in need;
    7: take reasonable steps to reduce need for care/supervision proceedings etc.;
    8: provision for children living with families;
    9: family centres;
   11: have regard to different racial groups;
   15: promote and maintain contact between child and family.

The partnership theme is continued in the care provisions. In particular I would draw attention to the following provisions:

s.1(5) : the presumption of no order
s.33(3)(b) : the continuation of parental responsibility when the child is in care
s.34(1) : the presumption of reasonable contact
s.34(2); (4) : orders for contact
s.34(5) : orders for contact without application
s.34(11) : court should consider arrangements before making a care order and invite parties to comment upon arrangements

s.43(13) : reasonable contact where there is an emergency protection order

There are clear examples in the Act also of partnership with children. For example:

> s.20(6) : the views of the child should be sought before s/he is accommodated
>
> s.20(11) : 16 and 17 year olds may be accommodated against the wishes of parents
>
> s.22(4) : ascertain wishes and feelings of child and parents before s/he is accommodated
>
> s.22(5) : give due consideration to wishes and feelings of child, parents and others and to the child's religion, racial origin and cultural and linguistic background
>
> s.38(6), s.43(8), s.44(7) : the *Gillick*-competent child's right to refuse examination and assessment.

The principle of partnership will not be easy to put into practice and it will not always work. It is important to realise that it will require skills in negotiation and in writing agreements. Both in negotiation and in formulating agreements the possibility that things will not work as hoped or anticipated must be borne in mind and provided for. Partnership will require decisions to be taken that maybe thought by some to court trouble. Partnership, however, anticipates that risks will be taken. Inevitably, there will be failures (and it must be assumed decisions which, in hindsight, were wrong). The emphasis on partnership, like that on parental responsibility, is in part an exercise in social engineering. As ever, it will be social workers who will take the blame if it does not work.

Notes

1. Compare Art. 3 of the UN Convention on the Rights of the Child.
2. *Re K* [1990] 2 FLR 64 (dispute between father and aunt and uncle).
3. *S* v. *S* [1978] 1 FLR 143; *C* v. *C* [1991] 1 FLR 223; *B* v. *B* [1991] 1 FLR 402. See now also *C* v. *C* (*No2*) [1992] 1 FCR 207.
4. *Re B and G* [1985] 1 FLR 134.

5. Lord MacDermott in *J* v. *C* [1970] AC 668, 710.
6. *May* v. *May* [1986] 1 FLR 325.
7. *T* v. *T* (1974) 4 Fam. Law 190.
8. *Painter* v. *Bannister* 140 NW 26 152 (1966) (discussed in Freeman (1983) pp. 202–4).
9. *Thompson* v. *Thompson* (1987) 17 Fam. Law 89. And see *Re H* [1991] 2 FLR 109.
10. *Re P* [1977] Fam. 25.
11. *Suter* v. *Suter and Jones* [1987] Fam. 111.
12. *Richards* v. *Richards* [1984] AC 174.
13. *Re D* [1977] Fam. 158.
14. *Re X* [1975] Fam. 47 (publication of a book); *Re C* [1991] 2 FLR 168 (refusal to compel a school to take a child).
15. *R* v. *Bolton MBC ex parte B* [1985] FLR 346.
16. *G* v. *G* [1985] 2 All ER 225.
17. *Allington* v. *Allington* [1985] FLR 586; *P* v. *P* (1975) 6 Fam. Law 75.
18. And see the Children's Legal Centre Survey (*Childright* No. 45).
19. *Re F* [1987] 1 FLR 269; *Re N* [1987] 1 FLR 290; *Re M* [1987] 1 FLR 293; *Re W* [1987] 1 FLR 297; *Re G* [1987] 1 FLR 310; *C* v. *C* [1987] 1 FLR 321; *Re H* [1987] 1 FLR 332; *Re X* [1989] 1 FLR 30; *Re E* [1991] 1 FLR 420; *Rochdale BC* v. *A* [1991] 2 FLR 192.
20. In *May* v. *May* [1986] 1 FLR 325.
21. *Practice Direction* [1985] 1 All ER 832.
22. *Re S* [1991] 2FLR 388; *Re A* [1991] 2 FLR 394.
23. *Plant* v. *Plant* [1982] 4 FLR 305. A good recent discussion of emotional needs (in this case for comfort after a mother's death) is *Re H* [1991] 2 FLR 109.
24. *Re M* [1988] 1 FLR 35.
25. See Masson, J (1990); Millham, S *et al.* (1986).
26. *R* v. *Bolton MBC ex parte B* [1985] FLR 346.
27. *Re S* [1991] 2 FLR 388; *Re A* [1991] 2 FLR 394.
28. *Re A* [1987] 2 FLR 429.
29. See Owen and Jackson (1983).
30. *Re P* [1990] 1 FLR 96. See also *Re N* [1990] 1 FL R 58.
31. Leading to a threat that agencies with a blanket approach might lose their approval (D. Mellor, Social Services Conference, September 1989). See also CI (90)2. And see now *Re JK* [1991] 2 FLR 340, where the local authority was said to be the 'prisoner' of its policy.
32. *Attorney-General ex rel Tilley* v. *L.B. of Wandsworth* [1981] 1 WLR 854.
33. Prohibition of Female Circumcision Act 1985.
34. *Re H* [1987] 2 FLR 12.
35. *Re T* [1975] 2 FLR 239.
36. *Wright* v. *Wright* (1980) 2 FLR 276 (psychological damage from indocrination feared); *Hewison* v. *Hewison* (1977) 7 Fam Law 207 (social isolation).
37. *Re H* [1989] 2 FLR 174, 184–5.
38. *L* v. *L* [1989] 2 FLR 16, 29.

39. *Re M* [1988] Adoption and Fostering, 49.
40. *Re DW* (1984) 14 Fam Law 17.
41. *Re K* [1977] Fam. 179.
42. *Re B.C.* [1985] FLR 638, 641 (Dunn L. J.); *S* v. *S* [1988] 1 FLR 213.
43. Of which wardship is a species. See below, p. 160.
44. *Gillick* v. *West Norfolk and Wisbech Area Health Authority* [1986] AC 112.
45. On which see Bainham (1986).
46. *Hansard*, HL vol. 502, col. 1351.
47. *Re R* [1991] 4 All ER 177 (and see Masson, 1991).
48. The Law Commission considered it impossible to list them (Law Commission, 1988, para. 2.6).
49. Where there is a conflict between the gestational and the genetic mother, the Human Fertilisation and Embryology Act 1990 gives priority to the gestational.
50. See s.2.
51. *D* v. *Hereford and Worcester CC* [1991] 1 FLR 205.
52. Ibid, p. 212.
53. *Idem.*
54. *Re H* [1991] 1 FLR 214. The importance of fathers using the new machinery is emphasised by Ward J. in *F* v. *S* [1991] 2 FLR 349, 355 (a man who had 'acted as a father' nevertheless powerless to prevent the child's removal from this country because he did not have parental rights [responsibility]).

References

Bainham, A. (1986) 'The Balance of Power in Family Decisions', *Cambridge Law Journal*, 45, 262.
Bevan, H. (1984) 'The Role of the Court in the Adoption Process', in P. Bean (ed.) *Adoption: Essays in Social Policy, Law and Sociology*, London, Tavistock.
Black, D. (1990) 'What Do Children Need from Parents?', *Adoption and Fostering*, 14(1), 43.
Bottomley, A. and Roche, J. (1988) 'Conflict and Consensus: A Critique of the Language of Informal Justice', in R. Matthews (ed.), *Informal Justice*, Beverly Hills, Sage.
Bowlby, J. (1971) *Attachment*, Harmondsworth, Penguin.
Chambers, D. (1984-5), 'Rethinking the Substantive Rules for Custody Disputes in Divorce' *Michigan Law Review* 83, 477.
Department of Health and Social Security (1985) *Review of Child Care Law*, London, HMSO.
Department of Health (1990) *Principles and Practice in Regulations and Guidance*, London, HMSO
Department of Health (1991) *Guidance and Regulations* (9 vols.), London, HMSO.

Eekelaar, J. (1991) 'Parental Responsibility: State of Nature or Nature of the State?', *Journal of Social Welfare and Family Law*, 37.

Eekelaar, J. and Clive, E. (1977) *Custody After Divorce*, Oxford, SSRC Centre for Socio-Legal Studies.

Elster, J. (1987), 'Solomonic Judgments: Against the Best Interest of the Child', *University of Chicago Law Review*, 54, 1.

Farmer, E. and Parker, R. (1991) *Trials and Tribulations: A Study of Children 'Home on Trial'*, London, HMSO.

Fisher, M. *et al.* (1986) *In and Out of Care*, London, Batsford.

Fratter, J. *et al.* (1991) *Permanent Family Placement: A Decade of Experience*, London, BAAF.

Freeman, M. D. A. (1983) *The Rights and Wrongs of Children*, London, Frances Pinter.

Freeman, M. D. A. (1990) 'Listening to Children and Representing Them – A Lawyer's View' in A. Bannister *et al.* (ed.), *Listening to Children*, London, Longman.

Freeman, M. D. A. (1992) 'In the Child's Best Interests?', *Current Legal Problems*.

Freud, A. (1958) 'Child Observation and Prediction of Development', *The Psychoanalytic Study of the Child*, 13,97.

Kellmer-Pringle, M. (1980) *The Needs of Children*, London, Hutchinson.

Law Commission (1988) *Guardianship and Custody*, Law Com. 172, London, HMSO.

Levy, A. and Kahan, B. (1991) *The Pindown Experience and the Protection of Children*, Stafford, Staffs CC.

MacFarlane, J. (1964) 'Perspectives on Personality Consistency and Change from the Guidance Study', *Vita Humana*, 7, 115.

Masson, J. (1991) 'Adolescent Crisis and Parental Power', *Family Law*, 21, 528.

Millham, S. *et al.* (1986) *Lost in Care*, Aldershot, Gower.

Mnookin, R. (1975), 'Child Custody Adjudication: Judicial Functions in the Face of Indeterminacy', *Law and Contemporary Problems*, 39(3), 226.

Poulter, S. (1986) *English Law and Ethnic Minority Customs*, London, Butterworth.

Roche, J. (1991) 'Once a Parent Always a Parent?', *Journal of Social Welfare and Family Law*, 345.

Rutter, M. (1981), *Maternal Deprivation Reassessed*, Harmondsworth, Penguin.

Skolnick, A. (1973), *The Intimate Environment: Exploring Marriage and the Family*, Boston, Little.

Thoburn, J. (1991) 'The Children Act 1989: Balancing Child Welfare with the Concept of Partnership with Parents', *Journal of Social Welfare and Family Law*, 331–44.

Thurgood, J. (1990) 'Active Listening – A Social Services Perspective' in A. Bannister *et al.*, *Listening To Children*, Harlow, Longman, 1990.

Trent, J. (1989) *Homeward Bound*, London, Barnardo's.

Tunnard, J. (1991) 'Rights and Duties', *Social Work Today*, 23(14), 21.

Utting, W. (1991) *Children in the Public Care*, London, HMSO.

3

The Courts' Powers in Family Proceedings

This chapter discusses the court's powers to make orders under Part II of the Act in, what are called, 'family proceedings'.[1] The orders are sometimes called 'private law orders' because they are mainly intended for use in disputes between parents, but, as we shall see, their application is wider. For example, on an application by a local authority for a care order, a residence order may be made instead in favour of grandparents.

The main private law orders are known as 'section 8 orders'. The other novelty is the family assistance order (s.16) which is also considered in this chapter.

This part of the Act is based largely on Law Commission recommendations (Law Commission, 1988). It identified three major difficulties. First, different courts had different powers (some could allocate 'custody', 'care and control' and 'access', others 'legal custody,' and 'access'). Secondly, the precise effect of orders was in doubt. Thirdly, the law was applied inconsistently: there was a custody lottery (Priest and Whybrow, 1986). For example, in some courts joint custody orders were common, in others they where a rarity. The Law Commission also recognised (1988, para. 4.5) that the children who coped best after their parents' separation were those able to maintain a good relationship with both parents (Wallerstein and Kelly, 1980). That the law should not obstruct co-operation is recognised in s.1(5) discussed, above). That orders should not have the legal and emotive significance of the old custody orders is the message conveyed both by the concept of parental responsibility (see above) and by the new orders which are more flexible and do not remove parental

29

responsibility from the parent with whom the child is not living. Section 8 orders concentrate on practical questions rather than the more theoretical matter of who has particular powers or duties.

There are *four* orders in section 8:

the residence order;
the contact order;
the prohibited steps order;
and the specific issue order.

The first two resemble custody and access orders, though they are by no means identical. The other two orders are new. They are modelled on the wardship jurisdiction and are intended to incorporate the most valuable features of that jurisdiction into the statutory scheme (Law Commission, 1988, para. 1.4). It means in effect that all three tiers of court will be able to make decisions that previously might have to have been taken by a High Court judge.

The orders (s. 8(1))

(a) *A residence order* means an order 'setting the arrangements to be made as to the person with whom the child is to live'. It focuses on arrangements for the child, not on who has authority over the child. This, by virtue of the concept of continuing parental responsibility, is retained by both parents. Although the Act says 'person', residence orders can be made in favour of more than one person (see Lord Mackay, *Hansard*, HL vol. 502, col. 1219). A residence order can thus be made in favour of two people (for example, a parent and a step-parent) or indeed more, though that is unlikely. Further, more than one residence order may be made in respect of one child (s.11(4)): for example, in favour of each parent. There is no reason why residence orders should not be made in favour of each parent and that parent's new partner.

Where a residence order is made in favour of two (or more) persons who do not themselves all live together, the order may specify the periods during which the child is to live in the different households (s.11(4)). This legitimates joint parenting arrangements (Wallerstein and Kelly (1980), Woolley (1978); Roman and Haddad 1978)) and overrules a 1986 Court of Appeal decision[2] which rejected such arrangements as prima facie wrong (though in the case it had worked well for over five years). The new provision will be useful where it is intended that a child will spend the week with one parent and the weekend with the other, and for situations where it is envisaged that school holidays will be spent with the parent other than the one the child lives with during the school year. Such arrangements can also be effected by a residence order to one parent, a defined contact order to the other, but a joint residence order seems more realistic. Despite the new provision it is not envisaged that too many joint residence orders will be made. First, because, as the Court of Appeal recognised, children may be thought to need the stability of a single home,[3] and secondly, because where shared care is appropriate the need for an order at all (s.1(5)) is less likely (and see *Guidance and Regulations* vol.1 (1991), para. 2.28). Under s.11(4) the court may only specify time; any other conditions that are needed (for example, to take the child to piano lessons) would have to be specified separately under powers in s.11(7).

The following features of a residence order should be noted:

(*i*)   As indicated, it can be in favour of more than one *person*. The persons need not be parents (they could be grand-parents, relatives, foster parents, older siblings) (s.11(4)).

(*ii*)   A residence order can be in general or defined terms (s.11(7)). For example, it could provide that the child lives with the father but only whilst he remains in a particular area.

(*iii*) A residence order confers parental responsibility on a person who does not already have it (s.12(2)). This applies also to the unmarried father (s.12(1)).

(*iv*)   Where a residence order is in force, the child's surname cannot be changed and the child cannot be removed from the United Kingdom for more than one month (s.13(2)) without the written consent of all persons with parental responsibility or with the leave of the court (s.13(1)). That leave can be granted by the court when making the residence order (s.13(3)). Where it is feared the child may be abducted from the country, a prohibited steps order can be sought.

(*v*)   A residence order expires when the parents live together for a continuous period of six months (s.11(5)).

(*vi*)   If there is a residence order in favour of one parent, the other cannot act in any way which is incompatible with it (s.2(8)), for example by removing the child from the parent with the residence order.

(*vii*) Where a residence order is in force the court may order either or both of the parents to pay the applicant for the benefit of the child or the child him or herself periodical payments. (Sch.1, para.1). This may be particularly useful where a residence order is made in favour of a non-parent.

The following consequences of a residence order will concern social workers particularly.

(*i*)   A local authority cannot apply for a residence order (s.9(2)). If it could, it would be able to frustrate the intention of the Act that the only way to intervene coercively into a parent-child relationship is through care (or emergency protection) and thus by proving a minimum condition (see s.31(2)). A residence order cannot be made in favour of a local authority.

(*ii*)   If the child is subject to a care order, an application for a residence order is a means of discharge. Those who had parental responsibility before the care order must be named as respondents to the application. This route is likely to be used by a person who does not have parental responsibility (e.g. an unmarried father or a grandparent) (see s.91(1)). A person with parental responsibility (and also the child) would use s.39 (see below).

(*iii*) Where the child is subject to a residence order (indeed, any s.8 order), the making of a care order discharges that order. (s.91(2)). That was not the case with custody orders in the past.

(*iv*)   One way of achieving a phased return would be to make a residence order in favour of foster parents with increasing contact to the parents (using s.11(4)).

A contact order is an order 'requiring the person with whom a child lives, or is to live, to allow the child to visit or stay with the person named in the order, or for that person and the child otherwise to have contact with each other'.

A number of features of the contact order may be noted. First, it is child-centred. Too often 'access', as it was called, was looked upon as an absent parent's right with non-custodial fathers often bargaining access for maintenance (Maidment, 1975). A *Gillick-*

competent child cannot be compelled to maintain contact. And courts will only make orders in relation to children over 16 in exceptional circumstances (s.9(7)).

As long ago as 1973,[4] access was described by a court as a child's right and this was reiterated in 1990.[5] The courts have stressed the importance of contact in cases where social workers might be rather more dubious. Cases of sexual abuse are one such example.[6] Another was the recent case where indirect contact was ordered to be established in the expectation that direct contact could be reconsidered when the children were older.[7] The mother was frightened of the father and the children (three and one at parting) could not remember him. There were also difficulties in making suitable arrangements. But it was said that without contact the children might fantasise about their father. The child's right to know his or her siblings has also been affirmed recently by the Court of Appeal.[8] Children should be considered independently, not collectively.[9]

Secondly, although most persons 'named' will be non-residential parents, anyone can be named in the order. This could be, for example, a relative, a former foster parent, a step-parent, even a former neighbour. Grandparents,[10] in particular, may be expected to take advantage of this provision, but they will require leave of the court before making an application (see below). More than one person can be named in the order. It should be stressed that the person named in the order is not under an obligation to maintain contact.

Thirdly, the word 'requiring' should be considered. In the past the enforcement of access orders was notoriously difficult. There were attempts to fine the recalcitrant parent,[11] threats to switch custody to the parent denied access,[12] and the occasional committal to prison for contempt.[13] All these problems were graphically illustrated in the widely-publicised *Morgan* v. *Foretich* case in the United States (Groner, 1991). Problems will continue, but the shift in emphasis from the adult to the child and the strong word 'requiring' may indicate that courts should take a stronger line with the obstructive parent.

Fourthly, contact is wider than access.[14] An order could permit contact by means of letters, telephone calls, Christmas, birthday presents etc. And it is for 'contact': if 'no contact' is required, a prohibited steps order should be sought.

Fifthly, if the contact order is in respect of a parent it expires after six months' continuous cohabitation (s.11(6)).

Sixthly, conditions can be attached (s.11(7)).

Lastly, it must be assumed that when contact orders are made they will be for defined contact. In the past courts have made orders for 'reasonable access'. It is suggested that where the parent can agree on reasonable contact, an order is itself unnecessary (and see s.1(5)). However, the *Guidance and Regulations* (1991 vol. 1, para. 2.29) does not agree, the suggestion being that the usual order will be for 'reasonable contact'.

The following consequences of a contact order will concern social workers particularly.

(*i*)   A local authority may not apply for a contact order (s.9(2), nor may a court make a contact order in its favour. If a local authority were able to apply for contact order, it would not need to apply for a supervision order (s.31) and prove the minimum condition (s.31(2)) for it.

(*ii*)   If the child is subject to a care order, a contact order cannot be made. Contact with children in care is provided for in s.34 (see below): there is a statutory duty to allow reasonable contact. Where the child is accommodated under s.20 and a dispute arises over contact, a contact order may be sought.

(*iii*)   A care order discharges a s.8 contact order (s.91(2)).

(*iv*)   On the discharge of a care order, the court can make a contact order.

A prohibited steps order is an order 'that no step which could be taken by a parent in meeting his parental responsibility for a child, and which is of a kind specified in the order, shall be taken by any person without the consent of the court'. This order (and the specific issue order) is culled from the wardship jurisdiction. But, in wardship, there was a requirement that no 'important step' should be taken as regards the child without the court's approval, which was at best vague. Here a specific restriction is imposed on the exercise of parental responsibility. Examples are prohibiting a child's removal from the United Kingdom where there is no residence order and therefore no automatic restriction on removal; or preventing a child's removal from home pending a determination as to where he should live; or prohibiting a named person (perhaps a Schedule 1 offender) from coming into contact with the child. A prohibited steps order can be sought in conjunction with a residence (or contact) order, or on its own.

A prohibited steps order can be made against anyone but can only prohibit a 'step which could be taken by a parent in meeting his parental responsibility'. So, it cannot be used to prevent a child being molested (this would require an injunction)[15] or to restrict publicity about a child (the court's inherent jurisdiction may have to be invoked to achieve this),[16] because neither are within the scope of parental responsibility.

A prohibited steps order can be undermined by the child him or herself. For example, a father could obtain a prohibited steps order against the mother to stop the fifteen-year-old son going potholing. But this would not stop the boy himself pursuing this activity.

There are two important restrictions on prohibited steps orders (these also apply to the specific issue order). First, the court cannot make a prohibited steps order 'in any way which is denied to the High Court (by section 100(2)) in the exercise of its inherent jurisdiction with respect to children' (s.9(5)(b)). Section 100(2) relates to the restrictions on the use of inherent jurisdiction which the Act imposes on local authorities. As we shall see (below), an authority may not invoke the High Court's inherent jurisdiction without leave and this will only be granted where the result the authority is trying to achieve could not be achieved under the statutory scheme. These restrictions cannot be circumvented by applying for a prohibited steps order.

Secondly, the court cannot make a prohibited steps order (or specific issue order) 'with a view to achieving a result which could be achieved by making a residence or contact order' (s.9(5)(a)), for example as regards the location of the child's home.

As far as local authorities are concerned three further matters should be noted:

(*i*)   A prohibited steps order cannot be made with respect to a child who is in the care of a local authority (s.9(1)).

(*ii*) A prohibited steps order cannot be used to prevent a child's removal from accommodation provided under s.20, but it could be sought to prevent a parent visiting a child in a foster home or children's home (if the child was accommodated, but not if the child is in care).

(*iii*) If a care order is made, this discharges the prohibited steps order (s.91(2)).

A specific issue order is 'an order giving directions for the purpose of determining a specific question which has arisen, or which may arise, in connection with any aspect of parental responsibility for a child'. It is intended 'not to give one parent or the other a general "right" to make decisions about a particular aspect of the child's upbringing, for example his education or medical treatment, but rather to enable a particular dispute over such a matter to be resolved by the court, including the giving of detailed directions where necessary' (*Guidance and Regulations* (1991) vol. 1. para. 2.32). The directions could be that an appropriate third party takes the decision: for example, leaving treatment to a doctor[17] or the question of contact to a welfare officer.[18]

In private disputes wardship remains an available option. But it is intended that specific issue orders (and prohibited steps orders) will largely take its place, though for wardship leave will not be required whereas it is required for many section 8 applications. If it is thought that the case should be heard at a senior level, the case could be transferred up to the High Court.[19]

As far as local authorities are concerned, the same considerations apply as for prohibited steps orders. It is, however, possible that a local authority could ask a court to require a parent to take a child to a doctor.

Family proceedings

The four orders may be made in any 'family proceedings' in which a question arises with respect to the welfare of any child (s.10(1)). 'Family proceedings' is wide-ranging and embraces:

    (*i*)   proceedings under the inherent jurisdiction of the High Court in relation to children (though not proceedings on an application for leave by a local authority under s.100(3));

    (*ii*)   proceedings under s.4 (parental responsibility orders);

    (*iii*) proceedings under s.5 (guardianship);

    (*iv*) proceedings under part II of the Act, that is
          (a) free-standing applications for an order (s.10(1), (2))
          (b) applications for leave (s.10(2)(b))
          (c) by court of its own motion (s.10(1)(b))
          (d) applications for financial provision for children (Sch.1);

    (*v*)   proceedings under part IV of the Act, that is
          (a) care and supervision proceedings (s.31)
          (b) proceedings for contact with children in care (s.34)

(c) proceedings relating to education supervision orders (s.36);

(vi) proceedings under the Matrimonial Causes Act 1973
    (a) divorce, nullity and judicial separation
    (b) applications for financial relief following divorce or neglect to maintain;

(vii) proceedings under the Domestic Violence and Matrimonial Proceedings Act 1976
    (a) applications for non-molestation orders
    (b) applications for exclusion orders by cohabitants[20] (so that the court may determine where a child lives and what contact he is to have with the excluded person, even if that person is not the parent);

(viii) proceedings under the Adoption Act 1976
    (a) adoption proceedings
    (b) applications for freeing orders;

(ix) proceedings under the Domestic Proceedings and Magistrates' Courts Act 1978
    (a) proceedings for financial relief
    (b) proceedings for personal protection and exclusion orders;

(x) proceedings under sections 1 and 9 of the Matrimonial Homes Act 1983
    (a) proceedings for ouster and related orders;

(xi) proceedings under part III of the Matrimonial and Family Proceedings Act 1984
    (a) proceedings for financial relief after an overseas divorce.

The principal area excluded from 'family proceedings' is emergency protection under part V of the Act. Also excluded are secure accommodation proceedings under s.25 of the Act.

It will be observed that section 8 orders can be made both in proceedings which relate directly to children (wardship, adoption, care etc.) and in certain proceedings which are primarily concerned with disputes between adults but in which the interests of children may be very important, such as divorce and domestic violence.

The implications of any of the four orders being made in any family proceedings need to be grasped. A few examples will illustrate. In adoption proceedings the court will be able to make a residence order instead of an adoption order. Custodianship has been abolished. Under the old law courts were directed to have regard to the alternatives of custodianship or divorce court custody in the case of adoption applications by relatives and step-parents (Children Act 1975 s.37(1) and (2) and Adoption Act 1976 s.14(3) and s.15(4)). Although the court had to satisfy itself of the test in this legislation, the view emerged that the court should decide between adoption and the other alternatives in terms of what would be best for the child.[21] This is also the position taken in the Act. By bringing adoption proceedings within family proceedings, the court is empowered to make a s.8 order whenever it believes that it would be better for the child than an adoption order. But the statutory directives (the meaning of which was disputed) have been removed, so that the courts are not encouraged to think in any particular way. A second example, also drawn from adoption, is the possibility of making an adoption order together with a contact order, as an alternative to attaching contact as a term or condition to the adoption order.[22] With more open-ended adoption (Rushton, 1988; Ryburn, 1990; Hall, 1991, Mullender, 1991) this strategy is bound to appeal. A contact order, could also be made in conjunction with a freeing order. The use of section 8 orders in the domestic violence context is also worth investigating. On an application for an ouster order, the court could make a residence order which, by settling the living arrangements of the children, would in effect determine where the other parent should live. This would have the advantage over an ouster order of (i) being governed by the paramountcy principle (s.1(1)),[23] (ii) not having any time restriction (ouster orders may be 'until further order'[24] but usually last for up to three months in the first instance; and (iii) where the applicant is not married to the respondent not having to satisfy the 'living together as husband and wife in the same household' test (Domestic Violence and Matrimonial Proceedings Act 1976 s.1(2)). This is a particular advantage in situations where there is a relationship but no household as such.[25] The principal disadvantage is that a power of arrest cannot be attached to a residence order.

Who can apply?

The rules as to who can apply for a section 8 order are complex. They are set out in section 10. There are a number of categories.

    (*i*)   Those with an automatic right to apply for any Section 8 order:

(a) Parent (including the unmarried father) and guardian (s.10(4)(a));
(b) Any person in whose favour a residence order (or custody order made before the Act came into operation) is in force (s.10(4)(b)).

(ii) Those with an automatic right to apply for a residence or contact order:
(a) Any party to a marriage (subsisting or not) in relation to whom the child is a child of the family (s.10(5)(a));
(b) Any person with whom the child has lived for a period of at least three years (s.10(5)(b));
(c) Any person who (i) where a residence order is in force with respect to the child has consent of each of the persons in whose favour the order was made; (ii) where the child is in the care of the local authority has the consent of that authority; or (iii) in any other case has the consent of each of those (if any) who have parental responsibility for the child (s.10(5)(c)).

Group (a) consists mainly of step-parents. The definition of 'child of the family' adopts that in the Domestic Proceedings and Magistrates' Courts Act 1978 s.88(1) (rather than that in s.52(1) of the Matrimonial Causes Act 1973), so that children formerly privately fostered are included. Groups (b) and (c) are broadly those who, under the previous law, were eligible to apply for custodianship. But the law and the procedure have been simplified. People who have the consent of those whose rights will be affected if any order is made can apply whether or not the child is currently living with them. Those who do not have the consent must have had the child living with them for a total of three years. This period need not be continuous but must not have begun more than five years before, or ended more than three months before, the making of the application (s.10(10)). There is no longer any provision (cf. Children Act 1975 sections 41 and 42) prohibiting the removal of a child who has been with the applicants for three years: if a child is removed against the applicant's wishes s/he has three months to make an application. The procedure has been simplified too: the local authority is no longer required to investigate and report to the court in every case. A welfare report may be called for from a probation officer or the local authority if the court thinks it will be helped by one (s.7).

(iii)   Those with an automatic right to apply to vary or discharge a s.8 order.

Any person (not within categories (i) or (ii)) is entitled to apply for variation or discharge of a s.8 order if either the order was made on his or her application or, in the case of a contact order, s/he is named in the order (s.10(6)).

(iv)   Those who have obtained the leave of the court (s.10(2)(b)).

This enables anyone with a genuine interest in the child's welfare to apply for any s.8 order with the leave of the court. The child him or herself can apply for leave, which may be granted if the court is satisfied that s/he has sufficient understanding to make the proposed application (s.10(8)). It is possible that a child refused leave could make him or herself a ward of court.[26]

Where the applicant is not the child concerned, the court must have regard to a number of factors in deciding whether to grant leave: the nature of the proposed application, any risk of the proposed application disrupting the child's life to such an extent that s/he would be harmed by it; and, where the child is being looked after by a local authority, the authority's plans for the child's future and the wishes and feelings of the child's parents (s.10(9)).

(v)   Local authority foster parents will *in addition* require the consent of the local authority.

A local authority foster parent cannot apply for leave to make an application for a s.8 order with respect to a child s/he has fostered at any time within the last six months without the consent of the local authority (s.9(3)), unless s/he is a relative of the child (defined as grandparent, brother, sister, uncle or aunt or step-parent (s.105(1))) or the child has lived with him or her for at least three years preceding the application.

This restriction only applies to local authority foster parents, and not, therefore, to private foster parents. The justification for this is to preserve confidence in the voluntary child care system: if foster parents were able to apply for residence orders without these restrictions, parents might be reluctant to enter into voluntary arrangements with local authorities. It might also frustrate local authorities in their efforts to make plans for children if premature applications from short-term foster parents were permissible. Different considerations, however, apply where the foster parents are also relatives. They will need leave from the court, but not the consent of the local authority.

Grandparents and section 8 orders

The position of grandparents has attracted a lot of attention (Douglas and Lowe, 1990). Under the previous law they could apply for access in certain circumstances under the Domestic Proceedings and Magistrates' Courts Act 1978 and the Guardianship of Minors Act 1971 but their rights were contingent on other proceedings having been taken. Now for the first time they can make free-standing applications. However, before the Act they did not require leave, which is now a precondition. They are thus both better off and worse off as a result of the Act. The Law Commission (1988, para. 4.41) thought the requirement of leave would 'scarcely be a hurdle at all to close relatives such as grandparents... who wish to care for or visit a child'. Lord Mackay however distinguished between cases where there is a 'close bond' in which leave will be a 'formality' and other cases where a grandparent's intervention might be less than 'benign, even if well-intentioned' (*Hansard* HL vol. 503, col. 1342). There is power under s.10(7) to add to the category of persons who may apply for orders as of right. The leave requirement for grandparents could, therefore, be dropped if it was thought to be causing unnecessary problems. Grandparents formerly used wardship as well[27] and they can continue to do so. But it is clearly intended that they will use the lower courts and apply for leave for s.8 orders. If the leave requirement becomes burdensome (if, for example, leave becomes difficult to obtain), it may be expected that there will be wardship applications. For this reason (if for no other), it is not expected that leave in the genuine case will constitute an impediment of any weight.

The child

The court is empowered (s.10(1) in 'family proceedings') (see above) to make a section 8 order in respect of 'any child', that is a person under the age of eighteen (s.105(1)). The court's powers are not limited to 'children of the family'. Nor are they limited to the biological children of the parties. But a s.8 order is not to be made in respect of a child who has attained the age of 18, nor should any order be expressed to have effect beyond a child's sixteenth birthday, unless the court is satisfied that the 'circumstances of the case are exceptional' (s.9(6), (7)). Orders not expressed to extend beyond the child's sixteenth birthday automatically end when s/he reaches the age of sixteen (s.91(10)). Where a direction is made, the order will cease to have effect when the child reaches the age of sixteen (s.91(11)). An example of exceptional circumstances might be where the child is mentally handicapped.

As already noted, a child can apply for a s.8 order with leave but the court must be satisfied that s/he has sufficient understanding to make the proposed application. Of course, the child may be seeking a s.8 order just because no one else is sufficiently interested in his or her welfare to take any steps to protect him or her. If the court then refuses leave, in effect it abdicates responsibility for the child. It may be that the very children who apply for leave will be those 'most in need of protection because they are immature, mentally retarded or otherwise vulnerable' (Bainham, 1990, p.49) – the very children who may lack the understanding to make the application. The insistence on *Gillick* competence may thus achieve a sort of catch-22 situation, with the children most in need of the court's protection not being in a position to apply for it.

When orders should be made

The court should not make any of the s.8 orders 'unless it considers that doing so would be better for the child than making no order at all' (s.1(5)).

When will it be better? If there is a dispute between parents, it is likely to be better for the child for the court to make an order (*Guidance and Regulations*, vol. 1, 1991, para. 2.56). Where there is no dispute, 'the child's need for stability and security may be best served by making an order' (*idem*). There are also situations where legal advantages may attach to an order. If there is fear that the child might be abducted, a court order is necessary for enforcement proceedings. But whether a residence order which confers parental responsibility gives 'rights of custody' (required for enforcement under the European Convention[28] and under the Hague Convention)[29] is debatable. Despite assurances of the Lord Chancellor (reported in *The Times*, 7 October 1991), I do not believe that it does. This could cause problems to an unmarried father or a relative wishing to enforce a residence order abroad.

The welfare principle in s.1(1) (discussed above) applies wherever a court is considering whether to make a s.8 order. It applies also when the question of a s.8 order arises in the context of other proceedings, for example adoption, where normally the child's welfare would not be paramount. In contested s.8 applications (and in applications for variation or discharge of s.8 orders), the court has to have regard to the checklist set out in s.1(3) (see above). The checklist does not apply to all family proceedings: a court therefore would not have to have regard to the checklist if the question of a residence order arose in ouster proceedings or a contact order in adoption proceedings (to use two examples from above). The 'general principle that any delay in determining the question is likely to prejudice the welfare of the child' (s.1(2), and see above) must also be borne in mind by the court.

Timetabling and directions

The court is required to draw up a timetable for s.8 proceedings and give such directions as it considers appropriate for the purpose of ensuring, so far as is reasonably practicable, that the timetable is adhered to (s.11(1)). By Rule 14 of the Family Proceedings Rules 1991 the timetable may be drawn up by magistrates, the court clerk, the judge or district judge, all or any of whom may give, vary or revoke the timetabling details at a directions hearing. The Rules circumscribe the provision in s.11: for example, Rule 9 requires that within 14 days of service of s.8 applications, each respondent shall file at the court an answer, and serve that answer on each other respondent and on the applicant. Whilst the answer does not appear to require a full statement of the respondent's case, it does clearly require more than merely an indication as to whether the application is to be opposed or not.

The Lord Chancellor has said that timetables should be 'realistic and take account of circumstances, otherwise it simply will not be adhered to '(*Hansard*, HL vol. 503, col.1347). They are, of course, enforceable as contempt, by a costs penalty and by the magistrates under the Magistrates' Courts Act (s.63).

The family assistance order

The new family assistance order is a way of providing short-term help to a family to overcome the problems and conflicts associated with their separation or divorce. According to the *Guidance and*

Regulations (vol. 1, 1991, para. 2.50), help may well be focused more on the adults than the child.

It must be distinguished from a supervision order under s.31 which is designed for more serious cases. The minimum conditions in s.31 must be satisfied before a supervision order can be made. Supervision orders will be sought where child protection rather than family assistance is called for, and where access to the local authority's services and facilities is needed.

The family assistance order (together with the supervision order) replace the courts' power to make a supervision order in private law proceedings including in wardship. Though intended mainly for private law proceedings, it can also be made in care proceedings and with a care order. The order will require a probation officer to be made available, or a local authority to make an officer of the authority available, to 'advise, assist and (where appropriate) befriend any person named in the order' (s.16(1)). The persons who may be named in the order are:

(a) any parent or guardian of the child;
(b) any person with whom the child is living or in whose favour a contact order is in force with respect to the child;
(c) the child him or herself (s.16(2)).

There are two restrictions on the making of a family assistance order. The court must be satisfied that the circumstances of the case are exceptional. It should therefore not be made as a matter of routine. There is, however, a big gap between the exceptional and the routine, and many cases in between where help would be of genuine assistance. Whether family assistance orders are made in these cases will depend on how broadly 'exceptional' can be interpreted, as well as on how the courts see their role and, crucially, on resources. The second restriction is that an order may only be made with the consent of every person to be named in the order except the child. This emphasises the voluntary nature of assistance. But excepting the child from this is not easy to understand in cases where s/he could be said to be *Gillick*-competent.

A further limitation is that no order can have effect for more than six months (s.16(5)), though there is no restriction on further orders.

The order may place obligation on the persons named in it to keep in touch with the welfare officer. It may also require any of the persons named to take specified steps with a view to enabling the officer concerned to be kept informed of the address of any person named in the order, and to be allowed to visit any such person (s.16(4)).

The order may only be made by the court acting of its own motion. It must be better for the child than no order (s.1(5)) and satisfy the welfare principle in s.1(1). It can only require a local authority to make an officer available with the authority's consent, or if the child lives or will live within the authority's area (s.16(7)). Where an order requires a probation officer to be made available, s/he shall be selected in accordance with the arrangements made by the probation committee for the area in which the child lives or will live (s.16(8)). There is no guidance as to which officer should be appointed. The Law Commission (1988, para. 5.19) suggested that, in private law proceedings, the welfare officer who has compiled the welfare report for the court is the most appropriate person to appoint. In care proceedings, it is more likely to be the social worker attached to the case. It cannot be the guardian ad litem (who is neither a probation officer nor an officer of the local authority). It is important that the court makes it clear why family assistance is needed and what it is hoped it will achieve. This may clarify the role the officer is expected to play (and see Law Commission, 1988, para. 5.20).

When both a family assistance order and a s.8 order are in force at the same time with respect to a child, the officer may refer to the court the question whether the s.8 order should be varied or discharged (s.16(6)).

It is difficult to predict how often family assistance orders will be made and how effective they will be. Sceptics may wonder how often the consent of all named persons will be obtained, but there are clearly cases where the short-term help of a family assistance order will be welcomed (for example, by a mother whose child has been sexually abused by the father who is now out of the home or by a parent having difficulty coping with a contact order that she believes is not in the child's best interests).

Section 37 directions

Although s.37 directions are to be found in part IV of the Act, they are essentially part of the private law provisions of the Act and are best considered here. Section 37 states:

'Where in any family proceedings in which a question arises with respect to the welfare of any child, it appears to the court that it may be appropriate for a care or supervision order to be made with respect to him, the court may direct the appropriate authority to undertake an investigation of the child's circumstances.'

The authority must comply with the direction. It must also specifically investigate whether it should:

(*i*)   apply for a care or supervision order;
(*ii*)   provide services or assistance for the child or his or her family;
(*iii*) take any other action with respect to the child (s.37(2))

It must do so within eight weeks unless the court otherwise directs (s.37(4)). The short timescale is consistent with other provisions in the Act (s.1(2), s.11(1), s.38(4)). The authority will have to consider whether compulsory intervention is necessary (is the child likely to suffer significant harm?) or whether the child's welfare can be adequately protected by other means (the provision of services including accommodation). If the authority is of the view that an order should not be sought, the court can do nothing even if it disagrees. The court cannot act of its own motion: the local authority is the final arbiter of whether care or supervision proceedings should be brought. But if the local authority decides not to bring care or supervision proceedings, it must inform the court of the reasons for its decision, of any service or assistance it has provided or intends to provide for the child and his family and any other action which it has taken or proposes to take in relation to the child (s.37(3)).

Whilst the investigation is taking place, the court may make an interim care or supervision order (see s.38(1)(b) and below).

Notes

1. See *Dipper* v. *Dipper* [1981] Fam. 31.
2. *Riley* v. *Riley* [1986] 2 FLR 429.
3. Said recently to be 'in general, quite inappropriate' (*J* v. *J* [1991] 2 FLR 385).

4. *M* v. *M* [1973] 2 All ER 81.
5. *Re S* [1990] 2 FLR 166; *Re H* [1992] 1 FLR 148.
6. *H* v. *H* [1989] 1 FLR 212; *L* v. *L* [1989] 2 FLR 16; *Re H* [1989] 2 FLR 174.
7. *Re M, The Times* 22 February 1990 (also *Childright* No. 65, p. 21).
8. *Re S* [1990] 2 FLR 166.
9. *Corkett* v. *Corkett* [1985] FLR 708. *Cf S* v. *S* [1988] 1 FLR 213, where there was sexual abuse of one and access was denied to all three.
10. For example see *Re N* [1974] Fam 40 (dispute with putative father); *Re W* [1985] AC 791 (dispute with local authority).
11. *I* v. *D* [1988] 2 FLR 286.
12. *V-P* v. *V-P* [1978] 1 FLR 336. Cf. *Re N* [1992] 1 FLR 134.
13. *C* v. *C* [1990] 1 FLR 462, 469 ('a weapon of last resort').
14. See *Allette* v. *Allette* [1986] 2 FLR 427.
15. Domestic Violence and Matrimonial Proceedings Act 1976.
16. *Re L* [1988] 1 All ER 418. But it may not be stopped (*Re X* [1975] 1 All ER 697; *Re M and N* [1990] 1 All ER 205; *Re W* [1992] 1 All ER 794).
17. *Re C* [1990] 1 FLR 252.
18. This practice was disapproved of under the previous law: *Orford* v. *Orford* [1979] 1 FLR 260.
19. Under the Children (Allocation of Proceedings) Order 1991.
20. A spouse has to use the Matrimonial Homes Act 1983 (*Richards* v. *Richards* [1984] AC 174.)
21. *Re D* [1981] 2 FLR 102; *Re S* [1987] Fam. 98.
22. *Re C* [1989] AC 1; *Re J* [1973] Fam 106; *Re S* [1976] Fam 1. An interesting comparison is *Re R* [1991] 2 FLR 78.
23. In ouster applications the child's welfare is only one consideration (*Richards* v. *Richards* [1984] AC 174.
24. *Galan* v. *Galan* [1985] FLR 905.
25. *Tuck* v. *Nicholls* [1989] 1 FLR 283; *Harrison* v. *Lewis* [1988] 2 FLR 339.
26. The application should be made through a 'next friend' (normally a parent) Bevan (1989, para. 8.13) suggests the Children's Legal Centre, where the parent would be inappropriate.
27. A good illustration of their problems is *Re L* [1991] FLR 14. Its sequel (*Re L (No 2)* [1991] 1 FLR 29) demonstrates one judge's willingness, even before the Act was implemented, to stress the importance of the natural family over adoption.
28. See part II of the Child Abduction and Custody Act 1985.
29. See part I of the Child Abduction and Custody Act 1985.

References

Bainham, A. (1990) *Children – The New Law*, Bristol, Family Law.
Bevan, H. (1989) *Child Law*, London, Butterworths.

Department of Health (1991) *The Children Act 1989: Guidance and Regulations, vol. 1, Court Orders*, London, HMSO.

Douglas, G. and Lowe, N. (1990) 'Grandparents and the Legal Process', *Journal of Social Welfare Law*, 89.

Groner, J. (1991) *Hilary's Trial*, New York, Simon and Schuster.

Hall, G. (1991) 'Adoption and Contact with Birth Families', *Adoption and Fostering*, 15(3), 40.

Law Commission (1988) *Guardianship and Custody*, Law Com. No. 172, London, HMSO.

Maidment, S. (1975) 'Access Conditions in Custody Orders', *British Journal of Law and Society*, 2, 182.

Mullender, A. (1991) *Open Adoption*, London, BAAF.

Priest, J. and Whybrow, J. (1986) Supplement to the Law Commission Working Paper No.96, London, HMSO.

Roman, M. and Haddad, W. (1979) *The Disposable Parent*, New York, Holt, Rinehart.

Rushton, T. (1988) *New Parents for Older Children*, London, BAAF, 1988.

Ryburn, M. (1990) 'Openness in Adoption', *Adoption and Fostering*, 14(1), 21.

Wallerstein, J. and Kelly, J. (1980) *Surviving the Breakup*, New York, Basic Books.

Woolley, P. (1978) 'Shared Custody', *Family Advocate*, 1, 6.

4

Family Support

This chapter is about Part III of the Act and the accompanying Schedule 2. It is that part of the Act which is most difficult to implement. But, if the Children Act is to be a success, it is the part to which most sustained attention must be given.

Section 17 gives local authorities a general duty to safeguard and promote the welfare of children in need, and to promote the upbringing of such children by their families, so far as this is consistent with their welfare duty to the child, by providing an appropriate range and level of services. These services include day care provision (s.18) and accommodation for children in need who require it (s.20). The latter replaces 'reception into care' (or 'voluntary' care) with its overtones of parental failure.

Schedule 2 contains a multiplicity of provisions designed to assist children in need to continue to live with their families. The intention is, wherever possible, to prevent the breakdown of family relationships. The guiding principle is partnership with parents. Wherever possible children too are to be consulted. The parents' parental responsibility is to be taken seriously, not undermined. A similar approach is to be adopted also when a child is in care, so long as his or her welfare is not jeopardised.

Values

In the belief that the implementation of this part of the Act will be improved if we understand the values which inform it, it is worth pausing momentarily to consider what these are. They are conveniently summarised by the In Need Implementation Group (1991), a collective of individuals from local authorities, voluntary organisations and the universities. They suggest that the following principles indicate wider values which should underpin work with children and their families (not just under the Act).

Universalism. We all use and need services, whether we are managing to lead relatively 'normal' lives or we are in crisis and under stress. Families of children in need have full rights to the wide range and diversity of universalist provisions (health, social security, employment, housing, education, leisure) as well as those more specialist services to help them over particular difficulties.

Equality and Equity of Access to Services. Everyone in our community has rights to accessible family support services; parents requesting help should not be stigmatised and their access to a wide range of services must be facilitated.

The Normality of Difficulties in Parenting. Services should support and supplement families' endeavours, especially when parenting difficulties are compounded by poverty and deprivation.

Participation. Parents usually know what their needs are and their views should be taken seriously.

These values must be visible in the day-to-day services provided by local authorities and not just by its social services departments. There are opportunities for the development of partnerships with voluntary child-care organisations: many of the latter may be especially responsive to ethnic or cultural dimensions of local need (MacDonald, 1991). There are also opportunities for creative thinking, for breaking down barriers in traditional practices, for budgetary innovation. There must be a commitment to assess need, including unmet need, and to publicise services. This 'should be viewed as a service in itself which empowers potential service users.... Information policies need to ask themselves "If I were a stranger here, how long would it take me to find out what is on offer for my child's needs?"' (In Need Implementation Group, 1991, p.20). Another key element is accountability. The Act provides for a representations and complaints procedure with an independent element (s.26(3)), but to feel confident about its accountability a local authority has to go beyond establishing such statutory mechanisms. It must have in place a system for monitoring, evaluating and promoting service quality.

Children in need

Children 'in need' is defined by statute for the first time. There was concern that this would stigmatise but, if policies of identification and service provision are informed by the values just articulated, this should not be a problem.

Section 17(10) defines 'children in need' thus:

'For the purposes of this Part a child shall be taken to be in need if:

(a) he is unlikely to achieve or maintain, or to have the opportunity of achieving or maintaining, a reasonable standard of health or development without the provision for him of services by a local authority under this Part;

(b) his health or development is likely to be significantly impaired, or further impaired, without the provision for him of such services; or

(c) he is disabled,

and "family", in relation to such a child, includes any person who has parental responsibility for the child and any other person with whom he has been living.'

The following sub-section (s.17(11)) defines, for the purposes of the Act, 'disabled' as 'blind, deaf or dumb' or suffering 'from mental disorder of any kind' or 'substantially and permanently handicapped by illness, injury or congenital deformity or any such disability as may be prescribed'. It also explains that, in this part of the Act, 'development' means 'physical, intellectual, emotional, social or behavioural development' and 'health' means 'physical or mental health'.

The definition of 'need' is wide: a clear indication of the emphasis of the Act on preventive support and services for families. Contrast the Child Care Act 1980 (s.1) where prevention concentrated on the negative (keeping children out of care rather than promoting their welfare). On the other hand, under the Act the duty is owed to restricted group of children. This, it has been rightly said, 'constitutes the new ideology of residualism' and will 'provide a challenge for good practices in child care' (Hardiker *et al.*, 1991, p. 357). There are three categories of need:

(*i*) for a reasonable standard of health and development;

(*ii*) not to have that health or development significantly impaired;

(*iii*) for support where disabled.

With resource deficiencies it is tempting to redefine 'need' or interpret it restrictively (Barber 1990). One way of restricting eligibility for services is to equate 'children in need' with 'children at risk'. Not only does this reduce numbers, but, by deterring and stigmatising, it reduces demand. The Department of Health, in a circular issued on January 17, 1991 (see White, 1991), informed local authorities that the practice is unlawful (see also *Guidance and Regulations*, vol. 2, 1991, para. 2.4). The Act is clear that children potentially at risk are not to be considered separately from children in need: note 'Every local authority shall take reasonable steps, through the provision of services under Part III of this Act, to prevent children within their area suffering ill-treatment or neglect' (Sch. 2, para. 4(1)). Inevitably, local authorities will set priorities. It cannot be said that this is desirable, but it is inevitable and it is not unlawful. But it must be clear that, though there are priorities (for example for children at risk), all children 'in need', as defined by the Act, are within the purview of the authority's preventive strategies. Should this not be done, the possibility of a successful application for judicial review cannot be discounted (and see below).

The child's needs include physical, emotional, social and educational needs and will depend on his or her age, sex, religion, culture and race and on the capacity of his or her parents (or other carer) to meet those needs. The Department of Health's *Guidance and Regulations* resists laying down firm criteria or setting priorities because 'the Act requires each authority to decide their own level and scale of services appropriate to the children in need in their area' (vol. 2, 1991, para. 2.4). The parents' incapacity to meet the child's needs may be because the parent is ill, temporarily or chronically, or him or herself disabled. The different ways of addressing this problem should be sensitively considered. Providing accommodation is an easy solution, but not necessarily the best one: support services in the home may be a better form of provision. The *Guidance and Regulations* direct (vol.2, para. 2.5) that 'children should not necessarily be identified as in need because one or both parents are disabled'. Clearly, ways of keeping the child at home should be considered by providing services under the Chronically Sick and Disabled Persons Act 1970 or under s.17(3) of this Act.

Section 17(3) provides that 'any service provided by an authority in the exercise of functions conferred on them by this section may be provided for the family of a particular child in need or for any member of his family, if it is provided with a view to safeguarding or promoting the child's welfare'. Family is defined (s.17(10)) to include 'any person with parental responsibility for the child and any other person with whom he has been living'. This could include a relative or a private foster parent. An unmarried step-parent could be regarded as a member of the child's family.[1] Services could thus be provided for a variety of persons in order to safeguard or promote a child's welfare: for example, home help or day care provision. Of course, there would be evaluation subsequently to determine whether it had met its objective.

Meeting needs

Section 17 and part 1 of Schedule 2 set out in considerable detail the duties, qualified duties and powers of local authorities in relation to support services for children with families. Under s.17(1) there is a general duty to provide a range and level of services appropriate to the children in their area who are 'in need' so as to safeguard and promote their welfare and, so far as is consistent with that aim, to promote their upbringing by their families.

Local authorities cannot be expected to meet every individual need, but they are to take 'reasonable steps' to identify the extent of need in their area and then to use their discretion reasonably and sensibly to make decisions about service provision in the light of the information they receive and their statutory obligations. They must ensure that a range of services is available to meet the need they identify. What is required will vary from area to area but is likely to include day care, foster care, some provision of residential care. They will need to offer a range of placements to reflect the racial, cultural, religious and linguistic needs of the children of their area (s.22(5)(c)). They will also have to have a range of short-term and longer term accommodation as well as permanent placements.

There are some absolute duties (see below) but most are qualified. Thus, for example, the local authority is to take 'reason-able' steps.... The local authority is to make such provisions 'as they consider appropriate'. The local authority is to offer an 'appropriate' range and level of services. There are, it can clearly be seen, a number of 'designer loopholes' (Gardner, 1990). The duties include the identification of the extent of need (Sch 2, para. 1), to prevent children suffering neglect and abuse (para. 4); to provide specific services including advice, activities, home helps including laundry facilities, assistance with travel, holidays (para. 8); family centres (para. 9); and, where the child is not living with his family, assistance to enable him or her to live with or be in contact with them (para. 10).

The duties to disabled children which derive from the National Assistance Act 1948 and the Chronically Sick and Disabled Persons Act 1970 are absolute. Local authorities must open and maintain a register of disabled children (para. 2) and provide services for them to minimise the effect on them of their disabilities and to give them the opportunity to lead as normal lives as possible (para. 6). Local authorities are also required to provide information to other authorities about children likely to suffer harm (para. 4(2)), and to take reasonable steps to reduce the need to bring various proceedings (including criminal proceedings) or take other steps in relation to children (para. 7). They are also (unbelievably) to take reasonable steps 'to encourage children within their area not to commit criminal offences' (para. 7(b)). In providing day care and in encouraging people to act as foster parents, local authorities are to have regard to the different racial groups to which children within their area who are in need belong (para. 11).

There is also a power to assist alleged abusers to obtain alternative accommodation (para. 5(1)). Such assistance may be in cash (para. 5(2)) and may be recouped, unless the recipient is in receipt of income support or family credit (s.17(9)).

Local authorities are also expected to act as facilitators of provision of the services covered by section 17, section 18 (day care), section 20 (accommodation), section 23 (accommodation and maintenance) and section 24 (advice and assistance to young persons under 21 by way of 'after-care'), as well as being the primary providers themselves (s.17(5)). These services must be publicised (para. 1(2)(a)(i)) and, where the authority considers it appropriate to do so, information is also to be published about the service provision by others including voluntary organisations (para. 1(2)(a)(ii)) Such steps 'as are reasonably practicable' must also be taken to ensure that those who might benefit from such services receive the information relevant to them (para. 2(b)). This clearly requires a proactive response with attention being paid also to the language problems of ethnic minorities. It will be important to monitor and evaluate services in order to be clear about which do actually promote the welfare of children in need and their families.

Studies (Packman *et al.*, 1986; Creighton, 1985) have suggested that families experiencing serious child care problems are distinguishable from other families along a number of dimensions, notably: social disadvantage and deprivation; personal vulnerability; and lack of social support. There is little evidence on how successful social services are in addressing these malaises. In one recent study (Gibbons, 1991), indicators of family needs, services received and outcomes were used to examine whether services were matched to needs and whether they had any effect on family problems in the short-term. This indicated that social workers are identifying most of those with the 'greatest (measured) needs at the time of referral and picking them out to receive help' (pp. 221–2) but not distinguishing between families in lower priority groups. The study also stressed that there was a close relationship between the provision of day care (for example, playgroup provision) and good outcomes. There was only a small majority (51 per cent) of parents who felt their problems had lessened as a result of social work intervention. The finding as to day care is significant in the light of the Act's new emphasis upon it. But the finding that social workers are having difficulty distinguishing cases of moderate and low priority may be of concern.

Assistance in cash

Assistance to families by way of cash payments can be traced to practice in the 1950s (Packman, 1981). The practice was legitimated in the Children and Young Persons Act 1963 s.1, and became known, as a result, as 'Section 1 money'. Although there is criticism of the practice, both its ethics and its utility (Heywood and Allen, 1971; Handler, 1973; Jackson and Valencia, 1979; Hill and Laing, 1979; see also Freeman, 1980), there has been no attempt to do away with it in the 1989 legislation.

But the new provision (will it be called 's.17 money'?) is different in a number of ways from the previous one. The new power (in s.17(6)) is part of the provision of support services and therefore must be seen in the same positive way as the remainder of the support package. No longer is it linked to keeping children out of care or away from juvenile courts. Nor should it be associated with parental shortcoming or attract stigma, as it may have done in the past. These are all changes for the better. One that may be considered in a less favourable light is that (see s.17(7)) laying down that assistance (and not just cash assistance) may be made subject to conditions including repayment. No person is to be liable to make any repayment of assistance or its value at any time when s/he is in receipt of income support or family credit (s.17(9)). Nevertheless, consonant with the ideology of the social fund and that expressed in the Health and Social Services and Social Security Adjudication Act 1983 (s.17), cash and other assistance is seen more as a loan, as something that should be paid for in appropriate circumstances. However, where the authority is satisfied that a person's means are insufficient for it to be 'reasonably practicable' for him/her to pay a charge for service, it should not require the payment of more than that person can reasonably be expected to pay (s.29(2)).

Cash assistance may only be paid in 'exceptional circumstances'. There is no guidance in the Act or in the case law as to what this means. As Masson (1990, p. 40) states: 'there are two possible interpretations: a restrictive one which requires the circumstances to be exceptional in the life of the individual recipient and another which requires them to be exceptional in the community'. In the past the latter, more liberal interpretation has prevailed in practice. There is no reason why it should not continue to do so.

It is clear from the case law[2] that 'assistance in kind' may include the provision of accommodation. The case from which this ruling comes offers insight also into the interface between child care and homelessness legislation. As the judge put it:

> 'in every case where there is a family without a home for whatever reason, the local authority is obliged to consider whether the welfare of the child requires that some attempt be made to keep the family together. The local authority should on each occasion ask, should this child be taken from its homeless parents and received into care, or does his welfare require that, if some accommodation can be found for his family, that he remain with his parents.'[3]

The case is also the clearest of denunciations that 'blanket' policies which fetter discretion are unlawful.

Section 1 payments were disregarded for the purpose of calculating means-tested social security payments and Housing benefit. It has been stated by the Lord Chancellor that this disregard will apply to the provision in the 1989 Act too (*Hansard*, HL vol. 502, col. 1298).

Children with disabilities

'A child is disabled if he is blind, deaf or dumb or suffers from mental disorder of any kind or is substantially and permanently handicapped by illness, injury or congenital deformity or such other disability as may be prescribed' (s.17(11)). This definition is very similar to that used for adults under the National Assistance Act 1948 (s.29(1)). The same people should thus qualify for services before and after the age of eighteen. It covers children affected by physical disability, chronic sickness, mental disability, sensory disability, communication impairment and mental illness. It is, however, surely somewhat unfortunate that the word 'dumb' should occur in legislation drafted at the end of the twentieth century.

The Act places a 'clear, positive and separate' (*Guidance and Regulations*, 1991, vol. 2 para. 2.18) duty on local authorities to provide services for children with disabilities in their area so as to minimise the effect of their disabilities and give such children the opportunity to lead lives which are as normal as possible (Sch. 2, para. 6). It is intended that these services should assist in the identification, diagnosis, assessment and treatment of children with handicaps (mental and physical) or mental disorder, in helping these children adjust and in overcoming their limitations (in communication, mobility etc.) in appropriate ways.

The *Guidance and Regulations* devotes a whole volume (vol. 6) to *Children with Disabilities* (1991). The following, which appears in the volume (para. 3.5) should be borne in mind:

'In deciding which services are needed by individual families, SSDs will need to give careful attention not only to families' stated preferences but to the contribution which other statutory and voluntary agencies might make. Co-ordinating packages of services from multiple service providers will require time and resources and the compatibility of services offered should be carefully assessed. Individual children and families will have very different levels of need which may fluctuate throughout the year according to other pressures of family life. The provision of education, respite care and day care will not be effective unless they are tailored to the needs of the child and family. Arrangements must be such that parents are reassured that the child will receive good quality care and that the child's interests are met. In some instances provision of a discrete service (e.g. aids and adaptations to a house or transport in order to use a local after school club) may assist the child and his family to lead fulfilling lives without other service provision.'

There is a duty on local authorities to maintain a register of disabled children (Sch. 2, para. 2). There is no corresponding duty on parents to agree to registration. It is voluntary for them to do so. Services must not be dependent on registration. The *Guidance and Regulations* (vol. 2, para. 2.19), however, stresses that local authorities, in collaboration with health authorities, local education authorities and voluntary agencies 'need to publicise widely and positively the existence and purpose of registers to relevant professionals, parents and young people' and stress the usefulness of the register as an aid to planning services to help parents with children with disabilities, and in the long-term to assist those children when they become adults to take advantage of resources and benefits (e.g. tax relief if registered blind, assistance with text telephones if registered deaf).

Under Schedule 2, paragraph 3, local authorities have the power to arrange for any assessment of a child with a disability, because s/he may be in need, to be combined with an assessment under the Chronically Sick and Disabled Persons Act 1970, the Education Act 1981, the Disabled Persons (Services, Consultation and Representation) Act 1986, or any other enactment. It is thus possible to arrange a unitary assessment for the several different services, where this is appropriate and in the child's best interests. This will avoid duplication of assessment procedures and provide an opportunity for effective co-ordination.

Although the only provisions in Schedule 2 directly relating to disabled children are paragraphs 2 and 6, it must be stressed that the new emphasis on integration of services means that local authorities must offer children with disabilities the benefit of those powers and duties which they have in respect of all children in need. In particular, the provisions applying to children being looked after by the local authority apply equally to children with disabilities. So requirements such as having to review the case of a child who has been living away from home, having to give paramount consideration to his or her welfare and to consult him or her and the parents before decisions are taken, apply to children with disabilities as to other children. In addition the special provisions that applied with disabilities before the implementation of the Children Act also apply.

Discussion of the subject of the relationship between these other provisions and the Act, and fuller treatment of the impact of the Act on disabled children should be sought in specialised publications. In particular the sixth volume of *Guidance and Regulations* (1991) is recommended, as are Lyon (1991), Shaw *et al.* (1990) and Sinclair (1991). The *Guidance and Regulations*, volume 6, also has a very full bibliography (see pp. 60–6).

Children living with their families

Schedule 2, paragraph 8 requires local authorities to make such provision 'as they consider appropriate' for the following services to be made available with respect to children in need in their area 'while they are living with their families' *viz.*

(a) advice, guidance and counselling;
(b) occupational, social, cultural or recreational activities;
(c) home help (which may include laundry facilities);
(d) facilities for, or assistance with, travelling to and from home for the purpose of taking advantage of any other service provided under this Act or of any similar service;
(e) assistance to enable the child concerned and his/her family to have a holiday.

The *Guidance and Regulations* (vol. 2, para. 2.23) stresses that it is important to have regard to this general duty when planning a service for an individual child.

Enforcing the local authority's duties

It has been seen that local authorities have a large number of duties imposed upon them by Part III of the Act (and further examples follow in later sections of this chapter). Can an aggrieved parent (or other interested person) enforce these duties? Are there remedies for breaches of the duties? Is there any redress when a person suffers harm as a result of a failure by a local authority to carry out any of its duties? These are important questions to which there are no definitive answers. But guidance may be sought in the attitudes and responses of the courts when confronted with these and similar questions under other cognate legislation.

The reluctance of the courts to interfere with the ways local authorities exercise their powers is demonstrated by the response of the House of Lords in *Puhlhofer* v. *Hillingdon London Borough Council*[4] (an application under homelessness legislation for accommodation by a couple with two young children living in one room of a guesthouse with no cooking or laundry facilities). Lord Brightman acknowledged that the plight of the homeless was desperate and commanded 'deepest sympathy'. But it was not, he said,

'appropriate that the remedy of judicial review, which is a discretionary remedy, should be made use of to monitor the actions of local authorities under the Act save in the exceptional case.'

He went on to express the hope that 'there will be a lessening in the number of challenges which are mounted against local authorities who are endeavouring, in extremely difficult circumstances, to perform their duties... with due regard for all their other housing problems'. It is significant that the number of applications halved in the year following this direction (Sunkin, 1987). Shortly afterwards the Court of Appeal[5] supported the view of the Lords, Purchas L. J. saying that it was 'clearly established' that the circumstances in which the court would intervene by judicial review were 'severely circumscribed'. It has also been said[6] that the local authority must have a proper administrative system for considering applications. Though said in the context of housing applications by the homeless, the message to social services coping with demands under part III of the Children Act is clear.

The aggrieved parents' position may be even weaker than that of the disgruntled homeless person. The Children Act has default powers (in s.84). If the Secretary of State is satisfied that any local authority has failed, without reasonable excuse, to comply with any of the duties imposed on it by the Act, an order may be made declaring the authority to be in default. S/he may give directions to ensure the duty is complied with (s.84(3)) and enforce any such direction by an application to the Divisional Court of the Queen's Bench Division for mandamus (s.84(4)). It is envisaged that this power will only be used in 'extreme circumstances', for example where a local authority 'fails to make requisite provision for a class of children' (Solicitor General, Standing Committee B, col. 492). These powers are rarely used (Logie, 1988), but they are there. The courts have said that default powers preclude reliance on any other remedy.[7] Of course, as Wade (1982) acknowledged, the default powers are suitable where there has been a general breakdown in the public service (for example, a local authority not providing accommodation for children in need), but they are 'quite unsuitable as a remedy for defaults in individual cases'. In a case concerning the Chronically Sick and Disabled Persons Act 1970 it has been held that a breach of duty by a local authority under that Act does not give rise to an action for damages.[8] It is worth recording what Geoffrey Lane L. J. said:

> 'A statute such as this which is dealing with the distribution of benefits – or, to put it perhaps more accurately, comforts to the sick and disabled – does not in its very nature give rise to an action by the disappointed sick person. It seems to me quite extraordinary that if the local authority, as is alleged here, provided, for example, two hours less home help than the sick person considered himself entitled to that that can amount to a breach of statutory duty which will permit the sick person to claim a sum of monetary damages by way of breach of statutory duty. It seems to me that eminently that is the sort of situation where [default powers are] appropriate and an action in damages is not appropriate.'[9]

However, more recently, the High Court,[10] as a preliminary issue, held that, where a local authority has acted so incompetently that a child's welfare has been seriously prejudiced, the authority is not entitled to immunity and that duties under the Child Care Act 1980 (sections 18 and 21) could found a claim to damages, but that the proper procedure would have been to apply for judicial review.[11] But, we have seen how reluctant the courts are to allow judicial review to be used against local authorities.[12]

Aggrieved parents (and others) may thus have to fall back on the new representations and complaints procedure (s.26(3), discussed below) to air grievances. Whether this will be adequate and satisfactory remains to be seen.

Provision of accommodation

Voluntary care or receptions into care (see Child Care Act 1980 s.2) have been replaced by the provision of accommodation (s.20). The Act does not distinguish between accommodation provided on a short-term basis (however this is defined) and long-term or permanent accommodation. Accommodation cannot be provided when anyone with parental responsibility who is willing and able to provide, or arrange for, accommodation objects (s.20(7), discussed below). Further, any person with parental responsibility may at any time remove the child from accommodation being provided. (s.20(8)). Notice is not required. The procedure whereby a local authority could convert 'voluntary care' into compulsory care by administrative action (the resolution to assume parental rights) has been abolished. Accordingly, the local authority may sometimes feel that it has a tenuous grasp on the child. But this is what the Act intends.

Accommodation is to be seen as a service which parents with a child in need may seek to take up so long as it is in the best interests of the child. It is intended as a voluntary arrangement. Section 20(1) provides

'Every local authority shall provide accommodation for any child in need within their area who appears to them to require accommodation as a result of –
(a)   there being no person who has parental responsibility for him;
(b)   his being lost or having been abandoned; or
(c)   the person who has been caring for him being prevented (whether or not permanently, and for whatever reason) from providing him with suitable accommodation or care.'

There is an additional duty to accommodate children over sixteen if the authority considers the child's welfare ' is likely to be seriously prejudiced if they do not provide him [or her] with accommodation' (s.20(3)). In effect this means that children 'in need' can be discharged from care at 16. The authority will still owe the children the duties imposed by s.17(1) (see above) and, if the child has been in care after 16, the 'after-care' duties found in s.24 (see s.24(2) and below). A local authority may also refuse to provide accommodation for children of 16 or over in need unless in the authority's view their welfare is likely to be seriously prejudiced. Such children, however, are amongst those who can initiate a complaint against the local authority (see s.26(3)(a)). With the dramatic increase in the number of the homeless young (Bradshaw, 1990), it is to be expected that these vulnerable young people will exploit the Children Act as a new resource (Lunn, 1991). Social services may enlist the help of the housing authority, but it only has to comply with a request for help if it is 'compatible with [its] own statutory or other duties and obligations and does not unduly prejudice the discharge of any of [its] functions' (s.27(2)). Unless social services departments define 'in need' restrictively, perhaps to encompass only abandoned children or children with disabilities, they are likely to be inundated with demands for accommodation. This could have an impact on the way accommodation is provided for younger children.

The provision of accommodation is to be arranged in voluntary partnership with parents. The original conception of this in the *Review of Child Care Law* (1985(a)) was for 'shared' care, 'a genuine and voluntary partnership' between parents and the authority (para. 7.4). There were to have been requirements for consultation and the giving of notice before a child cared for six months or more could be removed. Partnership is still emphasised, but the sharing of responsibility and the concomitant restrictions have gone. 'A high degree of co-operation' between parents and local authorities in negotiating and agreeing the 'form' of accommodation and the 'use' to be made of it is expected (*Guidance and Regulations*, vol. 2, para. 2.25). In every voluntary arrangement the service should be based on a voluntary decision by the parents to take up an appropriate service on offer and continuing parental participation in and agreement to the arrangements for the child' (ibid, para. 2.26).

The local authority does not acquire parental responsibility, which is retained by the parent or parents or whoever else had it at the time the child was accommodated. As a person (if a local authority is so regarded) without parental responsibility caring for the child, the authority may, subject to the provisions of the Act, do 'what is reasonable in all the circumstances of the case for the purpose of safeguarding or promoting the child's welfare' (s.3(5)). If there is no one with parental responsibility (for example, the child is illegitimate and the mother has died), the authority may use this provision to assist an appropriate person to apply for a residence order and thus acquire parental responsibility (s.12(2)). If there is such a person this may well be preferable to providing accommodation for the child.

Although the Act does not use the concept of 'respite care', it is clearly a resource consonant with the philosophy of the Act (Holman, 1988; Webb, 1990; Webb and Aldgate, 1991). Its existence is recognised in s.20(4). Webb and Aldgate ((1991), p.10) found that there was 'some confusion over the incorporation of respite care into the formal services that authorities can offer under the Children Act'. For example, when does 'respite care' become 'shared care' (also, of course, an expression not used in the Act)? Holman (1988, p.92) suggests that where a 'respite' placement lasts for over a month it should become 'shared care'. But it is doubtful whether it is helpful to impose this sort of dichotomy. The Act does not distinguish them, nor does the law attach different consequences in terms of rights and obligations. There may be problems if those involved are not clear about the aims and objectives, which makes the formulation of agreements between the authorities and the parents all the more important. Respite care has got to be situated within debates about different levels of preventing breakdown and disruption, and not merely in terms of giving parents and children a break from each other (Swanson, 1988). It is 'central to the principles of partnership' (Webb, 1990, p.26). Webb and Aldgate (1991) found that social workers were sympathetic to using respite care for families experiencing child care difficulties of an emotional/behavoural kind, but not in extreme or crisis-oriented cases where the child's welfare is at risk. They believe that respite care can also be used for child protection and refer to American practice (Subramanian, 1985). It may be assumed that, initially, it will not be used in such cases but will be found particularly useful in cases of parental illness and where family relationships are impaired. Above all its value may lie in preventing family breakdown (Aldgate *et al.*, 1989; Webb and Aldgate, 1991).

Central to all arrangements is the principle of partnership (Aldgate, 1991). The DHSS (1985(b)) has suggested that partnership arrangements will flourish if workers build in

'Honesty, naturalness, reliability. Keeping clients informed, understanding their feelings, and the stress of parenthood, offering combined practical and moral support. They will need actively to help vulnerable parents retain their role as responsible authority figures. They need to be actively involved with families.'

Partnership requires 'informed participation' (*Guidance and Regulations*, vol. 2, para. 2.28). The Act emphasises that, where possible, children should participate in decision-making about their future well-being (see s.22(4), (5)).

Section 20 of the Act must be read together with Schedule 2, in particular paragraphs 4(1), 5 and 7. The use of services, including accommodation, to prevent ill-treatment and neglect (para. 4(1)), in which is included 'alternative accommodation' for alleged abusers (para. 5), is crucial to understanding an Act which advocates orders only where they are 'better' for the child. (s.1(5), above). Where there is evidence that the child is suffering, or is likely to suffer, significant harm, the pros and cons of applying for a care or supervision order (s.31(2)) will need to be investigated. The *Guidance and Regulations* (vol. 2, para. 2.30) advises that 'in the majority of cases local authorities will be able to agree on an arrangement that will best provide for the needs of the child and safeguard and promote his welfare'. It is, the *Guidance* suggests (*idem*) where the parent is or becomes 'unco-operative or inconsistent in attitude or commitment to the child' that the need for care proceedings or emergency protection action should be considered. If the local authority decides to use compulsory measures, a care order may anyway be refused by the court, leaving it to fall back on a voluntary arrangement that may not be as easy to effect after compulsion has been tried.

Retaining a child in accommodation

There is understandable concern that local authorities may become 'dumping grounds'. The flexibility of accommodation arrangements could lead to children coming in and out of local authority accommodation at a parent's whim, with no opportunity for planning, and little attention to the needs of the child for security and stability.

Two provisions in particular have provoked disquiet amongst child care organisations. Section 20(7) states that a local authority may not provide accommodation under this section if a person with parental responsibility is 'willing and able' to provide accommodation (or arrange it) and 'objects'. The accommodation is not required to be satisfactory or even safe. The provision is understandable in the context of the parent who is, to use Packman's language (1986), a 'volunteer', but, as she found, many parent clients of accommodation are likely to be 'victims', or even 'villains'. 'Able' suggests that a homeless or inadequately housed parent could not object (but see also above). It will be noted that the sub-section refers to a person with parental responsibility. So, if a divorced mother asks for her child to be accommodated, the child's father can object (provided he can offer or arrange for accommodation). The unmarried father cannot object, unless he has acquired parental responsibility (see above). If the mother has a residence order and the father does not (or vice versa), her decision to ask the local authority to accommodate her child is effective whatever his objections (see s.20(9), and the authority can act on an agreement with her (*Guidance and Regulations* vol. 3, 1991, para. 2.65). In those circumstances if he objected, he would have to persuade the local authority to place the child with him (see s.17(1), s.23(6)), or would need to obtain a residence order himself.

The local authority which believes that a child is at risk and which cannot persuade the parent to use s.20 will have to seek an emergency protection order (s.44) or bring care proceedings (s.31). If there are no grounds (if the minimum conditions cannot be satisfied), it cannot seek permission to accommodate the child from the High Court by wardship (s.100(2)(b)).

More concern was felt at s.20(8). This states:

'Any person with parental responsibility for a child may at any time remove the child from accommodation provided by or on behalf of the local authority under this section.'

The repeal of the twenty-eight days notice provision must potentially leave children vulnerable to sudden removal, and may encourage some authorities to use compulsory measures where they do not trust parents.

A number of points about the sub-section should be noted:

(*i*)   Removal may be 'at any time'. A period of notice is said to be 'inappropriate' (*Guidance and Regulations* vol. 2, para. 3.28).

(*ii*)   A person with parental responsibility may remove the child even where that person cannot provide, or arrange for, accommodation (cf. s.20(7)).

(*iii*)   Where the parents are married, or were married, or where an unmarried father has acquired parental responsibility, each may exercise the powers under s.20(8): one could accordingly place, and the other remove, the child. The child could be removed by a parent with whom s/he has had no contact.

(*iv*)   In the written agreements parents will agree that they cannot remove their child inappropriately - for example in the middle of the night. But parents will behave irresponsibly – whatever the Act says.

(v)   What can the foster parent, etc., do when confronted with a demand for the child's immediate return? First, s/he will need to be certain that the person making the request is a person with parental responsibility. This may be difficult to establish in the middle of the night (Do parents take their children's birth certificates to the 'pub'?).

(vi)   Police protection may be invoked. Section 46 provides that where a constable has reasonable cause to believe that a child would otherwise be likely to suffer significant harm, he may remove the child to 'suitable accommodation' or take such steps as are reasonable to ensure the child is not removed from where s/he is then being accommodated (see, further, below). The constable could ensure this by using the arrest powers in s.25 of the Police and Criminal Evidence Act 1984.

(vii)   An emergency protection order may be applied for (s.44). The trigger for this is 'significant harm', which may be easier to establish where the child has been in accommodation for a lengthy period. This will create a 'breathing space',[13] giving time for the agreement to be renegotiated, or, if this is not desirable or feasible, for a care order to be sought. This could be granted – the assumption being that a hypothetical parent in the position of the parent would realise that uprooting a child who was well-settled would cause such harm.

(viii)   The foster parent could seek a residence order by entitlement after three years (s.10(5)(b)) or with the leave of the court (s.10(2)(b)). If the local authority applies for a care order, a residence order may be granted to the foster parent.

(ix)   The foster parent may ward the child and seek care and control. This is not prevented by s.100. It turns the clock back to case law of the 1960s.[14] The foster parent would cease to be a local authority foster parent and forfeit the boarding out allowance. (Sch.2, para. 15 would not apply unless a residence order was obtained.)

(x)   The foster parent (or other person with 'care' of the child – 'care' not being defined) could use s.3(5), to which reference has already been made. A person without parental responsibility but with care may do what is reasonable in all the circumstances of the case to safeguard or promote the child's welfare. This was prayed in aid by David Mellor

(Standing Committee B, col. 148) as enabling the local authority to refuse to hand over a child to an inebriated parent (see also *Hansard* HL vol. 503, col. 1412; vol. 505, col. 370). But, s.3(5) has to be read 'subject to the provisions of this Act' and these include s.20(8) which states the child may be removed 'at any time'. The inter-relationship of s.20(8) and s.3(5) will undoubtedly require litigation to clarify. Until it does, it may be relied upon to retain the child, at least temporarily. It must be 'reasonable' to refuse to hand over a child in the middle of night or during the day at a moment's notice or at any time to an unfit or incapacitated person. And it would be reasonable to hold a child long enough to seek advice or seek an emergency protection order. What is 'reasonable' both in terms of steps taken and time must depend upon the circumstances of the case.[15]

(*xi*) The situation may arise where there is a difference of opinion between the foster parent and the local authority, the former wishing to retain the child. If the foster parent refuses to hand over the child, what action can the local authority take? The foster parent will necessarily be in breach of his or her undertaking, but that is of no great assistance. In *Krishnan* v. *London Borough of Sutton*,[16] it was said that the local authority should not be compelled to take *habeas corpus* proceedings. It seems that it can merely remove the child.

(*xii*) Another question is the extent to which the *Gillick*-competent child can insist upon remaining in accommodation. The Act is clear as far as children of 16 are concerned. Neither s.20(7) nor s.20(8) applies where a child of 16 'agrees to being provided with accommodation' (s.20(11)). But what of the fourteen- or fifteen-year-old with sufficient maturity and understanding to make a rational decision that s/he is better where s/he is than at home? The *Krishnan* case[17] held that there was no absolute duty to return a child of nearly eighteen who did not wish to go back to her parents (who had arranged a marriage for her). But suppose the child is considerably short of sixteen? Under the old law, the answer may well have lain in instituting wardship proceedings (Bevan, 1989, p. 703). But is this a case where leave to seek the inherent jurisdiction of the court might be granted (s.100(3))? I think it unlikely (see further below). It might be possible that to argue that a child who refuses to go home is beyond parental control. If it could also be shown that s/he was likely to suffer significant harm attributable to this, a care order might be sought.

(*xiii*) Can a child of sixteen or seventeen discharge him or herself from accommodation? The Act is silent on this. But local authorities have no statutory power to detain such a child without a care order. The child could not be warded.[18] So it seems s/he could just leave. This is consistent with the *Gillick* principle.

Agreements

With accommodation a voluntary arrangement, the importance of agreements cannot be underestimated. 'Agreement' is preferable to contract because it is not a contract in law and is not enforceable (White, 1983), and because 'it implies a full negotiation of the partnership' (Aldgate, 1991, p. 7), though it seems unlikely that there will not be standard terms.

The *Guidance and Regulations* (1991, vol. 2, para. 3. 32) stress:

'Agreements reached will need to involve all those with parental responsibility and will require careful negotiation. The plan for the arrangements will set out (amongst other things) the reasons for, purpose and anticipated length of the child's stay in local authority accommodation (or accommodation provided by other agencies on behalf of the local authority), the arrangements for contact with the child and any delegation of parental responsibility which may be necessary. In a voluntary arrangement the local authority should explain that it will usually be in the child's interests for his return to be planned by all those concerned and that termination of the arrangement should be undertaken in that spirit wherever possible, in accordance with a planned timetable.'

The advantages of entering into written agreements are: (i) expectations are clearer; (ii) the client's viewpoint is recognised (Sheldon, (1980); (iii) success can be more easily measured; (iv) treatment focuses on key issues; and (iv) accountability (Nelken, 1987; Brady, 1982). But there are limitations in the approach too (Tunstill, 1989). How soon after a referral should a written agreement be made? How far do clients and workers hold ideas in common about the nature of the problems and the likely solution to them? (Rojek and Collins, 1987). Clients can be 'lumbered' with unreasonable burdens and responsibilities. The absence of teeth is a further problem: the agreement cannot be enforced. The client can use the complaints procedure (s.26(3)) and shortcomings by the authority will be used if legal proceedings (for example, for judicial review) are ever pursued. Talk of sanctions against clients seems misplaced where the main concern is the child's welfare. These issues can be pursued further in helpful Family Rights Group publications (1989, 1990).

The Children and Young Persons Arrangements for Placement of Children (General) Regulations 1991[19] provides for the first time in statutory form for agreements. Regulation 3, which governs the making of 'arrangements' requires that a responsible authority should draw up a plan in writing. Where a child is not in care, the responsible authority should reach agreement on the plan with the parents, other persons with parental responsibility or, if there is no such person, the person caring for the child. Regulation 4 governs the considerations to which the responsible authority is to have regard so far as reasonably practicable in making the arrangements. These are 'general considerations' and considerations concerning the child's health and education. Matters to be included in arrangements to accommodate children who are not in care include the type of accommodation, details of any services to be provided for the child, the respective responsibilities of the authority, the child, any parent and anyone with parental responsibility, arrangements for contact, the expected duration of arrangements and the steps which should apply to bring the arrangements to an end, including arrangements for rehabilitation of the child with the person with whom s/he was living before the voluntary arrangements were made.

The *Guidance* (vol. 3, para. 2.63) stresses that the agreement must set out the 'role for the parent in the day to day life of the child. This will have been discussed and agreed in negotiations between the responsible authority and the parents with the involvement of the carer'.

The responsible authority must produce a written copy of the agreement which incorporates details of the plan for the child, and the arrangements made (Regulation 5(3)). There is no requirement for the agreement to be signed by the parent. The *Guidance* (vol. 3, para. 2.64) suggests that the authority 'will wish to sign the document to indicate their commitment to the plan for the child'.

Copies are to be sent to the person with whom the agreement is made and to the child 'in a form appropriate to his understanding'. The *Guidance* suggests (vol. 3, para. 2.64) that a child of 16 or over should be encouraged to sign the agreement when s/he has referred him or herself to the local authority and is to be provided with accommodation by the authority by virtue of its powers under s.20(3), (4) and (11). There is, however, no requirement that the agreement should be signed.

The agreement should include arrangements for the child leaving accommodation. The *Guidance* (vol. 3, para. 2.66) advises that these should include 'a period of notice to allow time for preparation of the child for this event and to ensure that the child's wishes and feelings are taken into account'. It explains: 'Where a child is provided with accommodation . . . for a substantial period and has become attached to the carer, this will be important if the child and the carer are to have a sense of stability and security'. The agreement should also provide for the steps to be taken if a party to the agreement decides to change it (for example, the authority changes its mind about a service promised or the parent does something during contact which harms the child). In the latter case, the agreement might actually draw to the parent's attention in advance the consequences of so doing (the possibility of the authority making an application for an emergency protection order).

Accommodation for children in police protection, on remand, etc.

Section 21 requires local authorities to receive and provide accommodation for certain specified children. These children are:

(*i*) children removed or kept away from home under emergency protection orders (s.44) or children being assessed away from home under a child assessment order (s.43) (s.21(1));

(*ii*) children who have been taken into police protection (s.46) (s.21(2)(a);

(*iii*) arrested juveniles (those apparently under 17 arrested with or without warrant) (Police and Criminal Evidence Act 1984 s.37(15), as amended by this Act, Schedule 15) (s.21(2)(b)). The obligation to place arrested children in the hands of the local authority has been strenghened by amendments to the 1984 Act s.38(6) (see schedule 13, para. 53);

(*iv*) children remanded to care or children subject to a supervision order with a residence requirement under s.12AA of the Children and Young Persons Act 1969, as inserted by Sch. 12, para. 23 (s.21(2)(c)).

Where these children are accommodated they are owed the duties in part III and Schedule 2 (s.105(5)) (see below).

Duties to children looked after

The duties to children being 'looked after' by the local authority, laid down by s.22, apply to children accommodated[20] under sections 20 and 21 and to children subject to care orders (s.22(1)). The duties are the same whether or not the children are subject to care orders, though where there is a care order the local authority has parental responsibility (s.31(3)) and thus greater control.

It is the duty of a local authority looking after a child to 'safeguard and promote' the child's welfare and to make such use of services available for children cared for by their own parents 'as appears to the authority reasonable' (s.22(3)). These need not be services provided by the local authority itself. It should be noted that this provision is different from its predecessor (s.18 of the Child Care Act 1980) in three important respects. Section 18(1) of the 1980 Act directed that 'first consideration' should be given to the child's welfare.[21] The importance of 'first consideration' was that children were to be prioritised over other potential clients of the local authority.[22] This emphasis has gone (Lyon, 1989). Secondly, section 18 required promotion of the child's welfare 'throughout his childhood'. These words have been removed but the change is of no consequence since 'welfare' must require consideration of long-term needs. Thirdly, there is no longer a requirement to consider welfare in relation to 'any' decision, as before. Section 18 was used to challenge the closure of children's homes.[23] It may be assumed that an authority which ignores the welfare of children in homes when deciding to close a home is in breach of s.22(3). But the argument, which was once accepted,[24] that the authority is now able to consider how to safeguard a child's welfare *after* it has decided to close the home may be tenable.

Before making any decision about a child they are looking after, or proposing to look after, a local authority is, so far as is reasonably practicable, to ascertain the wishes and feelings of the child, his parents, persons with parental responsibility and any other person whose wishes and feelings the authority considers relevant regarding the matter to be decided (s.22(4)). 'Child' is not qualified by a test as to understanding, so that any child who can communicate wishes and feelings should be listened to. Much will depend on the skills of the person talking to the child. But the child should not be made to feel that the burden of decision-making has fallen on him or her. 'Parent' includes the unmarried father. Other persons include persons who have looked after the child or been in close contact with him or her. They also include all the relevant statutory agencies which have been involved with the child. The child's G.P. and school may be consulted (*Guidance*, vol. 4, para. 2.51). It is not reasonably practicable to ascertain wishes and feelings of those (for example, a parent who has disappeared or is unknown) who cannot be communicated with. Where there is a guardian ad litem, s/he should also be consulted.[25] The guardian may assist the local authority to ascertain the child's views.

In making decisions 'due consideration' is to be given to the wishes and feelings of the child, such as have been ascertained (having regard to age and understanding), to such wishes and feelings of parents, persons with parental responsibility and others the authority considers relevant and 'to the child's religious persuasion, racial origin and cultural and linguistic background' (s.22(5)).

The question of race, religion, culture and language

Racial origin

The provision in s.22(5)(c) (above) must be read together with Schedule 2, para. 11.

'Every local authority shall, in making any arrangements –
(a) for the provision of day care within their area; or
(b) designed to encourage persons to act as local authority foster parents,
have regard to the different racial groups to which children within their area who are in need belong.'

It should be considered in conjunction with Principle 21 in the *Principles and Practice In Regulations and Guidance* (Department of Health, 1989). This states:

'Since discrimination of all kinds is an everyday reality in many children's lives, every effort must be made to ensure that agency services and practices do not reflect or reinforce it.'

The race question is contentious: this is one of the reasons that courts will not give preference to it over other aspects of a child's welfare.[26] There have been highly controversial cases where black or mixed race children have been moved from white foster families to black ones.[27] A good summary of one authority's same race placement policy is Heywood (1990). Current research seems to show that:

'black children adopted into white families are usually brought up as if white; that all black people are sooner or later exposed to racism; that up to their mid-teens, transracially adopted children appear to be doing quite well, that breaking emotional attachments of young children is risky, but re-attachment is not impossible under favourable circumstances.' (Rowe, 1990, p. 8)

It is suggested that all agreements with families from ethnic minorities include a positive statement against agency racism as a basis for partnership with clients from minorities (see also MacDonald, 1991, p.100). Giving 'due consideration' to racial origin means both understanding the connection between race and decision-making and applying that understanding to the individual child. As Macdonald puts it (1991, p. 103):

'paying due consideration to their racial origin involves more than simply working out whether same race foster carers are available or whether the residential home staff know anything about the political situation in Ethiopia, or can cook rice and peas. It means that all staff and carers must know why this question is important and be prepared to take action, whatever their job, to tackle the inequalities which arise.'

The *Guidance* (vol. 4, 1991, paras 2.40–2.42) regards ethnic origin, cultural background and religion as 'important factors for consideration'. It stresses that where re-uniting the child with his or her family is the goal, there is a greater chance of success if the foster parents are of similar ethnic origin. But it acknowledges that 'there may be circumstances in which placement with a family of different ethnic origin is the best choice for a particular child' (para. 2.41).

Examples are where there are strong links with prospective foster parents or a relationship; a child's preference and need to remain close to school, friends and family where ethnic appropriate foster parents cannot be found in the locality; children with special needs. In addition siblings or step-siblings who are not of the same ethnic origin may need placement together (and see s.23(7)(b)).

In relation to children of mixed ethnic origins, the *Guidance* (para. 2.42) advocates 'placement in a family which reflects as nearly as possible the child's ethnic origins'. It adds that the choice should be influenced by the child's 'previous family experience'. This is at best cautious, at worst ambiguous advice. Most of such children will regard themselves and will be regarded as black, and placements with black families will in most cases be best for the children. The recruitment of black foster parents must be a major priority of local authorities with substantial black populations. For indications as to how this might be achieved see Arnold and James (1989). The recruitment of black families is also discussed by the British Agencies for Adoption and Fostering (1991).

'Racial origin' is not defined by the Act. In other contexts Sikhs have been regarded as an ethnic group.[28] Gypsies have also been so regarded.

Religious persuasion

It is arguable that 'religious persuasion' is not as important a consideration in the Act as 'racial origin'. There is no equivalent to Schedule 2, para. 11. On the other hand, social workers already had a legal obligation, before the Act, to place children with foster parents of the same religion or, if that were not practicable, with people who undertook that the child would be brought up in that religion.[29] Racism and religious prejudice will often go in tandem. Intolerance towards minority religions and to minority interpretations of Christianity (Pentecostalism, Plymouth Brethren) has to be avoided when placements are made. The problem of recruiting black foster parents may otherwise be aggravated.

The Act does not define what is meant by religious persuasion. The courts have held that religion must involve the worship of a deity.[30] This precludes Scientology.[31] It could preclude Buddhism but it was expressly stated in *Segerdal*'s case that, despite the fact that a deity is not revered, Buddhism is a religion.[32] On this test Rastafarians are a religion (they believe in the divinity of Emperor Haile Selassie of Ethiopia) (Williams, 1981).

Cultural background

'Cultural background' is not defined in the Act. To take it into account positively requires a recognition that there are different cultures, that stereotyping should be avoided and that appropriate connections should be made with race and religion. Social workers should be able accurately to 'recognise cultural clues, link them with other vital information, and understand how the accommodation to be provided must be part of work which:

(*i*)   'avoids furthering any discrimination children have suffered, and

(*ii*) promotes a healthy pride and awareness in children of their cultural identity, and hence their healthy and assertive development' (Macdonald, 1991, p. 107).

'Culture' is a broad concept. It can include dress (important when placing a child who dresses traditionally in a family of the same ethnicity who may not do so); food (important where the child is a vegetarian or only eats halal or kosher food); the celebration of festivals (which in a secularised society may only be marginally connected with religion). A heightened awareness of culture does not, it must be stressed, require us to tolerate manifestations of that culture which can reasonably be regarded as harmful: female circumcision is a good example.

Linguistic background

'Linguistic background' can be interpreted broadly. Obviously, it requires sensitivity to the languages spoken by the families. But it includes also awareness of the communication needs of those, in particular the deaf, with special needs. 'Linguistic background' includes sign language (Edwards, 1990). Thus provision should be looked at together with s.23(8) with its cack-handed direction that accommodation for the disabled should be 'not unsuitable' to that person's particular needs. The deaf child needs accommodation where people have an understanding of deafness and an ability to communicate with deaf people. The deaf community has often been passed by as a resource when considering the needs of a deaf child. But it also should not be forgotten that many deaf children are being brought up successfully in the hearing world: to place one of them with a deaf, signing family would be equally inappropriate.

It is imperative that no one is prevented from understanding and taking part in work with the authority because of a language barrier. The availability of interpreters and translators becomes an important resource in many authorities. Serious consideration must be given to drawing up agreements in languages understood by families. Other matters to consider are the employment of multi-lingual staff and the appointment of independent visitors, where the criteria apply, with similar cultural and/or linguistic background.

Protecting the public

Section 22(6)–(8) allows a local authority to derogate from its duties to protect the 'public' from 'serious injury'. 'Public' does not include other children accommodated by the authority: s.22(3)(a), which requires a local authority looking after a child 'to safeguard and promote his welfare' does this. There is no reason why social workers themselves should not be regarded as members of the public (but cf. Masson, 1990, p. 51). 'Serious injury' necessarily excludes minor injury and damage to property.

The Secretary of State may, if s/he considers it necessary to protect the public from serious injury, give directions to a local authority with respect to the exercise of these powers (s.22(7)). The authority must comply 'even though doing so is inconsistent with their duties under this section' (s.22(8)).

These provisions must be looked at in connection with secure accommodation (s.25). This is discussed (below).

The local authority and accommodation

A duty is imposed on local authorities to provide accommodation and to maintain children they are looking after (s.23(1)). There are in addition four qualified duties:

(*i*)   to place a child with relatives or friends, unless not reasonably practicable or consistent with the child's welfare (s.23(6));   .

(*ii*)   to secure that any accommodation is near the child's home, so far as is reasonably practicable and consistent with the child's welfare (s.23(7)(a));

(*iii*)   to accommodate siblings together, so far as is reasonably practicable and consistent with welfare (s.23(7)(b));

(*iv*)   to secure that accommodation for the disabled child is, so far as is reasonably practicable, not unsuitable to the child's particular needs (s.23(8)).

The latter two duties are new: the others are similar to duties in the previous legislation.

The types of accommodation which can be used are listed in s.23(2). There is complete discretion over placement but the authority must comply with the duty to safeguard and promote the child's welfare (s.22(3)(a)), the provisions in Schedule 2, part II and the Foster Placement (Children) Regulations 1991,[33] the Placement of Children with Parents Regulations 1991,[34] and any other regulations that are made. (There is also full *Guidance* in volume 3 (1991), chs 3–5). In addition to the types of accommodation listed in s.23(2), the authority may make 'such other arrangements as seem appropriate to them' and comply with (as yet unmade) regulations. Half-way houses and hostels for teenagers are two examples.

Schedule 2, part II, amongst other things, empowers the local authority to make payments to allow visits between children they are looking after and parents, relatives and friends (para. 16). It requires the local authority to appoint a visitor (and pay reasonable expenses) for children they are looking after who are not being visited and whose welfare demands it (para. 17). The local authority may guarantee apprenticeships for children they are looking after (para. 18). The local authority can arrange for a child to live outside England and Wales, but must obtain the approval of the court, which will only be given if it it is the child's best interests and the child and every person with parental responsibility have consented to the child living in that country (para. 19(1),(3)–(5)). Where approval is granted the child may be adopted (para. 19(6)). If the court gives its approval, the order may be stayed pending an appeal (para. 19(7)–(8)). Arrangements may be made for a child who is looked after by the local authority, but not in care, to live outside England and Wales with the consent of everyone with parental responsibility (para. 19(2)). There is also a provision detailing the authority's powers and duties where a child who is being looked after dies (para. 20).

Foster placements

Foster placement is defined as placement with

(*i*)   a family
(*ii*) a relative
(*iii*) any other suitable person (s.23(2)(a), (3)).

Any person with whom the child is so placed is a 'local authority foster parent' (s.23(3)), unless s/he is a parent of the child, a person with parental responsibility for the child or, where the child is in care, a person in whose favour there was a residence order in force immediately before the care order was made (s.23(4)). It will be observed that the statute preserves the now-controversial 'foster parent' expression: the Government was unwilling to substitute 'foster carer'.

Accommodation must be 'suitable' because of the duty in s.22(3) (and see also the reference to suitability in s.23(2)). This is reinforced by the Foster Placement (Children) Regulations 1991 r.5:

'A responsible authority is not to place a child with a a foster parent unless it is satisfied that –
(a) that is the most suitable way of performing their duty under (as the case may be) section 22(3) or 61(a) and (b) of the Act; and
(b) placement with the particular foster parent is the most suitable placement having regard to all the circumstances.'

Reference should also be made to the Arrangements for Placement of Children (General) Regulations 1991, r.3, which requires local authorities, as far as is reasonably practicable, before they place a child to 'make immediate and long-term arrangements for that placement, and for promoting the welfare of the child who is to be placed.' The *Guidance* advises (vol. 3, 1991, para. 4.2) that 'hasty or immediate placements should be avoided as far as possible'. Regulation 5 of the Foster Placement Regulations also requires authorities to place a child, where possible, with a foster parent of the same religious persuasion as the child or with a foster parent who will undertake to bring the child up in that religious persuasion. According to the *Guidance* (vol. 3, 1991, para. 4.3) it also requires local authorities to satisfy themselves that the child's needs arising from his racial origin and cultural and linguistic background will be met. In fact the Regulation omits this but, given s.22(5)(c), the instruction is anyway clear. The *Guidance* also stresses (para. 4.4) the child's need for 'continuity in life and care', which suggests'a need for placement with a family of the same race, religion and culture in a neighbourhood within reach of family, school or day nursery, church, friends and leisure activities. Continuity also requires placement in a foster home which a child can find familiar and sympathetic and not remote from his own experience in social background, attitudes and expectations '(*idem*).

In making any decision the authority is to have regard to the wishes and feelings of the child subject to the child's understanding. This applies to all decisions in relation to foster care. However, the ultimate responsibility lies with the authority: the Guidance wisely advising that children should not be allowed ('made' might be a better way of expressing it) to feel that the burden has fallen totally upon them (para. 4.5). Foster parents must be approved (r.3(1)). This changes the previous law under which 'households' were to be approved. Approval is not to be given unless the prospective foster parent has supplied names and addresses of two referees and interviews with them have been arranged (the interviews strangely need not have taken place) (r.3(4)(a)) and the authority has obtained so far as practicable information relating to the foster parent and has or her family listed in Schedule 1 of the Regulations. (r.3(4)(b)). These are:

1. His age, health (supported by a medical report), personality and marital status (including any previous marriage).
2. Particulars of the other adult members of his household.
3. Particulars of the children in his family, whether or not members of his household, and any other children in his household.
4. Particulars of his accommodation.
5. His religious persuasion, the degree of his religious observance and his capacity to care for a child from any particular religious persuasion.
6. His racial origin, cultural and linguistic background and his capacity to care for a child from any particular origin or cultural or linguistic background.
7. His past or present employment or occupation, his standard of living and leisure activities and interests.
8. He previous experience of caring for his own and other children and his ability in this respect.

9. (If any, and subject to the Rehabilitation of Offenders Act 1974(b)) his previous criminal convictions and those of other adult members of his household.
10. The outcome of any request or application made by him or any other member of his household to foster or adopt children or for registration under section 71 of the Act or any previous enactment of that section.
11. Particulars of any previous approval under regulation 3, or refusal of approval or termination of approval under regulation 4, relating to him or any other member of his household.

Regulation 5(6) requires the authority to enter into a written placement agreement with the foster parent. The matters to be covered in the foster placement agreement are set out in Schedule 3. These are:

1. The provision by the responsible authority of a statement containing all the information which the authority considers necessary to enable the foster parents to care for the child and, in particular, information as to –
   (a) the authority's arrangements for the child and the objectives of the placement;
   (b) the child's personal history, religious persuasion and cultural and linguistic background and racial origin;
   (c) the child's state of health and need for health care and surceillance;
   (d) the child's education needs
   including a requirement for the statement to be provided either at the time of the signing of the agreement or, where this is not practicable, within the following 14 days.
2. The responsible authority's arrangements for the financial support of the child during the placement.
3. Any arrangements for delegation of responsibility for consent to the medical or dental examination or treatment of the child.
4. The circumstances in which it is necessary to obtain in advance the approval of the responsible authority for the child to live, even temporarily, away from the foster parent's home.
5. The arrangements for visits to the child, in connection with the supervision of the placement, by the person authorised by or on behalf of the responsible authority or area authority and the frequency of visits and reviews under the Review of Children's Cases Regulations 1991(a).

6. The arrangements for the child to have contact with his parents and other persons, including any arrangement in pursuance of section 34 of the Act (parental contact, etc., for children in the care of local authority in relation to a child in care, or any contact under (as defined in section 8(1) of the Act)).
7. Compliance by the foster parent with the terms of the agreement set out in Schedule 2.
8. Cooperation by the foster parent with any arrangements made by the responsible authority for the child.

Regulation 6 provides a framework of requirements, including visits, for the social worker's task of supervising the placement and working with the child and foster parent towards the objective of the placement and the achievement of the plan for the child. The requirements for supervision are:

(i)   visits. The child must be seen on each visit;
(ii) advice to the foster parent
Also under the Review of Children's Cases Regulations 1991[35] r.2
(iii) reviews of the plan for the child.

Minimum visiting requirements are one visit within the first week of placement, and then at intervals of not more than 6 weeks during the first year of placement, and thereafter visits at intervals of not more than three months. The authority must arrange a visit 'whenever reasonably requested by a child or foster parent' (*Guidance*, para. 4.20). The need to see the child alone will be decided upon by the responsible authority during the course of the placement (r.6(3). After each visit the authority must ensure that the social worker who made the visit produces a written report (r.6(4)). *Guidance* directs that the 'report should indicate that the child was seen and if not why not, and if the child was seen alone. It should also comment on the child's welfare and the success of the placement including any comments made by the child or the carer' (para. 4.20). Matters of concern or difficulties should be highlighted so that any necessary action can be discussed with the social worker's supervisor. *Guidance* urges that visits should not be neglected because a placement is going well (para. 4.22). But if, in a long term placement, 'visits and support seem genuinely superfluous and parents are no longer involved with the child, the case for a residence order application [by the foster parent] could be considered' (para. 4.22) (and see above).

A placement of a child cannot continue 'if it appears to [the responsible authority] that the placement is no longer the most suitable way of performing their duty under section 22(3) or s.61(1)(a) and (b)' (if a voluntary organisation) (Regulation 7(1)). Where the child is at risk of harm, the child should be removed immediately (*Guidance*, vol. 3, para. 4.42), but the aim should be to bring placements to a 'planned conclusion' (para. 4.43). Immediate placements (by local authorities, not voluntary organisations) are provided for by Regulation 11. In an emergency this Regulation allows a child to be placed with a person who is an approved foster parent for a period not exceeding 24 hours, even though the requirements relating to the placement agreement (in r.5(6), and above) have not been met. Before such a placement, the local authority should satisfy the provisions of Regulation 5(1)(a) (suitability) and obtain a written agreement covering the details in Regulation 11(4)(a)–(e). These duties are:

'(a) to care for the child as if he were a member of the foster parent's family;
(b) to permit any person authorised by the local authority...to visit the child...at any time;
(c) where regulation 7(1) or (2) applies, to allow the child to be removed from the home of the foster parent at any time by the local authority...;
(d) to ensure that any information which the foster parent may acquire relating to the child, or to his family or any other person, which has been given to him in confidence in connection with the placement is kept confidential and is not disclosed except to, or with the agreement of, the local authority and
(e) to allow contact with the child in accordance with s.34 of the Act...,[36] any contact order (as defined in s.8(1) and with the arrangements made or agreed by the local authority.'

Regulation 11(3) allows immediate placement with a relative or friend, after the fullest checks possible in the circumstances and, where possible, after taking into account the parents' views. These powers are intended to be used 'exceptionally in unforeseen circumstances' (para. 4.26). Inappropriate use of these powers should be guarded against. The *Guidance* recommends authorisation at a senior level (para. 4.26). An immediate placement may last no longer than six weeks (r.11(3)), unless during that period the relative or friend is approved as a foster parent. The child must be visited at least weekly.

Regulation 9 tackles schemes variously known as 'respite care' (see above), 'phased care' and 'family link' schemes. It allows for a series of pre-planned short-term foster placements of a child with the same foster parents to be treated as a single placement for the purpose of these Regulations. No single placement may exceed 4 weeks and all the placements must occur within a period which does not exceed one year. The total duration of time in the placement during the arrangement must not exceed 90 days. The authority is required to visit a child as circumstances require and when reasonably requested by the child or foster parent. The minimum visiting requirements are one visit during the first placement in the series, followed by a second visit if more than six months pass from the beginning of the first placement in the series while the child is in the placement. The *Guidance* expects that once organised there will need to be 'minimal involvement from a social worker' (para. 4.30).

A local authority may arrange, or assist in arranging, for a child for whom it is providing accommodation by voluntary agreement to live outside England and Wales (Sch. 2, para. 19(2), and see above). Voluntary organisations cannot place a child outside the British Islands (r.19). Both local authorities and voluntary organisations may place a child outside England and Wales but within the British Islands. The question of placement outside England and Wales may arise (for example) where a foster parent is moving or is going abroad to work or where it would be in the interests of a child to be placed with a relative or other person in Scotland, Northern Ireland, the Isle of Man or the Channel Islands. Appropriate arrangements for supervision need to be made with the relevant authorities in these countries. The *Guidance* directs (para. 4.36) that a decision to allow a foster parent to take a child overseas, except for a holiday, should not be made except where there are 'exceptional circumstances and adequate and realistic arrangements can be made to safeguard the child's welfare and meet the requirements of the Regulations'.

The Arrangements for Placement of Children (General) Regulations 1991 contain requirements for a register of all children placed in a local authority area and for children's case records. Reference may be made to volume 2 of the *Guidance and Regulations*. The following Regulations in the Foster Placement (Children) Regulations 1991 should also be noted:

r.12 : Keep a register of all approved foster parents and of persons not approved with whom a child is placed pursuant to r.11 (above) (an index also of resources)

r.13 : Keep a case record for each approved foster parent and for persons not approved with whom a child is placed pursuant to r.11 (above)

r.13(5) : Keep a record for each prospective foster parent who, after assessment, has been issued with notice that he cannot be approved.[37]
The *Guidance* (vol. 3, para. 4.52) recommends that personal details of the child and the family should not be kept on the foster parents' case record, and the personal details of the foster parent should not be kept in the child's case record.

r.24 : Keep foster parents' case records for at least ten years from the date approval is terminated, or the death of the foster parent if earlier.

Day care and family centres

Section 18(1) of the Act imposes a duty on local authorities to provide 'such day care for children in need within their area who are aged five or under and not yet attending schools as is appropriate'. 'Day care' means any form of care or supervised activity provided for children during the day, whether or not on a regular basis (s.18(4)).

Section 18(5) imposes a duty to provide care or supervised activities outside school hours and during school holidays for children in need, as is appropriate. A supervised activity is any activity supervised by a responsible person (s.18(7)). 'Responsible' is not defined, but presumably means 'responsible' for children.

These services may be provided for other children (those not in need) (s.18(2),(6)).

The local authority is also empowered to provide facilities, including training, advice, guidance and counselling for those caring for children in day care, and for those who accompany such children while they are in day care (s.18(3)). This includes family aides (*Guidance*, vol.2, para. 3,39).

These are services the need for which has been long recognised (Bone, 1977).

Charges can be levied for any of these services, other than advice, guidance or counselling (s.29(1)). Where the service is provided for a child under 16, each of the parents can be charged. Where the child is 16, s/he can be charged. Where it is provided for a member of the child's family, that member can be charged (s.29(4)). There will be situations where it is ambiguous for whom the service is provided: for example, is a place in a day nursery a service for the child or the parent?

How the local authority discharges its duties and carries out its powers is up to it (note the 'as is appropriate'). Volume 2 of the *Guidance* (1991) gives examples of the services that can be provided under this section. It lists:

(*i*)   day nurseries;
(*ii*)   playgroups;
(*iii*)   childminding;
(*iv*)   out of school clubs and holiday schemes;
(*v*)   supervised activities;
(*vi*)   befriending services (the Home-Start Consultancy and NEWPIN are referred to);
(*vii*)   parent/toddler groups;
(*viii*) toy libraries;
(*ix*)   drop-in centres;
(*x*)   play-buses (paras 3.8 – 3.17).

Schedule 2, paragraph 9(1) gives local authorities a general duty 'to provide such family centres as they consider appropriate within their area'. The Act defines family centres as places where a child, his parents, anyone who has parental responsibility for or is looking after him or her may go for 'occupational, social, cultural or recreational activities', or 'advice, guidance or counselling' or the person may be 'provided with accommodation while s/he is receiving advice, guidance or counselling' (Sch. 2, para. 9(2), (3)).

The duty is not confined to children in need. It thus follows the research finding (Gibbons, 1991(b)) which stressed the importance of family centres being open to neighbourhoods rather than restricted to referrals. The *Guidance* (vol. 2, 1991, para. 3.19) advises that local authorities should decide whether to discharge this duty through providing such facilities themselves or facilitating other organisations to do so. The *Guidance* (vol. 2, 1991, para. 3.20) identifies three main types of family centre (therapeutic, community and self-help). It suggests that local authorities should consider whether family centres of the therapeutic type would provide an effective way of discharging some of their part III duties. 'In particular', it notes, 'attendance at a family centre might form one element of a package of services put together for a family with a child in need. These facilities...provide a place where parents and children of all ages can go...[and] provide a place where adult members of a family can go to take part in activities which may help to improve their confidence and their ability to cope more effectively with their difficulties' (ibid, para. 3.21).

Under section 19 local authorities are under a new duty to review the day care they provide, the extent to which the services of child minders are available within their area for children under eight, and the provisions for day care within their area for children under eight by persons other than the authority. The review must be carried out with the local education authority as a 'joint exercise' (*Guidance*, vol. 2, (1991), para. 9.2), and at least once every three years (s.19(2),(5)). The first review has to be carried out by October 14, 1992. It must take account of other provisions for under-fives in schools and hospitals (s.19(5)). They must take account of representations by health authorities and others, for example 'local authority groups, parents and employers' (David Mellor, Standing Committee B, col. 523). Examples of local groups include lone parent organisations and ethnic minority groups. The results of the review must be published (s.19(6)).

The review duty is explained further in chapter 9 of *Guidance and Regulations*, volume 2 (1991), to which reference should be made. The concept of 'review' involves 'measurement or assessment' (para. 9.10). This is not possible, the *Guidance* continues, 'without agreed aims and objectives for the service or services in question so that the review is undertaken within a framework' (*idem*).

The report, it is suggested (see *Guidance*, vol. 2, para. 9.19) should cover the following matters:

(i)   basic data on services in the area;

(*ii*)   a map of the area with the location of facilities marked;

(*iii*) policies on day care and early years education, children in need, services for children with special educational needs, policies on equal opportunities including race, gender and disability and how developed and monitored;

(*iv*) centres of excellence and those with innovative or unusual features;

(*v*)   known problems – for example, mismatch of supply and demand, difficulties in staff recruitment, shortage of child minders or difficulties in the organisation of the registration system;

(*vi*)   training opportunities;

(*vii*) range of other support services for families (by libraries, home visiting schemes, parent/toddler groups, information services);

(*viii*) methods of conducting the review with details about whether members and senior officers were involved and in what way and the consultation procedures used;

(*ix*) numbers of local authority staff involved in services for under-fives and out of schools and in what capacity;

(*x*)   changes in provision and plans for the future and monitoring arrangements.

Co-operation and consultation

Section 27 provides that, where it appears to a local authority that another authority, a local education authority, a housing authority, a health authority or any other person authorised by the Secretary of State could help in the exercise of any of their functions under part III, they may request such help, and the authority whose help is so requested is to comply so long as it is compatible with their statutory or other duties and does not prejudice the discharge of any of their functions.

Local authorities are also to assist local education authorities with the provision of services for any child within the local authority's area with special educational needs (s.27(4)).

Section 28 imposes new duties on local authorities to consult the appropriate local education authority before they accommodate a child at an establishment which provides education (s.28(1)), and to inform them of the placement (s.28(2)) and when it ends (s.28(3)). This applies to placements in boarding schools and homes which are also schools.

Notes

1. By analogy with similar interpretations in other areas of law *e.g.* Housing Act 1988 s.39 and *Dyson Holdings* v. *Fox* [1976] QB 503.
2. *Att-Gen. ex rel. Tilley* v. *Wandsworth LBC* [1981] 1 All ER 1162.

3. Ibid p. 1168.
4. [1986] 1 All ER 467.
5. *R* v. *Tower Hamlets LBC ex parte Monaf* [1987] 19 HLR 577 and [1988] 20 HLR 529.
6. *R* v. *Camden LBC ex parte Gillan* [1989] 21 HLR 114.
7. *Southwark LBC* v. *Williams* [1971] Ch.734; *Wyatt* v. *Hillingdon LBC* [1978] 76 LGR 727.
8. *Wyatt* v. *Hillingdon LBC* [1978] 76 LGR 727.
9. Ibid, p. 733.
10. *Guevara* v. *London Borough of Hounslow, The Times*, April 17, 1987. See also [1987] Journal of Social Welfare Law 374.
11. Because of *O'Reilly* v. *Mackman* [1983] 2 AC 237 and *Cocks* v. *Thanet District Council* [1983] 2 AC 286.
12. But the existence of default powers does not prevent an application for judicial review (*R* v. *Secretary of State for the Environment ex parte Ward* [1984] 1 WLR 834).
13. See *Wheatley* v. *L.B. of Waltham Forest* [1979] 1 All ER 289,293.
14. *Re S* [1965] 1 All ER 865.
15. But note in *Lewisham LBC* v. *Lewisham Juvenile Justice Court* [1980] AC 273 the opinion of Lord Salmon (p.290) and Lord Keith (p.301) that the local authority had no right to retain a child whose return was demanded. Though an interpretation of different legislation, it has persuasive force.
16. [1970] Ch. 181, 186.
17. [1970] Ch. 181
18. *Cf Re SW* [1986] 1 FLR 24.
19. SI 890 (1991) (Annex A of *Guidance and Regulations*, vol. 3).
20. For a continuous period of more than 24 hours (s.22(2))
21. Interpreted in *M* v. *H* [1988] 3 WLR 485 by Lord Brandon as no different from 'first and paramount' consideration to the child's welfare, as then required by the Guardianship of Minors Act 1971 s.1.
22. *Liddle* v. *Sunderland BC* (1983) 13 Fam. Law 250, 252–3 (*per* Latey J.)
23. See the *Liddle* case and Freeman, 1984.
24. *A-G* v. *Hammersmith and Fulham LBC The Times*, 18 December 1979, criticised by Freeman, 1980.
25. *R* v. *North Yorkshire CC ex parte M* [1989] 1 All ER 143. See also *Guidance*, vol. 4, 1991, para 2.51.
26. *Re A* [1987] 2 FLR 429.
27. *Re P* [1990] 1 FLR 96 generated considerable controversy in 1989.
28. *Mandla* v. *Dowell Lee* [1983] 2 AC 548.
29. The Boarding Out of Children (Foster Placement) Regulations, 1988, r.5(4).
30. *R* v. *Registrar General ex parte Segerdal* [1970] 2 QB 697.
31. Ibid. See also *Re B and G* [1985] 1 FLR 134 (Ron Hubbard apparently will not do!).
32. Op. cit., note 30 p. 707. Buddhists do recognise a supreme being.
33. SI (1991) 910.

34. SI (1991) 893.
35. See Courts and Legal Services Act 1990 Sch. 16. para. 12(2), inserting a new s.23(5A) into the Children Act and reversing the effect of the decision in *R* v. *Newham LBC ex parte P* [1990] 2 All ER 19.
36. SI (1991) 895.
37. This only applies where there is a care order. See ch. 6.

References

Aldgate, J. (1991) 'Partnership with Parents: Fantasy or Reality?', *Adoption and Fostering*, 15(2), 5.
Aldgate, J. *et al.* (1989) 'Using Care Away from Home to Prevent Family Breakdown', *Adoption and Fostering*, 13(2), 32.
Barber, S. (1990) 'Heading Off Trouble', *Community Care*, 840, 23.
Bevan H. (1989) *Child Law*, London, Butterworths.
Bone, M. (1977) *Pre-School Children and the Need for Day Care*, London, HMSO.
Bradshaw, J. (1990) *Child Poverty and Deprivation in the UK*, London, National Children's Bureau.
Brady, J. (1982) 'Briefly Stated Advantages and Problems of Using Written Contracts', *Social Work*, 27,275.
British Agencies for Adoption and Fostering (1991) *Recruiting Black Families*, London, BAAF.
Creighton, S (1985) 'An Epidemiological Study of Abused Children and their Families in the UK', *Child Abuse and Neglect*, 9, 441.
Department of Health (1985(a)) *Review of Child Care Law*, London, HMSO.
Department of Health (1985(b)) *Social Work Decisions in Child Care*, London, HMSO.
Department of Health (1989) *The Care of Children: Principles and Practice In Regulations and Guidance*, London, HMSO.
Department of Health (1991) *Guidance and Regulations*, vol. 2: *Family Support*, London, HMSO.
Department of Health (1991) *Guidance and Regulations*, vol. 3: *Family Placements*, London, HMSO.
Department of Health (1991) *Guidance and Regulations*, vol.4: *Residential Care*, London, HMSO.
Department of Health (1991) *Guidance and Regulations*, vol.6: *Children with Disabilities*, London, HMSO.
Edwards, J. (1990) 'Silent Rights', *Community Care*, 843 (Supplement p.6).
Family Rights Group (1989) *Using Written Agreements with Children and Families*, London, FRG.
Family Rights Group (1990) *Written Agreement Forms for Work with Children and Families*, London, FRG.

Freeman, M. (1980) 'The Rights of Children and the Closure of Children's Homes', *Justice of the Peace*, 144,38.

Freeman, M. (1980(b)) 'Rules and Discretion in Local Authority Social Services Departments', *Journal of Social Welfare Law* 84.

Freeman, M. (1984) 'Recent Cases – *Liddle* v. *Sunderland BC*', *Journal of Social Welfare Law*, 44.

Gardner, R. (1990) 'Children in Need', *Community Care*, 841, 28.

Gibbons, J. (1991(a) 'Children in Need and their Families', *British Journal of Social Work*, 21, 217

Gibbons, J. (1991(b)) *Child Care Policies and Prevention*, London, HMSO.

Handler J. (1973), *The Coercive Social Worker*, Chicago, Rand McNally.

Hardiker, P. *et al.* (1991) 'The Social Policy Contents of Prevention in Child Care', *British Journal of Social Work*, 21, 341.

Heywood, S. (1990) 'Putting Same Race Placement Policy into Practice', *Adoption and Fostering* 14(2), 9.

Heywood, J. and Allen, B. (1971) *Financial Help in Social Work*, Manchester, Manchester University Press.

Hill, M. and Laing P. (1978) *Money Payments, Social Work and Supplementary Benefits*, SAUS, University of Bristol.

Holman, R. (1988) *Putting Families First: Prevention and Child Care*, London, Macmillan.

In Need Implementation Group (1991) *The Children Act and Children's Needs*, London, NCVCCO.

Jackson, M. and Valencia, E. (1979) *Financial Aid Through Social Work*, London, RKP.

Logie, J. (1988) 'Enforcing Statutory Duties: Courts and Default Power', *Journal of Social Welfare Law*, 185.

Lunn, T. (1991) 'Children Act – Hidden Duties' ,*Social Work Today*, 22(23), 21.

Lyon, C. (1989) 'Legal Developments Following the Cleveland Report', *Journal of Social Welfare Law*, 200.

Lyon, C. (1991) *The Implications of the Children Act 1989 and Young People with Severe Learning Difficulties*, London, Barnardo's.

Macdonald, S. (1991) *All Equal Under the Act?* London, National Institute of Social Work.

Masson, J. (1990) *The Children Act*, London, Sweet and Maxwell.

Nelken, D. (1987) 'The Use of "Contracts" as a Social Work Technique', *Current Legal Problems*, 40, 207.

Packman, J. (1981) *The Child's Generation*, Oxford, Blackwell.

Packman, J. (1986) *Who Needs Care?* Oxford, Blackwell.

Rojek, C. and Collins, S. (1987) 'Contract or Con Trick', *British Journal of Social Work*, 17, 199.

Rowe, J. (1990) 'Research, Race and Child Care Placements', *Adoption and Fostering* 14(2), 6.

Shaw, M. *et al* (1990) *Children in Need and their Families: A New Approach*, Leicester, University of Leicester.

Sheldon, B. (1980) *The Use of Contracts in Social Work*, Birmingham, BASW.

Sinclair, R. (1991) *Residential Care and the Children Act 1989*, London, National Children's Bureau.

Subramanian K. (1985) 'Reducing Child Abuse Respite Center Intervention', *Child Welfare* LXIV, 501.

Sunkin, M. (1967) 'What is Happening to Applications for Judicial Review?', *Modern Law Review* 50, 432.

Swanson, M. (1988) 'Preventing Reception into Care' in Freeman, I. and Montgomery, S. (eds), *Child Care Monitoring Practice*, London, Jessica Kingsley.

Tunstill, J. (1989) 'Written Agreements: An Overview' in Family Rights Group, *Using Written Agreements with Children and Families*, FRG, London.

Wade, H. (1982) *Administrative Law*, Oxford, Clarendon Press.

Webb, S. (1990) 'Preventing Reception into Care: Literature Review of Respite Care', *Adoption and Fostering,* 14(2),22.

Webb, S. and Aldgate J. (1991) 'Using Respite Care to Prevent Long Term Family Breakdown', *Adoption and Fostering,* 15(1), 6.

White, R. (1983) 'Written Agreements with Families', *Adoption and Fostering,* 7(4), 24

White, R. (1991) 'Assessing Children's Needs', *New Law Journal,* 141, 433.

Williams, K. (1981) *The Rastafarians*, London, Ward Lock.

5

The Public Care System – I

This chapter (and chapter 8 which deals with emergency protection) investigate the question of compulsory intervention into family, the ways this can be done and the limits on such coercion. In the past child care legislation was designed primarily to control delinquents, not to protect children from abuse and neglect (Dingwall *et al.*, 1984). A concern with the latter has occurred all too rarely. It should not be forgotten that child abuse was only rediscovered in the 1960s and that as recently as 1980 a DHSS Circular on registers did not recognise the existence of sexual abuse. The phenomenon of organised abuse (Tate, 1991) is only just now beginning to be recognised as a social problem (the new edition of *Working Together*, 1991, para. 5.26 gives official guidance on it for the first time).[1]

Child Abuse

The categories of abuse are never closed. It is striking that, although the new edition of *Working Together* (the previous one was published in 1988) gives the same four categories of abuse (in relation to registration) (see 1991, para. 6.40) new phenomena have been included (for example, Munchausen's syndrome by proxy, which got a lot of media attention after the *Tameside* case in November 1987). *Working Together* (1991, para. 6.40) now lists four categories of abuse (for the register and statistical purposes). They are, however, a convenient summary of the official view of what constitutes abuse. They are:

'*Neglect*: The persistent or severe neglect of a child, or the failure to protect a child from exposure to any kind of danger, including cold or starvation, or extreme failure to carry out important aspects of care, resulting in the significant impairment of the child's health or development, including non-organic failure to thrive.

Physical Injury: Actual or likely physical injury in a child, or failure to prevent physical injury (or suffering) to a child including deliberate poisoning, suffocation and Munchausen's syndrome by proxy.

Sexual Abuse: Actual or likely sexual exploitation of a child or adolescent. The child may be dependent and/or developmentally immature

Emotional Abuse: Actual or likely severe adverse effect on the emotional and behavioural development of a child caused by persistent or severe emotional ill-treatmant or rejection. All abuse involves some emotional ill- treatment. This category should be used where it is the main or sole form of abuse.'

It is pointed out (para. 6.41) that these categories do not fit precisely into the definition used in the Children Act, where the trigger for intervention is 'significant harm' (see s.31). *Working Together* (1991, para. 6.41) also observes that the courts may provide a definition of 'sexual abuse', which, as we shall see, the Act does not define, different from the above, in which case, it is advised, 'their definition should be used'. It has to be said that it is unlikely that the courts will advance a definition as such, though a greater understanding of what they consider to be sexual abuse will emerge as cases are tested and the parameters refined.[2]

Child protection and the courts

Most child protection cases will not come before the courts. But where there is a need for intervention the courts will be more actively involved and more pro-active.

Before the case is heard, there may be an initial hearing (a 'directions appointment') involving all those concerned in the case. At this the following may occur:

(*i*)   directions may be given as to how the case should proceed;
(*ii*) a timetable may be set (and see s.32, below);
(*iii*) a guardian ad litem to represent the child in court will probably be appointed;

(*iv*) a decision may be taken to transfer the case to another court (reasons are discussed below);

(*v*) the question as to whether the child should attend may be considered (see s.95 and below);

(*vi*) other directions as appropriate may be given, for example as to contact and assessment.

It is also important to stress that there will be greater access to information before the case is heard. Everyone involved will be expected to reveal their arguments and evidence in advance in writing. For example, all the parties will have seen the guardian ad litem's report in advance of the final hearing (see The Family Proceedings Courts (Children Act 1989) Rules 1991, r.11(7)).[3]

The conference and the register

The child protection conference

The Child Protection Conference is 'central' to child protection procedures (*Working Together*, 1991, para. 6.1). But is '*not* a forum for a formal decision that a person has abused a child. That is a matter for the courts' (*Working Together, idem*). The CPC brings together the professionals concerned and the family. It 'symbolises the inter-agency nature of assessment, treatment and the management of child protection' (*idem*).

Working Together advises that a CPC should be called only after an investigation under s.47 has been made into the incident or suspicion of abuse which has been referred (para. 6.4). If a decision to register is made a 'key worker' must be appointed and recommendations for a 'care group' of professionals to carry out the inter-agency work made (para. 6.5).

Working Together stresses 'the need to ensure that the welfare of the child is the overriding factor guiding child protection work' (para. 6.11). The importance of professionals working in partnership with parents and the concept of parental responsibility, so much the keys to an understanding of the philosophy of the Act, are also emphasised in this context.

The first edition of *Working Together* (1988, para. 5.45) advocated parents being invited to 'case conferences' where 'practicable' and unless 'in the view of the Chairman... their presence [would] preclude a full and proper consideration of the child's interests'. The courts followed this by deciding that it was not a breach of natural justice not to invite them.[4] The 1991 edition sees the exclusion of the parent from a CPC as 'exceptional' (para. 6.15), so that it needs to be 'especially justified'. The example is given of 'a strong risk of violence, with supporting evidence, by the parents towards the professionals or the child ... or evidence that the conference would be likely to be disrupted' (*idem*). But 'the possibility that one of the parents may be prosecuted for an offence against the child does not in itself justify exclusion' (*idem*). The decision to exclude should rest with the 'chair' (as the Chairman of 1988 vintage has become!). If parents are excluded or cannot or will not attend, 'it is important that they are encouraged to find a method of communicating their views to the conference' (para. 6.17).

As far as children are concerned, they are to be encouraged to attend CPCs whenever they have sufficient understanding and are able to express their wishes and feelings and participate in the process of investigation and assessment, planning and review (para. 6(3)). If the child's attendance is inappropriate or s/he does not wish to do so, a 'clear and up-to-date account of the child's views by the professionals who are working with the child' (*idem*) is to be provided.

Working Together stresses also that the interests of parents and children may conflict; in which case the child's interests should take 'priority' (para. 6.12).

Ways of encouraging participation by children and adults in the family are also suggested in *Working Together* (para. 6.23).

It must be stressed that the decision to initiate care proceedings lies with the agencies with statutory powers (that is with local authorities and the NSPCC: s.31(1), (9)), and not with the child protection conference (see also *Working Together*, para. 6.20).

The Child Protection Register

The Child Protection Register is 'not a register of children who have been abused but of children for whom there are currently unresolved child protection issues and for whom there is an inter-agency protection plan' (*Working Together*, para. 6.36). Registration is not to be used for the ulterior purpose of obtaining resources for a family which might 'otherwise not be available' (*idem*). The purpose is to provide a record and ensure that plans are formally reviewed every six months (para. 6.37). Only a CPC can place a child's name on a register (para. 6.35) Before a child is registered the CPC must decide that

'there is, or is a likelihood of, significant harm leading to the need for a child protection plan. One of the following requirements needs to be satisfied:
(i) there must be one or more identifiable incidents which can be described as having adversely affected the child. They may be acts of commission or omission. They can be either physical, sexual, emotional or neglectful. It is important to identify a specific occasion or occasions when the incident has occurred. Professional judgment is that further incidents are likely; or
(ii) Significant harm is expected on the basis of professional judgment of findings of the investigation in this individual case or on research evidence.' (para. 6.39).

The CPC will need to establish as far as possible 'a cause of the harm or likelihood of harm' (*idem*). *Working Together* advises (*idem*) that 'this cause can also be applied to siblings or other children living in the same household so as to justify registration of them'.

The four categories of abuse for the purposes of registration have been listed (see above). *Working Together* recommends that in some cases more than one category of registration may be appropriate (para. 6.40) but cautions (*idem*) 'that multiple abuse registration should not be used just to cover all eventualities'.

The data to be included on the register is listed in Appendix 4 of *Working Together* (p. 107). This should be consulted. Included is information on relevant offences (that is offences established by a criminal conviction which is 'relevant to the reasons for which the child is thought to be at risk and the child's name entered on the register' (para. 6.53). In the light of the *Norfolk* case,[5] care should be taken with case records which contain information about adults suspected but not convicted of offences against children and a list of such people should not be held (para. 6.54). The consequences of registration are sufficiently serious to impose a legal duty on the C.R.C. to act fairly. Not to do so is to risk successful challenge by judicial review.[6] *Working Together* (para. 6.54) advises that where there is information about an abuser s/he must be informed and told of the possibility of 'questioning the details or making representations about the entry'.

Applying for a care or supervision order

Only the local authority and authorised persons may apply for a care order or supervision order (s.31(1)). The only authorised person is the NSPCC (and its officers), though others may be so authorised by order of the Secretary of State (s.31(9)).[7] The police, the local education authority and the parents can no longer bring (or in the case of parents since 1963 activate) care proceedings.

The police were able to commence proceedings where the commission of a criminal offence by the child was the basis of the application. But the abolition of the offence condition (see below) has removed the rationale of police applications. Similarly, the removal of the 'school refusal' ground takes away the basis for applications by LEAs. The status and position of the parent is further considered in the section on 'beyond parental control' children (below).

Where the NSPCC, or other 'authorised person', proposes to make an application, it is required, where reasonably practicable and before it makes an application, to consult the local authority in whose area the child is ordinarily resident (s.31(6)). This is to avoid duplication. Concerns, information and thinking should be shared. The court cannot entertain an application by the NSPCC (or other authorised person), if, at the time when it is made, the child concerned is the subject of an earlier application, which has not been disposed of, or is already the subject of such an order (s.31(7)).

An application may be made in 'care proceedings or by intervening in any 'family proceedings' (s.31(4)). The meaning of 'family proceedings' was explained above (p. 36), and is wide.

The child must be under seventeen (or sixteen if married under 16, as is possible where both spouses are domiciled abroad).[8] The *Guidance* advises that 'the court is likely to look particularly keenly at a case for making an order for a young person who is approaching his seventeenth birthday (or sixteenth, if married)' (vol.1, 1991, para. 3.15). Nor is there the fall back of wardship in such a case.[9] An order ceases to have effect at the age of eighteen unless brought to an end earlier (s.91(12)). It is no longer possible to extend the period of care to nineteen in certain circumstances.

The *Guidance* advises (vol. 1, para. 3.12) that before proceeding with an application, the local authority should always seek legal advice, preferably within the contexct of a multi-disciplinary, multi-agency child protection conference[10] on the following matters:

(a) whether the minimum conditions will be satisfied and the order should be made after applying the s.1(5) test and having regard to the checklist in s.1(3);

(b) the implications of another party to the proceedings opposing the application and applying for a section 8 order instead;

(c) whether the application ought to be transferred upwards to a higher court;

(d) whether the court should be asked for an interim order (care or supervision), the desired length and what directions should be sought;

(e) the matters to be provided for in the authority's advance statement of case, including copies of witness statements that can be made available and a broad outline of the authority's plans for the child;

(f) notification and other procedural requirements and matters likely to be considered and the 'directions appointment';

(g) whether the court is likely to consider in all the circumstances of the case that a guardian ad litem does not need to be appointed (this will be comparatively rare);

(h) whether use of a residence order linked with a supervision order would be an appropriate alternative to a care order.

The new minimum conditions

Under the old law a care or supervision order required proof of one or more of seven conditions and of the overriding condition that the child was 'in need of care or control which he [was] unlikely to receive unless the court [made] the order' (Children and Young Persons Act 1969 s.1(2)).[11]

These conditions are swept away and there is now just one 'ground', or set of 'criteria' or 'minimum' or 'threshold' conditions.[12] This is the only 'trigger' for state intervention into the family. Without proof of these minimum conditions no compulsory or coercive measures can be taken against a family. The Lord Chancellor explained (1989, p. 508) that 'the integrity and independence' of the family are the 'basic building blocks of a free and democratic society'. Accordingly, he argued that 'unless there is evidence that a child is being or is likely to be positively harmed because of a failure in the family, the state, whether in the guise of a local authority or the court, should not interfere' (*idem*).

There is now only one route into care, requiring proof (on a balance of probabilities) of the minimum conditions, which are set out in section 31(2). The fall back of wardship, so long positively encouraged by the courts[13] where local authorities felt the statutory framework did not offer children sufficient protection, is now extensively restricted (see section 100 and below). It is possible that, as a result, some cases may fall through the safety net. The Act may, indeed, fail to protect some children whom the previous legislation would have protected (Cretney, 1990, Freeman, 1990, 1992). But this is legislation which emphasises legality and rights rather than broad welfarist notions.

The new minimum conditions create a threshold for intervention, a hurdle which must be surmounted before coercive intervention into child-rearing can be countenanced. The conditions or 'criteria' as the *Guidance* calls them – vol. 1, para. 3.12 – are found in s.31(2). This sub-section contains the most complex interpretational problems in the whole Act (Freeman, 1990; Bainham, 1991). The conditions state:

> 'A court may only make a care order or supervision order if it is satisfied —
> (a) that the child concerned is suffering, or is likely to suffer, significant harm; and
> (b) that the harm, or likelihood of harm, is attributable to —
>   (i) the care given to the child, or likely to be given to him if the order were not made, not being what it would be reasonable to expect a parent to give to him; or
>   (ii) the child's being beyond parental control.'

The minimum conditions are the same for a care order and a supervision order. References, unless otherwise specified, to a care order apply equally to a supervision order. It should be pointed out, however, that a supervision order cannot be 'upgraded' to a care order without proof again of the minimum conditions. Whether this will discourage applications for supervision orders (Eekelaar, 1991) we can only wait and see.

The following observations may be made on the new minimum conditions.

The temporal dimension

They are forward-looking, applying to the future as well as present harm, thus obviating much recourse to the wardship jurisdiction. A care order may be sought where the prognosis is that the child is likely to suffer significant harm. Hitherto, this has not been possible, as is clear from a case[14] where the local authority failed to obtain a care order to prevent a serving soldier taking his two children out of voluntary care, where they had been for two years, to live with him and his new wife in Northern Ireland. The authority believed the removal would be disturbing to the children. It could (perhaps it should) have applied for wardship, but then all significant moves in the children's lives would have required judicial approval.[15] Under the Act an application for a care order could be made: if granted the authority, not the court, would be in the 'driving seat' (David Mellor, Standing Committee B, col. 232). The new provision also overcomes the hurdles authorities have had to confront in the past when faced with mothers who cannot cope with newborn babies (Freeman, 1980). It is inconceivable that, in the light of the philosophy of this Act, the practice of removing babies will continue save in the rarest case, but, should it do so, an application for a care order is now possible. A care order might also be sought where a surrogate mother plans to hand over her newborn child to the commissioning parents (Hayes and Bevan, 1988).

The past is not specifically included but the admonition of Butler-Sloss J. in *M* v. *Westminster City Council*[16] remains pertinent. 'A child's development is a continuing process. The present must be relevant in the context of what has happened in the past, and it becomes a matter of degree as to how far in the past you go'. It is, however doubtful whether a court today could come to the same conclusion as it did in the *Westminster* case. An interim order had been made but the child was allowed to return home. At the time of the final hearing the parents were looking after him without any further harm. The court held that because of their earlier conduct the condition was satisfied. It is difficult to see how this conclusion could be reached either within the letter of s.31(2) or the spirit of the whole Act.[17] Nevertheless, it must be stressed that the cutting off of the past must not be taken too literally: if it were, no removed child could ever be the subject of care proceedings. The words must be applied with reference to the circumstances prevailing at the time when the parent last had the child living with him or her.[18]

One of the more intriguing dilemmas in the child care field in recent years has centred on the mother who harms her child, notably by the ingestion of dangerous drugs, before the child is born. The *cause célèbre* was the 'heroin addict mother' in Berkshire.[19] The

House of Lords sanctioned the removal of a baby (Victoria) born with foetal drug syndrome because the harm done to her before her birth was continuing at the time compulsory measures of care (a place of safety order) were initiated. Most commentators (Masson, 1990; Bainham, 1990) are in no doubt that the courts will reach the same conclusion in interpreting the new Act. But I am more doubtful. It would have to be shown that the significant harm, which Victoria was undoubtedly suffering, was attributable to the care given her not being what it would be reasonable to expect a parent to give. But what steps are open to the addicted mother who becomes pregnant? If she comes off the drugs or drug substitutes it is likely that she will spontaneously abort (Tylden, 1983). The test is what a hypothetically reasonable woman in the position of the mother would have done. Is it better to be born drug-addicted (or HIV-infected to use another example) or not to be born at all? If we conclude the former, it is difficult to see how the new provision could lead to the same conclusion as the old.

Significant harm

The linchpin of care is 'significant harm'. But what is 'significant' harm? The DHSS *Review of Child Care Law* (1985, para. 15(15)) states:

'Having set an acceptable standard of upbringing for the child, it should be necessary to show some substantial deficit in that standard. Minor shortcomings in the health and care provided or minor defects in physical, psychological or social development should not give rise to any compulsory intervention unless they are having or likely to have, serious and lasting effects upon the child.'

The focus is thus on 'substantial deficit'. The *Guidance* (vol. 1, para. 3(9)) quotes the dictionary definition of 'considerable, noteworthy or important'. It is, I think, a lesser standard than would have been imported by the word 'serious' (cf. the test in Goldstein *et al.*, 1979, p.72; and see Freeman, 1983, pp. 253–5). It is clearly also a lesser standard than 'severe'. Harm may be significant in a number of ways: in amount, in effect, in importance. The *Guidance* adds that significance can exist 'in the seriousness of the harm or in the implications[20] of it' (vol. 1, para. 3.19). But this can hardly be said to clarify overmuch. It adds that 'this will be a finding of fact for the court' (*idem*) but it offers the courts little guidance. In a recent case,[21] where a four-year-old boy had been sexually abused by his father, the judge referred to a 'spectrum of abuse' and an 'index of harm' in a judgment of sensitivity which offers insight into what is meant by 'significant' harm. The fact that it was a loving, stable home, that there was an excellent relationship between the mother and the boy, both of whom were devastated by the rupture caused by the abuse, led the judge to conclude that the boy could be safely reintegrated into the family. 'Significant' has to be situated within relationships. It is necessary to look at *this* child in the context of *this* home: abuse in one context is not necessarily abuse in another. And context must also include culture. Clearly, there are limits to this: we cannot exculpate practices we believe to be objectively harmful merely because they are common amongst a particular group (female circumcision amongst certain African peoples is a good example). But what is 'significant' must depend in part upon what is expected and different cultures have different expectations of acceptable child-rearing behaviour.

The Act uses 'significant harm' as the trigger (and not just in the context of care). But it must not be forgotten that insignificant harm may betoken risk of significant harm, and so cannot be overlooked. A good example is the infliction of moderate corporal chastisement which we know can all so easily lead to child abuse (Freeman, 1988; Newell, 1989). Too many of the notorious child death cases are exercises of discipline which have gone badly wrong. Parents who use physical punishment excessively should be sounding warning bells to those engaged in the protection of children.

Harm explored

'Harm' itself is broadly defined in the Act. It means 'ill treatment' or 'the impairment of health and development' (s.31(9)). The *Guidance* (vol. 1) advises that these (though there are three) are 'alternatives' (para. 3.19) and, more importantly, informs that 'only one of these conditions needs to be satisfied but the proceedings may refer to all three' (*idem*). The Lord Chancellor explained 'ill-treatment' thus: it 'is not a precise term and would include, for example, instances of verbal abuse or unfairness falling a long way short of significant harm' (*Hansard*, HL vol. 503, col. 342). The examples he gives may be instructive, but this statement cannot be taken at face value: if the acts fall short of significant harm, they cannot form the basis of a care application.

The Act itself defines 'ill-treatment' as including sexual abuse and forms of ill-treatment that are not physical (s.31(9)). It includes physical abuse by implication. 'Ill-treatment is sufficient proof of harm in itself and it is not necessary to show that impairment of health or development has followed, or is likely to follow (though that might be relevant to later stages of the test)' (*Guidance*, vol.1, para. 3.19).

Although not specifically mentioned, 'emotional abuse' is clearly an example of non-physical ill-treatment. Emotional abuse was recognised as coming within the umbrella of 'being ill-treated' in s.1(2)(a) as far as the 1969 Act was concerned.[22] Since then our awareness of, and understanding of, emotional abuse has increased considerably, despite the argument in the highly influential *Beyond the Best Interests of The Child* (Goldstein *et al.*, 1979, p. 72) that emotional abuse should not be a ground for intervention into parent/child relations. A commonly-used example of emotional abuse is the refusal to recognise a child's gender, making him/her dress in the clothes of the other sex. It has been suggested by a leading child psychiatrist that three things should be looked for (Wolkind, 1988); parental behaviour that is deviant; a form of child behaviour that is persistently and severely impairing the child's full attainment of mental health (for the child psychiatrist the central factor); appropriate treatment offered and rejected by the parents. It will be observed that the focus is on the child's abnormal behaviour, not the abnormal parenting. This distinguishes emotional abuse from other forms of abuse. Since proof of emotional abuse will usually require psychiatric evidence, there may be problems with social workers and lawyers emphasising parental behaviour and the psychiatric evidence pointing to no disturbance in the child.

Sexual abuse is specifically included within 'ill-treatment' but not as such defined. In a recent case[23] the father was said to have indulged in 'vulgar and inappropriate horseplay' with his daughter. Where is the line to be drawn, and by whom? Our attitudes to sexual abuse clearly differ, as the battle-lines drawn over *Cleveland* indicate (cf. Bell, 1988 and Campbell, 1988; see also Freeman, 1989; and Richardson *et al.*, 1991). Some sexual abuse is gross physical abuse, in addition to being sexual abuse. All sexual abuse is emotional abuse (but see Wolkind, above). Is exposing a child to pornographic material sexual abuse? Does it depend upon what effect this has on the child's behaviour? There is, not surprisingly, no universally accepted definition of what constitutes child sexual abuse (Finkelhor, 1984; Haugaard and Reppucci, 1988; Faller,

1988). The intention of the abuser is critical, so that the inclusion within the definition of anything that gives him sexual gratification is meaningful. A useful working definition, put forward by the Standing Committee on Sexually Abused Children in 1984 (see Glaser and Frosh, 1988, p. 9) is:

'Any child below the age of consent may be deemed to have been sexually abused when a sexually mature person has by design or by neglect of their usual societal or specific responsibilities in relation to the child, engaged or permitted the engagement of that child in any activity of a sexual nature which is intended to lead to the sexual gratification of the sexually mature person. This definition pertains whether or not this activity involves explicit coercion by any means, whether or not initiated by the child, or whether or not there is discernible harmful outcome in the short term.'

Proof of harm may be difficult to establish. Indeed, the courts seem to believe that the standard of proof in child sexual abuse cases should be higher than in other abuse cases.[24]

The Act also does not define what is meant by ill-treatment. It includes sexual abuse and non-physical ill-treatment. But what else? The previous legislation had a separate category of 'neglect'. It will be observed that 'neglect' is not specifically mentioned in s.31. Under the old law failure to obtain medical treatment would have been considered 'neglect'.[25] It would surely now be regarded either as 'ill-treatment' or the impairment of health or development, depending on what form the neglect took. When is corporal punishment ill-treatment? English law draws the line between the two by permitting 'moderate and reasonable chastisement',[26] but this test is vague and value-laden and is continually changing. Amendments to the Children Bill to make it unlawful for parents and for foster parents to administer physical punishment failed.[27] The Swedes who, along with the Norwegians, Danes, Finns and Austrians, have made it unlawful to hit children did so partly because of its links with child abuse (see their Minister of Justice quoted in Newell, 1989, pp. 24–5). We will do so eventually too. In the meanwhile hitting children is not ill-treatment so long as it does not exceed (in intensity, in duration) what a reasonable parent might do. This is also clearly age-related. We cannot tell parents in advance whether their conduct is 'moderate and reasonable'. But they may discover after the event that it is not so considered.

The 'similar child'

Section 31(10) states:

> 'Where the question of whether harm suffered by a child is significant turns on the child's health or development, his health or development shall be compared with that which could be reasonably expected of a similar child.'

As the *Guidance* acknowledges (vol. 1, para. 3.20) the meaning of 'similar' will require judicial interpretation. We may note the reference is to 'a similar child', not a child of similar parents, and that the standard of care below which parents must not fall is that which can be reasonably expected to be given to similar children. It follows that only rearing below this threshold level may attract state intervention. There will be need for expert advice: the guardian ad litem may be a useful source, but in difficult cases, specialist expert advice may be necessary.

But what is a 'similar child'? According to the Lord Chancellor it is a child with the same physical attributes as the child concerned, and not a child of the same background. On this test, the development of a two-year-old has to be compared with that of other two-year-olds, and not with other two-year-olds from similar backgrounds. (*Hansard* HL vol. 503, col. 354). If this interpretation is right, a child from a deprived background is expected to achieve intellectual growth and emotional maturity comparable to children who come from well-ordered, materially comfortable and stimulating environments. The *Guidance* says (vol. 1, para. 3.20) that we 'may' need to 'take account of environmental, social and cultural characteristics of the child'. Clearly, we *ought* to do so for to ignore the impact of poverty and deprivation on, for example, intellectual development is to take a myopic view of what can be achieved in such circumstances. Neither the statement of the Lord Chancellor nor the corrective of the *Guidance* has legal authority. The judges will have picked up the Lord Chancellor's statement from commentaries on the Act. They are not supposed to read *Hansard* as an interpretative guide. The *Guidance* is just that: the judges are not supposed to be influenced by the interpretation it puts on the meaning of words in the Act. So we have before the Act even comes into operation a conflict of interpretation between two government limbs. We must await the courts' interpretation. But why should this be uniform when those behind the legislation cannot agree on its meaning?

There are thus problems with 'similar child'. But what the phrase does achieve is the comparison of *this* child with children like him/her: that is to say, children who have the same attributes. The development of (for example) a deaf four-year-old boy, who may only speak a few words, is to be compared with what is to be expected of other four-year-olds who are deaf, and not with other four-year-olds. But the value of this may be more apparent than real. First, even within the context of a physical disability like deafness, it is not apparent what the appropriate comparison is. Is a four-year-old, whose deafness was only diagnosed late, to be compared with a four-year-old, who was being appropriately treated before he reached his first birthday? And secondly, what is appropriate treatment? Is a deaf child to be integrated into the hearing world or specially educated at a school for the hearing-impaired? Should he be taught to speak or encouraged to sign? Intense conflicts rage over these matters (Sacks, 1989). Thirdly, there is the matter of amount of hearing loss, type of deficiency, particular type of loss (Tucker, 1986). Is a child of deaf parents a 'similar child' to a deaf child of hearing parents? If we take account only of the characteristics of the child, as the statute requires, a deaf child of deaf parents is like a deaf child of hearing parents. But is he? His rearing will have taken place in a different environment. His parents, with experiences of deafness, may well have attitudes to deafness and to the education of the deaf very different from parents who have not themselves suffered the disability.

This extended example of deafness could be replicated for other handicaps. What it illustrates is that, however laudatory the goal of the 'similar child' notion in emphasising the special needs of handicapped children, it overlooks the essential individuality of families and their problems. By concentrating on the child it also ignores the impact of interaction between the child and his parents, the effect such interaction can have on handicaps and on parents. Thus, to take one further example, there is evidence that mothers of Down's Syndrome children suffer disproportionately from depression (Gath, 1978) and that the birth of a Down's Syndrome child can turn a moderately successful or shaky marriage into a poor or dysfunctional one, with obvious concomitant effect on the child's development and health. It also ignores those cases where the source of a child's problems may lie in early family history (the emotionally frozen child may be one such example) (Jeffries, 1981; Del Priore, 1984).

The quality of care

The second limb of the minimum condition requires the court to be satisfied that

'the harm or likelihood of harm, is attributable to —
(i) the care given to the child, or likely to be given to him if the order were not made, not being what it would be reasonable to expect a parent to give to him; or
(ii) the child's being beyond parental control.'

Paragraph (1) of the limb is considered in this section. But it is first necessary to draw attention to the phrase 'attributable to'. I would suggest that 'attributable to' is different from, and wider than, 'caused by'. Parliament could have used the words 'caused by' and did not do so. It may therefore be taken to indicate that the care provision may be activated when the relationship between the harm and the parent's quality of care is linked other than causally. The *Guidance* (vol. 1, para. 3.23) states that 'harm caused solely by a third party is...excluded (unless the parent has failed to prevent it)'. The reason is that the harm in such a case is attributable to the quality of the parent's care, but it is not caused by it. This might also apply if the parent is psychiatrically sick and not responsible for his or her behaviour: harm could be attributed, even if it was not 'caused by' the parent (cf. Bainham 1991).

The quality of care must fall below what it is reasonable to expect of a parent. 'Care' is not defined but must include catering for the child's total needs (physical, emotional, intellectual, behavioural, social) and not just having physical charge (see also *Guidance*, vol. 1, para. 3.23). The care given to the child is not what it would be reasonable for *this* parent to give (in her high-rise flat, living on income support, with three children under five and a partner in prison), but what it would be reasonable to expect *a* parent to give. The standard is objective. It concentrates on the 'needs of the child...rather than on some hypothetical child and the hypothesis is transferred to the parent' (Lord Chancellor, *Hansard*, HL vol. 512, col. 756). The emphasis is on *this* child, given this child's needs. If he has asthma or brittle bones,[28] he may need more care, or a different type of care, from a 'normal' child. If *a* parent could provide this, then this parent is failing if s/he cannot. The *Guidance* points out (vol. 1, para. 3.23) that 'the court will almost certainly expect to see professional evidence on the standard of care which could reasonably be expected of reasonable parents with support from community-wide services as appropriate where the child's needs are complex or demanding, or the lack of reasonable care is not immediately obvious'.

The 'likely'element in the second limb provides for cases where the child is not being cared for by the parents at the time of the application (perhaps the child is being accommodated and his or her return has been demanded – see above), but there is reason for concern about his or her welfare if they were to start looking after him or her.

The extent to which cultural pluralism should be taken into account is a matter of contention. Bainham's view (1990, p. 101) is that the different situations of ethnic minority groups become relevant at the point where, the minimum conditions having been proved, without reference to cultural difference, s.1(3) comes into play with its checklist, including the 'background' of the child (see also Bainham, 1991). But, in legislation committed to cultural pluralism (see, for example, s.22(5)(c)), it ought to be asked whether the hypothetically reasonable parent has to be located within the dominant white English Christian culture. It might not be reasonable to expect *a* parent to have a male baby circumcised, but it would be unreasonable to expect a Jewish parent to do anything else (cf. Miller, 1990). As indicated above, what is 'significant harm' also depends upon cultural context. There is a line-drawing exercise involved. The courts have had to confront this very problem when dealing with the chastisement practices of ethnic minority groups. Thus, in one case,[29] the practices of a mother who was by origin Vietnamese was judged against the 'reasonable objective standards of the culture in which the children have hitherto been brought up', but the judge was careful to add, 'so long as these do not conflict with our minimal acceptable standards of child care in England'.

Beyond parental control

Under the old law 'being beyond parental control' was one of the primary conditions for a care order, and care proceedings (on that ground) could be activated (latterly, indirectly only) by a parent. There are thus changes, both substantive and procedural, in the new law.

First, the procedural change. No longer will parents be able to request the local authority to bring their child before the court or to apply by complaint to the juvenile court for an order directing an authority to do so, where the authority refuses or fails to comply within twenty-eight days. Whether this harms irreparably or strengthens a relationship was debated over 30 years ago (Ingleby, 1960). There was all-party support this time for an amendment that would have allowed an application for a care order by any person with parental responsibility (Standing Committee B, cols. 218–22). A parent can still request that the local authority provides accommodation for a child with whom they cannot cope (using s.20). But this may cause problems where authorities have adopted policies not to use accommodation for children over a particular age (thirteen was the example given of one London authority in Standing Commitee B, col. 227). But, if such policies continue, they are clear examples of the fettering of discretion and thus are potentially amenable to challenge by judicial review.[30] This is the ultimate remedy upon which a parent might have to rely.

The substantive change is that being beyond parental control survives as a 'ground' only where there is significant harm to the child (or this is likely) that it is attributable to the child's being beyond parental control. Children who are beyond parental control often wreak significant harm (vandalism, burglary etc.), but this is not the test. Proving that the sexually promiscuous teenager or the glue-sniffing child is likely to suffer significant harm should not be difficult but attributing it to their being beyond parental control may be less easy.

It is not entirely clear whether control is an objective standard (is the child beyond the control of a reasonable parent? In other words it is the child's fault) or a subjective one (is he beyond the control of his parents who are in some way at fault?). Since this limb of the section makes no reference to reasonableness, it has to be assumed that the subjective test applies. And that would be consistent with the minimum conditions as a whole which are about limiting state interference with parental autonomy. It would be right to interfere when *these* parents cannot control their child. But the *Guidance* (vol. 1, para.3.25) says it is immaterial whether it is the fault of the parents or the child, suggesting, somewhat equivocally, that 'beyond parental control' can be looked at in both ways.

A final point to note centres on the meaning of 'parental'. It must be assumed, given the nature of this Act, that the word 'parental' is wide enough to embrace all those who are exercising parental functions and responsibilities. So, if a mother, who cannot cope, asks the child's grandparents to care for the child and they cannot control the child, the possibility of recourse to care proceedings ought to be open. If it is not, a curious gap has been created.

Gaps?

Since the minimum conditions in s.31(2) are the precondition for intervention to protect children from abuse or neglect, it is worth pondering whether any gaps are created (Freeman, 1990). The inability of local authorities to assume parental rights and thus provide stability and planning for a child may mean that it will be impossible to prevent a parent who is capable of providing adequate facilities for a child from removing that child from a foster home where s/he has lived for a considerable time. There may be no difficulty in proving that such a child would be likely to suffer significant harm, but it may be rather more difficult to demonstrate that such harm is attributable to the care likely to be given to the child not being what it would be reasonable to expect a parent to give. Much will depend on how the courts interpret 'care given to the child'. A parent can give 'care' without day-to-day physical contact by showing love and affection, visiting, remembering birthdays and so on. If the courts interpret care to include these manifestations, then a parent who, for whatever reason, fails to offer this 'parenting' may not surmount the hurdle of s.31(2). But, interpreted more literally, it could lead to children being removed by 'unimpeachable' parents, where the trauma of removal from foster parents to whom they have become attached is likely to cause significant harm, and where the minimum conditions will not be satisfied.

Another gap is the one created by the removal of the abandonment grounds in section 3 of the Child Care Act 1980. The new Act lacks an equivalent of the concept of 'statutory abandonment' (deemed to occur if parents, with a child in voluntary care did not notify their address to the local authority for 12 months). This may lead to children remaining in limbo with no prospects of rehabilitation and, in some cases, no way in which a permanent plan can be devised. It may be possible to argue that 'care' expected from a parent would include notification of change of address. But, short of this, if a care order is not available, the foster parents will, after 3 years of caring for the child, be able to apply for a residence order (which will give them parental responsibility). They may also apply without fulfilling the time requirements with the local authority's consent. The court's leave will also be required, and it is to have 'particular regard' to the authority's plans for the child's future, and the wishes and feelings of the parents. Given these hurdles, whether there is sufficient in the legislation to protect the child from 'drift' will depend upon how local authorities and courts interpret these provisions.

The relevance of section 1

The provisions in section 1 and their importance have been explained in chapter 2. But it must be stressed again that proof of the minimum conditions in s.31(2), without more, will not satisfy a court that a care (or supervision) order should be made. It is necessary to show also:

(*i*) that the care order is in the child's best interests (s.1(1));
(*ii*) that regard has been had, in particular, to the matters in the checklist (s.1(3)); and
(*iii*) that the order would be better for the child than making no order at all (s.1(5)).

To satisfy these tests the local authority must have a clear idea of what the care order is designed to achieve and the ways it is hoped it will advance the child's welfare. A care order is no panacea and by itself achieves nothing. The authority will need to present to the court a plan for the future care of the child. This should address the checklist of factors in s.1(3), in particular the child's wishes and feelings, the likely effect on him or her of any change in his or her circumstances, any harm suffered or at risk of suffering, and the range of powers available to the court (which include 'private law' powers such as residence orders). The plan should also keep in mind the presumption of non-intervention, now enshrined in s.1(5). The *Guidance* advises (vol.1, para. 3.28) that, given this presumption, the plan will need to be 'more than embryonic'.

Procedural requirements

Parties

The local authority (or other authorised person) applying for a care or supervision order is required to serve a copy of the application on all the parties to the proceedings (Family Proceedings Courts (Children Act 1989) Rules 1991 r.7, Sch.2 column (iii)). These are:

(a) every person whom the applicant believes to have parental responsibility for the child;
(b) in the case of an application to extend, vary or discharge an order, the parties to the proceedings leading to the order which it is sought to have extended, varied or discharged.

The child will automatically be given party status. The court may also direct that others be joined to the proceedings (r.7(5)). A person may also file a written request that s/he be joined as a party or cease to be one (r.7(2)). The court may grant this with or without a hearing or representations (r.7(3)). But, where the person has parental responsibility, the court must grant this request (r.7(4)). Previously, it was specifically provided that grandparents could apply for party status in certain circumstances. There is no specific mention of them now, but, under rule 7, they can apply for party status. So, of course, can other relatives. It is grandparents and other close relatives who are most likely to request (and be granted, where appropriate) party status. It is possible that foster, or former foster, parents may also be looked upon favourably by courts hearing requests for party status.

The application

The application must be made on the Prescribed Form (this is Form 19, found in the Family Proceedings Courts (Children Act 1989) Rules 1991). A separate application must be made for each child. This has been designed to encourage the preparations of documentary evidence and early advance disclosure of relevant evidence to the court and other parties. It will be noted that the applicant is required to submit details of plans for the future care of the child and any requests for directions, including restrictions on contact (see s.34 and below). As the *Guidance* (vol. 1, para. 3.28) observes: 'the level of details given will be determined to some extent by the stage reached in the investigation of the child's circumstances'. The checklist in s.1(3) should be borne in mind when considering the plan, as should the presumption of no order in s.1(5). A plan which does not address itself to this presumption may well not substantiate the case for a care (or supervision) order.

The application must be served at least 3 days before the hearing or directions appointment on all the respondents (r.4(1)(b)), and notice in writing must be given to:

    (a) every person whom the applicant believes to be a party to pending relevant proceedings in the respect of the same child;

    (b) every person whom the applicant believes to be a parent without parental responsibility for the child.

Transfer of proceedings

On receipt of the application, the clerk of the court will consider whether the proceedings should be transferred to a higher court. Advice on the appropriate forum may be given by the guardian ad litem (r.11(4)(c)). The criteria for this (set out in the Allocation and Transfer Rules)[31] are:

    (a) A case may be transferred to *another magistrates'* court where it is in the interests of the child because
        – it will avoid delay
        – for the purposes of consolidation
        – for some other reason.

The receiving court's justices' clerk must consent to the transfer (Rule 6).

    (b) A case may be transferred to a *county court care centre* where it considers it is in the interests of the child to do so having regard to the following
        – the case is of exceptional gravity, importance or complexity
        – for the purposes of consolidation
        – where the case is urgent, delay would seriously prejudice the welfare of the child, and no other magistrates' court can take the case. (Rule 7(1)).

Gravity, importance and complexity are further explained as, in particular, cases where there is complicated or conflicting evidence about the risks involved to the child's physical or moral welfare, or where there are many parties, or an issue of private international law is involved, or there is a novel or difficult point of law involved or because of some question of general public interest (r.7(1)(a)). The vast majority of cases will start in the magistrates' court and finish there.

Directions appointment

On receipt of the application, the clerk of the court will also consider whether a directions appointment should be held in advance of the first hearing. At a directions appointment (which may be held at any time during the course of the proceedings), directions may be issued on any of the following matters (see Family Proceedings Courts (Children Act 1989) Rules 1991, r.14):

(a) the timetable for the proceedings;
(b) varying the time within which or by which an act is required;
(c) the attendance of the child;
(d) appointment of a guardian ad litem or of a solicitor;
(e) the service of documents;
(f) submission of evidence, including experts' reports;
(g) the preparation of welfare reports (see s.7);
(h) transfer of the proceedings (see above);
(i) consolidation with other proceedings (see above).

Directions may be given (as well as varied and revoked) either of the justices' clerk's or court's own motion or on the written request of a party specifying the direction which is sought (r.14(5)). In an urgent case the request can be made orally (r.14(6)).

The *Guidance* points out (vol. 1, para. 3.30) that the court usually will not be able to decide the application for a care order or supervision order at the first hearing. It directs that the applicant should be ready to tell the court at the directions appointment:

(a) whether s/he is applying for an interim order and if so, any directions under s.38(6);
(b) what plans the authority have made for safeguarding and promoting the child's welfare while the interim order is in force and, where an interim care order is sought, what type of placement is envisaged;
(c) in the case of an interim order, what proposals the authority has for allowing the child reasonable contact with his parents and others under s.34 (and see below).

Timetable requirements

Section 1(2) states that any delay in determining a question relating to a child's upbringing is likely to prejudice the welfare of the child.

But, as indicated above, this is not always necessarily so. Indeed, the new structure of care proceedings (extending the role of the guardian ad litem, widening access to party status) may be thought to protract proceedings. It is, however, hoped (though only experience will tell) that the new requirements on the advance disclosure of the case and witness statements by all parties, and the emphasis on agreeing facts at the directions appointment will more than balance this. There will normally be adjournments because a court hearing an application will not be in a position to decide it, even when it is not contested. For example, the guardian ad litem will need time to make enquiries, establish the views of the child and others, investigate the applicant's plans and prepare a report and recommendations for the court. And other parties will need to prepare their case.

Section 32 directs that a court hearing an application under part IV of the Act[32] is to draw up a timetable with a view to disposing of the application without delay and to give directions to ensure, so far as reasonably practicable, that it is adhered to. The guardian ad litem is expected to assist and advise the court in timing of the proceedings (see r.11(4)(d)). The applicant for the order 'should regard it as part of his responsibilities to help both the court clerk and the guardian ad litem identify and deal with difficulties likely to cause delay' (*Guidance*, vol. 1, para. 3.33).

There is evidence that in some places there has been a 'culture of acceptable delay' (Murch and Mills, 1987). It is this that s.32 and the accompanying Rules wishes to remove. The *Guidance* (*idem*) insists that local authorities should ensure that all staff are aware of directions on timetabling and do 'whatever is necessary' to ensure directions are complied with.[33] Timetabling and adjournments must be looked at in the context of the powers of the court to make an interim order under s.38. This is discussed in the next chapter.

Notes

1. For a more sceptical view see Mellon and Clapton (1991) (an attempt to divert the issue away from men as abusers to 'witches'). A very full discussion is in *Rochdale BC* v. *A* [1991] 2 FLR 192.
2. See, for example, *C* v. *C* [1988] 1 FLR 462 and *Re B* [1990] 2 FLR 317 both discussed below.
3. SI (1991) No. 1395.
4. *R* v. *L.B. of Harrow ex parte D* [1989] 2 FLR 51.

5. *R* v. *Norfolk CC ex parte X* [1989] 2 FLR 120.
6. But it was said in the *Norfolk* case that judicial review would not be granted if the procedure adopted represented a genuine attempt to reconcile the duty of child protection and the duty of fairness to the alleged abuser. For a further example of a failure to do so see *R* v. *Lewisham LBC ex parte P* [1991] 2 FLR 185. But recourse to judicial review in respect of decisions which did not involve removing a child from the care of parents should be rare and adopted only in exceptional cases (*R* v. *East Sussex CC ex parte R* [1991] 2 FLR 358).
7. It is not envisaged that other persons will be authorised.
8. An example is *Mohamed* v. *Knott* [1969] 1 QB 1.
9. As in *Re SW* [1986] 1 FLR 24.
10. Still then called a 'case conference'. There was a change of thinking between the writing of volume 1 and *Working Together*.
11. After *Re S* [1978] QB 120, the distinction between the primary conditions and the general conditions was blurred, since the Court of Appeal said 'care' included 'education', which a child being kept away from school was not receiving.
12. The Lord Chancellor (Mackay, 1989) describes them as the 'minimum circumstances'.
13. See *Re D* [1977] Fam 158; *Re R* [1987] 2 FLR 400.
14. *Essex CC* v. *TLR and KBR* (1978) 9 Fam Law 15.
15. *Re CB* [1981] 1 All ER 16.
16. [1985] FLR 325.
17. The original Bill said 'has suffered', not 'is suffering'. It was changed to prevent an order being made 'on the basis of significant harm suffered several years previously, and which is not likely to be repeated' (David Mellor, Standing Committee B, col. 221).
18. See *H* v. *Sheffield CC* [1981] JSWL 303.
19. *D* v. *Berkshire CC* [1987] AC 317.
20. The *Guidance* actually says 'implication'.
21. *Re B* [1990] 2 FLR 317.
22. *F* v. *Suffolk CC* (1981) 2 FLR 208.
23. *C* v. *C* [1988] 1 FLR 462.
24. *Re W* [1987] 1 FLR 297; *Re G* [1988] 1 FLR 314; *Re H; Re K* [1989] 2 FLR 313.
25. Bevan (1989, p.626) thinks 'ill-treatment'.
26. *R* v. *Hopley* (1860) 2 F and F 202.
27. There were debates in the House of Lords on 28 January 1989, 16 February 1989 and 16 March 1989.
28. *Re P* [1988] 1 FLR 328.
29. *Re H* [1987] 2 FLR 12, 17. In the particular case the mother's cruelty was grossly excessive by any standards. See, further Neate, 1991.
30. *Attorney-General (on the relation of Tilley)* v. *Wandsworth LBC* [1981] 1 All ER 1162.
31. SI 1677. See also Joint Lord Chancellor's Guidance/Home Office Guidance (Home Office Circular No 45/91). Both are reproduced in *Guidance and Regulations vol. 7*, 1991.

32. And therefore it applies also to education supervision orders under s.36, interim orders under s.38 and orders pending appeals under s.40.
33. A vivid illustration is *Manchester CC* v. *S* [1991] 2 FLR 370, a case study almost of the need for firm court control, such as is envisaged by the Act.

References

Bainham, A. (1990) *Children – The New Law*, Bristol, Family Law.
Bainham, A. (1991) 'Care After 1991 – A Reply', *Journal of Child Law*, 99.
Bell, S. (1988) *When Salem Came to the 'Boro*, London, Pan.
Bevan, H. (1989) *Child Law*, London, Butterworths.
Campbell, B. (1988) *Unofficial Secrets*, London, Virago.
Cretney, S. (1990) 'Defining the Limits of State Intervention: the Child and the Courts' in D. Freestone (ed), *Children and the Law*, Hull, Hull University Press.
Del Priore, C. (1984) 'Assessing Needs of the Handicapped Child', *Adoption and Fostering*, 8(4), 38.
Dingwall, R. *et al.* (1984) 'Childhood as a Social Problem', *Journal of Law and Society*, 11, 207.
Eekelaar, J. (1991) 'Parental Responsibility: State of Nature or Nature of the State?' *Journal of Social Welfare and Family Law*, 37.
Faller, K. (1988) *Child Sexual Abuse*, New York, Columbia University Press.
Finkelhor, D. (1984) *Child Sexual Abuse*, London, Sage.
Freeman, M. (1980) 'Removing Babies at Birth: A Questionable Practice', *Family Law* 10, 131.
Freeman, M. (1983) *The Rights and Wrongs of Children*, London, Frances Pinter.
Freeman, M. (1988) 'Time to Stop Hitting Our Children' *Childright*, 51, 5.
Freeman, M. (1989) 'Cleveland, Butler-Sloss and Beyond', *Current Legal Problems*, 42, 85.
Freeman, M. (1990) 'Care After 1991' in Freestone, D (ed.), *Children and The Law*, Hull, Hull University Press.
Freeman, M. (1992) 'In the Child's Best Interests? Reading the Children Act Critically', *Current Legal Problems*.
Gath, A. (1978) *Down's Syndrome and the Family: the Early Years*, London, Academic Press.
Glaser, D. and Frosh, S. (1988) *Child Sexual Abuse*, London, Macmillan.
Goldstein, J. *et al.* (1979) *Before the Best Interests of the Child*, New York, Free Press.
Haugaard, J. and Reppucci, N. (1988) *The Sexual Abuse of Children*, San Francisco, Jossey Bass.
Hayes, M. and Bevan, V. (1988) *Child Care Law*, Bristol, Jordans.
Jeffries, B. (1981) 'Art Therapy with the Emotionally Frozen', *Adoption and Fostering*, 106, 9.

Mackay, Lord (1989) 'Joseph Jackson Memorial Lecture', *New Law Journal*, 139, 505.

Mellon, M. and Clapton, G. (1991) 'Who[m] Are We Protecting?' *Community Care*, 854, 22.

Miller, A (1990) *Banished Knowledge: Facing Childhood Injuries*, London, Virago.

Murch, M. and Mills, R. (1987) *The Length of Care Proceedings*, London, DHSS.

Neate, P. (1991) 'Bridging the Cultural Divide', *Community Care*, 890, 12.

Newell, P. (1990) *Children are People Too*, London, Bedford Square Press.

Richardson, S. and Bacon, H. (eds) (1991) *Child Sexual Abuse: Whose Problem? Reflections from Cleveland*, London, Venture Press.

Sacks, O. (1989) *Seeing Voices*, London, Picador.

Tate, T. (1991) *Children for the Devil*, London, Methuen.

Tucker, I. (1986) 'Deafness' in S. Curtis (ed.) *From Asthma to Thalassaemia*, London, BAAF.

Tylden, E. (1983) 'Care of the Pregnant Drug Addict', *MIMS* (June 1).

Wolkind, S. (1988) 'Emotional Signs', *Journal of Social Welfare* Law, 82.

Working Together (1988), London, HMSO.

Working Together (1991), London, HMSO.

6

The Public Care System – II

The effect of a care order

The local authority designated in the care order must be the authority in whose area the child is ordinarily resident, or, where the child does not reside in the area of a local authority (for example, a child from outside England and Wales), the authority within whose area any circumstances arose in consequence of which the order is being made (s.31(8)).

Under the old law the effect of a care order was far from clear (Maidment, 1981; Freeman, 1982). Section 33, which sets out the powers and responsibilities of the various parties when a care order is made, is much clearer, though the compromises it effects may distort expectations.

When a care order is made the local authority is under a duty to receive the child into their care and keep him or her there while the order is in force (s.33(1)). An authorised person (in effect the NSPCC) may keep the child in their care until s/he is received by the local authority but only if the local authority was not informed of the application under s.31(6) (above) (s.33(2)).

A care order vests parental responsibility in the local authority. The White Paper (1987, para. 35) contemplated that parental powers and responsibilities would pass 'from the parents to the authority'. But the Law Commission (1988, para. 2.11) took a different view: 'the parents remain the parents and it will be important in many cases to involve the parents in the child's care'. The Law Commission accepted that the care order would leave the parents little scope to exercise their responsibilities 'save to a limited extent while the child is with them, because the local authority will be in control of so much of the child's life'. But it,

120

nevertheless, concluded that 'parents should not be deprived of their very parenthood unless and until the child is adopted or freed for adoption'. It is significant that the Law Commission used the word 'parenthood': it did not say 'parental responsibility' (Eekelaar, 1991).

These changes in thought and nuances of language are reflected in the compromise of section 33. The parents retain parental responsibility but can only exercise it in accordance with

- s.2(8): they are not entitled to act incompatibly with any order under the Act
- s.33(3) and (4): which give the local authority the power to determine, in accordance with the child's welfare, the extent to which the parents may exercise their responsibility.

However, a parent with care (that is physical control) of the child may do what is reasonable to safeguard or promote his or her welfare (s.33(5)).

So, both parents and the local authority have parental responsibility. But the local authority has the whip hand (and see David Mellor, Standing Committee B, col. 232). What is the effect of parents retaining powers they can only exercise at the discretion of the local authority? The *Official Guide* to the Children Act (1989, para. 5.4) says:

'if, while the child is staying with him a parent wants to take his child to visit a particular relative, he may do so, even if the local authority disapproves. However, the authority may prevent a parent or guardian from exercising his parental responsibility if it is necessary to do so to safeguard or promote the child's welfare. If, in the above example, the authority considers that seeing the relative in question was likely to put the child at risk, they could require the parent not to go through with his plan.'

Eekelaar (1991), pp. 44–5) suggests the authority in these circumstances could seek a prohibited steps order, but this cannot be right because the child is in care (s.9(1)). In practice, as he admits, the authority's remedy would lie in taking the child back. There is concern that we are saying parents have responsibility but giving them no way of challenging the exercise by a local authority of its discretion to take that responsibility away. That the authority can only do if satisfied that it is necessary to do so to safeguard or promote the child's welfare is of no great significance, because the authority will not have to satisfy anyone other than itself. The parent can use the new complaints procedure (s.26(3) and below), but has no recourse to any court. It is difficult, therefore, to gauge the significance, beyond the ideological, of the parent retaining parental responsibility when there is a care order. But 'parental responsibility' is clearly a 'civil right' and, since the European Convention on Human Rights and Fundamental Freedoms (Article 6) gives the right to 'a fair and public hearing within a reasonable time by an independent and impartial tribunal established by law' to determine 'civil rights and obligations', there is the distinct possibility of a challenge to the new law before the European Commission and Court in Strasbourg.

Accommodating the child with parents

The law on provision of accommodation was discussed above. Of particular significance (and therefore considered in this context rather than in the general discussion of accommodation) is accommodation with parents or 'home on trial'.

Section 23(5) of the Act lays down that 'Where a child is in the care of a local authority, the authority may only allow him to live with' a parent, a person with parental responsibility or a person in whose favour a residence order was in force before the care order was made 'in accordance with regulations made by the Secretary of State'. After the *Newham* decision,[1] the Courts and Legal Services Act, Schedule 16, para. 12(2) defined 'living with a person' as staying with that person for a continuous period of more than 24 hours. Lesser periods would be regarded as 'contact' (and thus governed by s.34).

Regulations have been made (the Placement of Children with Parents etc. Regulations 1991).[2] Before a placement is made, enquiries have to be conducted about the health of the child, the suitability of the person with whom placement is proposed, suitability of the proposed accommodation (including sleeping arrangements), the educational and social needs of the child, and the suitability of all the members of the household, aged 16 and over, in which it is proposed a child will live (r.3(1)). A police check is advised (*Guidance*, vol. 3, para. 5.25). The decision to place the child has to be taken by the Director of Social Services or an officer nominated in writing for that purpose by the Director (r.5(2)).

Where an immediate placement is necessary (perhaps there has been an unforeseen breakdown of a foster placement and it is thought the least traumatic move is to a parent), only the following basic checks have to be carried out before the placement:

(i) the parent must be interviewed;

(ii) the accommodation must be inspected; and

(iii) information about other persons living in the household must be obtained (r.6).

The other provisions of the Regulations concerning matters which should be investigated in other cases before a placement is made should be carried out as soon as possible after the placement. It is the view of the Department of Health (*Guidance*, vol. 3, para. 5.11) that the remaining enquiries should be completed within six weeks of the immediate placement.

A series of short, preplanned placements with the same carer are, under Regulation 13, to be treated as a 'single placement'. Typically, these placements may be for 'regular staying contact or to allow the carer or the child to have a break' (*Guidance*, vol. 3, para. 5.12). To be treated as a single placement, all the placements must occur within one year, no single placement must last more than four weeks, and the total duration of the placements must not exceed ninety days (r.13(1)).

If it appears to an authority that a placement is no longer in accordance with the duty laid down by s.22(3) (see above) or would 'prejudice the safety of the child', where, for example, there is suspicion of abuse, an inability to cope, or a lack of co-operation by the carer, the placement should be terminated and the child removed forthwith (r.11(1)). Where a placement is being terminated the authority is, so far as is reasonably practicable, to give written notice in advance of termination to, amongst others, the child (having regard to his or her understanding) and the person with whom the child is placed (r.12). The *Guidance* advises (vol.3, para. 5.58) that in most cases it will be possible to 'plan for removal and so minimise stress to the child and counteract a sense of failure in the carer or child'. (Chapter 5 of *Guidance and Regulations*, 1991, should be consulted further for a more detailed analysis of placement of children in care with their parents.)

Disputes between parents and local authorities

Many disputes will, as in the past, centre on the question of contact. This is addressed below in the next section. As far as other disputes are concerned, there is the new representations and complaints procedure in s.26(3). This is discussed later in this chapter.

Other methods of challenging the local authority's decision-making are severely curtailed. A court cannot make a specific issue or prohibited steps order with respect to a child who is in the care of a local authority (s.9(1)). Nor can the parent use wardship to challenge the local authority's decision.[3] Despite the recommendation of the *Cleveland* report,[4] the House of Lords' decisions denying parents the use of wardship have not been reversed by the Act. Perhaps it is one of the contradictions of the Act that, in strengthening the position of parents in so many ways, it has not taken this to its logical conclusion and restored to them the challenge of wardship. But judicial review remains available if the parent can establish one of the grounds for this.[5] The grounds are (i) irrationality or unreasonableness;[6] in short, has the authority acted as no reasonable authority would by taking into account matters that reasonable authorities would not or by failing to consider matters that reasonable authorities would?[7] (ii) Illegality or *ultra vires*; has the authority exceeded powers conferred upon it by statute (by this Act or Regulations or other legislation or statutory instruments)?[8] and (iii) breach of natural justice: has the authority failed in its duty to act fairly?[9] If the court (the Divisional Court of the Queen's Bench Division, but often staffed for these purposes by judges from the Family Division) finds against the local authority, its decision can be quashed by *certiorari* and the local authority can be ordered to carry out its statutory duty by *mandamus*. The matter is then remitted to the local authority to act properly. This is quite unlike the procedure in wardship, where the court would then take the decision as it saw it in the best interest of the child.[10] It also remains possible for the parent to refer a matter to the Commission for Local Administration (or Ombudsman),[11] but only where maladministration can be proved. The procedure is somewhat cumbersome, can be prolonged and, although it may lead to the authority having to change its policy (which may assist other parents), is unlikely to be very satisfactory for the parent who makes the complaint. Finally, if it can be shown that there is a breach of the European Convention on Human Rights and

Fundamental Freedoms,[12] there is recourse to the European Commission and, if it is satisfied, to the European Court of Human Rights. There have been many successful applications in recent years[13] but the procedure is once again cumbersome and slow and a judgment against the authority may come years after the matter in dispute has flared up.

Contact with children in care

Contact between parents and others and children in care has long been a bone of contention. It was about this that the litigation, which finally decided that wardship could not be used to challenge local authority decision-making, centred.[14] Appeals to the European Court were taken over denial of access[15] and eventually legislation was passed in 1983[16] providing for applications to the juvenile court for an access order where access was 'terminated' or the local authority refused to make arrangements for it. 'Terminate' did not preclude 'regulate restrictively'.[17] There was concern that 'family links [were] seldom given much consideration. As a result circumstantial barriers to access [went] unrecognised and little practical help [was] offered to encourage parents' visits' (Department of Health, 1985, p. 10). Parents felt 'totally devalued' (Rowe *et al.*, 1984). In another study about this time (Millham *et al.*, 1986), 40 per cent of children in care for three years or more had lost contact with their parents by the time two years had elapsed, yet there were no social work reasons for the exclusion of the family in two-thirds of the cases.

Section 34, which must be read together with Schedule 2, paragraph 15, and the *Guidance* in volume 3 (chapter 6) constitutes a complete shift in attitude about contact between children in care and their families. The Act reflects the view that contact is 'a right of the child'.[18] Note the language: 'the authority shall allow the child reasonable contact'. And note also that the child may apply for an order to be made (s.34(2)) and, significantly, for one to be refused (s.34(4)) and the child does not have to be *Gillick*-competent to do this. In theory a child of three could make an application to have contact with a parent or anyone else if that person had a residence order or care under the inherent jurisdiction of the High Court (wardship) immediately before the care order was made.

Under the old law a local authority could stop access and the parent could use the juvenile court to get it going (unless the authority forestalled this by 'regulating' rather than 'terminating' access). Now the local authority can only refuse to allow contact if satisfied that to do so is necessary to safeguard or promote the child's welfare and the refusal is decided upon as a matter of urgency and does not last for more than seven days (s.34(6)). Authorities have often given the child's need to settle down as a reason for refusing contact but there is no evidence that contact with the family damages the child's ability to settle: indeed, the most recent evidence is to the contrary (Berridge and Cleaver, 1987). Litigation may well test the meaning of 'urgency'. In the absence of decided cases it is suggested that where there is contact to stop it would only be justified where an incident has occurred, or a reasonable suspicion has been aroused, that the child is at serious risk. In the light of the evidence referred to above (Berridge and Cleaver, 1987), a change of placement should not constitute urgency. Nor necessarily will the fact that the plan is to free the child for adoption. If there has been no recent contact it may be easier to justify refusal, but the court (after the seven days have elapsed) may well want to know why there has been no contact, particularly in the light of Sch.2, para. 15 which states that 'where a child is being looked after by a local authority, the authority shall, unless it is not reasonably practicable or consistent with his welfare, endeavour to promote contact between the child and – (a) his parents'.

There is a presumption of reasonable contact (s.34(1)). The authority has a *duty* to allow the child reasonable contact with:

(a) his parents;
(b) any guardian of his;
(c) any person who, before the care order was made, has a residence order;
(d) any person who had care of the child under the inherent jurisdiction[19] of the High Court before the care order was made.

The parents include the unmarried father.

Subject to any court order, it is for the authority to decide what is reasonable contact in the circumstances. The authority's view of what is reasonable must safeguard and promote the child's welfare because of the duty in s.22(3) (see above). The *Guidance* (vol. 1, para. 3.75) advises that the degree of contact should not necessarily remain static; the local authority may 'plan for the frequency or duration of contact to increase or decrease over time'. The local authority should indicate its intentions in the plan which is submitted to the court before the care order is made and, where possible, should have discussed this with the child and the parents. If there are disagreements these can be resolved by the court making an order as to the degree of contact. An order may improve such conditions (for example, as to time, place, amount and supervision) as the court considers appropriate (s.34(7)).

The court can make an order of its own motion if it considers that the order should be made (s.34(5)). But it cannot do this until there is a care order or interim care order (s.34(10)). The court may also make an order 'as it considers appropriate' on an application made by the authority or the child (s.34(2)) or by parents (including the unmarried father),[20] guardians and persons who had a residence order or care and control under the High Court's inherent jurisdiction before the care order was made[21] (s.34(3)(a), (1)), or by any person who has obtained the leave of the court (the most likely applicants for leave being grandparents (s.34(3)(b)). A parent, or other person, who wants to restrict contact between the child and other people, for example grandparents, can only do so by requesting the local authority or the child to seek an order refusing contact. It would be a ground for complaint (using s.26(3); see below) if the authority refused to do this.

Only the local authority and the child (who does not have to be of sufficient understanding) may apply for an order for contact to be refused (s.34(4)). There is no duty on the child to maintain contact and s/he can refuse to see a person named in an order even without applying to the court. As a result, the child will only need to apply to the court where there is no other way of avoiding contact. The local authority only has to get the court's consent to refuse contact to those persons in respect of whom it has a duty to maintain contact (that is, those persons listed in s.34(1)). So, it can refuse contact to others, for example grandparents, without the need to obtain an order.

If the court makes an order for contact, the local authority may refuse to comply for seven days, provided it is satisfied that this is necessary to safeguard or promote the child's welfare and it is a matter of urgency (s.34(6) and above). The *Guidance* (vol. 1, para. 3.81) describes this as a 'serious step which should not be undertaken lightly'. When an authority has decided under s.34(6) to refuse contact, otherwise required (either by s.34(1) or a court order), it has 'as soon as the decision has been made' to notify the following persons in writing –

(a) the child, if of sufficient understanding;
(b) the parents;
(c) any guardian;
(d) where there was a residence order in force before the care order was made, the person in whose favour that order was made;
(e) where a person had care by virtue of an order made by the High Court exercising its inherent jurisdiction, that person;
(f) any other person whose wishes and feelings the authority considers relevant;

(see Contact with Children Regulations 1991, r.2[22]).

The written notification must contain: the decision, its reasons; its duration (if applicable); remedies available in case of dissatisfaction and the date (Contact with Children Regulations 1991, Schedule).

There is also provision in the Regulations (see r.3) for a local authority to depart from the terms of a court order when all concerned are agreeable to the new arrangement. This may be done when:

(a) there is agreement between the local authority and the person in relation to whom the order was made;
(b) the child, if of sufficient understanding, also agrees;
(c) written notification is provided within seven days to all the persons listed in Regulation 2 (above). The *Guidance* (vol. 3, para.6.31) says this notification should be on 'need to know basis'.

This provision allows for 'flexibility and partnership in contact arrangements' and obviates the need to go back to court when all concerned 'agree' a new arrangement (*idem*).

Repeat applications for orders under s.34 are controlled by s.91(17). If an application for an order has been refused, the person concerned may not reapply for the same order in respect of the same child within six months without the leave of the court. The court, it is expected, will not grant leave save where there has been a change of circumstances. This provision applies also to local authorities. However, as the *Guidance* (vol. 1, para. 3.83) acknowledges, since they are expected to carry out good child care practice, leave will be sought 'as appropriate' and, presumably, will be given.

Orders made under s.34 may be varied or discharged by the court on the application of the authority, the child and the person who is named in the order. (s.34(9))

The effect of a supervision order

The supervision order puts the child under the supervision of a designated local authority or a probation officer (selection is dealt with by Schedule 3, para. 9). Children will continue to be supervised by local authority social workers unless para. 9(2) applies (that is, the authority requests supervision by a probation officer and probation have been involved with the household before). The supervisor is given three duties (s.35(1):

(a) to advise, assist and befriend the child;
(b) to take all steps that are reasonably necessary to see that the order is given effect;
(c) to consider whether to apply for variation or discharge of the order where it is not being wholly complied with or s/he considers that the order may no longer be necessary.

The supervisor must also refer back to the court on medical treatment should the need arise (Sch.3, para. 5(6)).

There has been a concern that very few supervision orders are made in care proceedings and a belief that this is because they are thought to be ineffective (House of Commons, 1984, para.150). They had been designed to deal with delinquency (the first orders dating from about 1820) and, because of this, were directed towards the child with few requirements imposed on parents. Under the Act the principal change is that requirements may be imposed on a 'responsible person', who is defined in Schedule 3, para.1 as any person with parental responsibility for the child, or any other person with whom s/he is living. With that person's consent, a supervision order may contain requirements:

(a) that s/he take all reasonable steps to ensure that the supervised child complies with the supervisor's directions;
(b) that s/he take all reasonable steps to ensure that the supervised child complies with any requirement as to psychiatric or medical examination made by the court;

(c) that s/he complies with the supervisor's directions requiring him/her to attend a specified place (e.g. a clinic or play group).
(d) that s/he keeps the supervisor informed of his/her address, if this differs from the child (para.3(3)).

These requirements (which last for a maximum of ninety days: para. 7) cannot be imposed on adults without their consent, but it is likely that this will be readily obtained where it becomes apparent that the alternative is a care order. But, as Eekelaar and Dingwall (1990, p. 135) stress 'social workers, and indeed, courts, should be wary about being drawn into a kind of "plea bargaining" where a supervision order is seen as a "compromise"'. The plan should clearly envisage a supervision order and the reasons for seeking one.

Requirements may be imposed on the supervised child (para. 2), also for a maximum period of ninety days (para. 7), to:

(a) live at a place specified in directions;
(b) participate in education or training activities;
(c) report to particular places at particular times;
(d) submit to psychiatric or medical examination or treatment under court directions;
(e) make him or herself available for monitoring visits by the supervisor at the place where s/he is living.

With the exception of (d) (and this only where the child is of 'sufficient understanding to make an informed decision':[23] paras. 4(4), 5(5)), the child's consent is not required. Regulations as to treatment are wholly the responsibility of the court and have to be specified in the order itself (para. 5): requirements as to examinations may be specified by the court in the order or by the supervisor (para. 4).

Health examinations and treatment are governed by Sch 3, paras. 4 and 5. The child may be required to submit to a medical or psychiatric examination by the court through the order or by direction of the supervisor (if the order gives authority for this). Examinations may be carried out at a hospital or mental nursing home with the child attending as a resident patient only if the court is satisfied by medical evidence that the child requires treatment and may be susceptible to it, and that a stay as a resident patient is necessary (para. 4(3)).

Paragraph 5 on treatment requires all directions to be given by the court, not the supervisor. It imposes different conditions for directions on psychiatric treatment (see para. 4(1) and (2)) and physical treatment (para. 5(3) and (4)). The court has to be satisfied, on the basis of advice from clinical experts, that the treatment is needed, and it must specify in the order how it is to be provided. The medical practitioner responsible for the treatment must report in writing to the supervisor if s/he is unwilling for the treatment to continue, or considers that the treatment should continue beyond the period specified, or that the child needs different treatment, is not susceptible to treatment or does not require further treatment (para. 5(6)). On receiving such a report, the supervisor must refer it to the court, which may then vary or cancel the requirement (para. 5(7)).

There is no remedy as such in the Act for breach of a requirement or direction. If the supervisor is prevented from visiting the child or having reasonable contact with him or her under paras 8(1)(b) and (2)(b), s/he may apply to the court for a warrant under section 102 (s.102(6)(b)). This is intended to enable the supervisor to exercise his or her powers and authorises the police to assist. If the supervisor believes that refusal of reasonable contact requires urgent action to be taken, consideration should be given to applying for an emergency protection order (s.44 and below) or asking the police to use their powers under s.46 (below). The *Guidance* (vol. 1, para. 3.95) suggests that the authority ought to explain to the child, the responsible person and the parents the consequences of non-cooperation and try to regain it. 'Failure to work closely with those concerned with the child's welfare, in particular the parents may lead to breakdown in the local authority's relationship with the parents, and consequent deleterious effects on the welfare of the child'.

Supervision orders will last for one year, unless brought to an end earlier (Sch. 3, para. 6) and can be extended on application by the supervisor so that in total it lasts for up to three years. The one-year time limit is new: it is intended to ensure that the effectiveness of the order and the circumstances of the child are reviewed and decisions are taken about what further steps, if any, are necessary.

A supervision order is brought to an end by:

(*i*) the court discharging the order (s.39(2));
(*ii*) the making of a care order;
(*iii*) the child reaching the age of 18 (s.91(13))
(*iv*) an order for the child's return or the registration of a decision under the Child Abduction and Custody Act 1985 (ss.16,25(1)(a), (b)) (as amended by Sch. 13, para. 57).

Interim orders

The *Review of Child Care Law* (1985) identified three problems with interim orders: (i) there were no statutory criteria; (ii) repeated hearings and a large number of interim orders were not uncommon; (iii) it was impossible to make an interim supervision order. The Act addresses these problems.

First, there is a new power to make an interim supervision order. This may be linked to a short-term residence order (see above).

Secondly, the court is now directed not to make an interim order unless it is satisfied that there are reasonable grounds for believing that the 'minimum conditions' in s.31(2) (see above) are met[24] (s.38(2)).

Thirdly, there are new provisions on the duration of orders (s.38 (4)), which should be read together with s.1(2) (on delay) (see above). But the possibility of an excessive number of interim orders cannot be ruled out.

Interim orders may be made in two situations (s.38(1)):

(a)   in any proceedings (including applications for care orders in 'family proceedings') for a care or supervision order where the proceedings are adjourned;

(b)   where the court orders an investigation under s.37(1) (see above).

In both cases the court must be satisfied:

(a)   that there are reasonable grounds for believing that the 'minimum conditions' of significant harm in s.31(2) are satisfied (s.38(2)). The evidence of the child or medical evidence may be sufficient to establish 'reasonable grounds'.

(b)   that an order will be better for the child than no order (s.1(5), above).

(c)   that the paramountcy test is satisfied (s.1(1)) and the checklist has been addressed.

There is a third situation in which the court must make an interim supervision order, unless satisfied that the child's welfare will be satisfactorily safeguarded without one. This is when on an application for a care or supervision order, the court makes a residence order (s.38(3)). The test in s.38(2) needs to be satisfied. If it cannot be, a family assistance order (s.16, above) may be considered a suitable alternative, but those named in such an order, with the exception of the child, must consent.

In the past courts have varied considerably in the amount of evidence they required to be satisfied that the circumstances justified the making of an interim order (Jones, 1984; Bean, 1987). With statutory criteria now provided for, there should be greater uniformity of approach. There is unlikely to be full evidence, but the local authority (or other authorised person) must be prepared to produce some evidence of 'significant harm' or its likelihood and demonstrate a link between this and the quality of the parents' care. If the application is contested, the court will have to evaluate the evidence, but the applicant's case will not need to be fully proved. Both cross-examination and the evidence should be restricted to the essential issues, so that a dress rehearsal of the full hearing is avoided.[25] If the application is not opposed, the court does not have to receive evidence but must still have sufficient material to enable it to exercise its judicial discretion whether or not to make an interim order.[26] On repeated applications there should not be rubber-stamping.[27] The court must satisfy itself that the criteria in s.38(2) and s.(1(5)) (above) are 'still satisfied – not by going over the evidence again but by considering any change in the circumstances, any new evidence that may have come to light and any other relevant matter that may cast doubt on the benefit of a new order' (*Guidance*, vol. 1, para. 3.44).

There are new time limits. Under the old law the court could make interim orders for any period up to twenty-eight days. An initial interim order can now be made for up to eight weeks. The *Guidance* vol. 1, para. 3.44 recognises that this should avoid 'unproductive' returns to court before the parties are ready to proceed, but it also cautions against eight week orders as standard practice. The length of each order should be decided having regard to the presumption against delay (s.1(2)), timetabling directions and the time limits in s.38(4). These limits are:

in adjourned proceedings
— an initial interim order may last for up to eight weeks beginning with the date on which it was made;
— a second or subsequent order may last for up to four weeks beginning with the date on which it was made, or where it was for less than eight weeks, from the date the initial order was made.

where in family proceedings a direction is given under s.37(1).

— the end of the eight week period or such other period as the court directs for the authority to report on its investigation (s.37(4)), subject to no care order or supervision order application having been made.

— if an application is made and proceedings on it are adjourned, an interim order made then would be the second order (and so would last for a maximum of four weeks).

There is no limit to the number of interim orders but the *Guidance* (vol. 1, para. 3.46) stresses that 'a balance will have to be struck between allowing sufficient time for enquiries, reports and statements, and risking allowing the child to continue in interim care or supervision for so long that the balance of advantage is distorted in favour of continued intervention'. The guardian ad litem will have a 'key role' (*idem*) in advising the court on interim orders. The *Guidance* (*idem*) urges the applicant to make his or her views known to the guardian. The guardian will also have to find out the views of others, including the child.

The Act gives the court a new power when making an interim order to give directions it considers appropriate about medical or psychiatric examination or other assessment of the child (s.38(6)). The court can prohibit examination or assessment altogether or make this subject to its specific approval (s.38(7)). Directions can be made when the order is given or at any time while it is in force and may be varied on an application by any person who was a party to the proceedings in which the directions were given (s.38(8)). Where an interim care order is made, the local authority has parental responsibility and can, without court directions, make decisions about the child's medical treatment.

If the child is of sufficient understanding, s/he may refuse to submit to an examination or assessment, both to one directed by the court (s.38(6)) and to one required by a local authority. The latter is not provided for by the Act but is the result of the *Gillick* decision,[28] though if 'consent can be given by someone else who has parental rights and responsibilities',[29] as the Court of Appeal has recently held, doubt must be cast upon the efficacy of s.38(6) (if the child refuses, can the local authority now consent on behalf of the child?) and as to how far the *Gillick* ruling extends. These matters may not have been finally resolved until there has been considerable litigation.

Repeated medical examinations solely for evidential purposes are to be avoided (Cleveland, 1988). An examination may have taken place before care or supervision proceedings are commenced, perhaps by agreement with the parents or under a child assessment order (s.43 and below). The *Guidance* (vol.1, para. 3.49) advises that in other cases the applicant should 'consider whether satisfactory arrangements can be made without the need for an interim order and court directions'. It advocates discussion with a view to securing the agreement of all concerned to a single programme of examination or assessment 'which could if necessary be observed by, or conducted jointly with, a medical practitioner nominated by the parents'. However, 'if there are any doubts or where any aspect of the assessment is likely to prove contentious – for example, a possibility that if the examination found abuse the parents would want a second opinion requiring further examination of the child[30] – the better course in the child's interests may be to seek an interim supervision order and court control by directions' (*idem*).

One problem in the recent past which first case law[31] and now the Act appears to have solved is the request for adjournments (and therefore a succession of interim orders) because criminal proceedings are pending.[32] The courts had stated that, in deciding whether to adjourn care proceedings, the guiding principle is the paramountcy of the child's welfare, so that delay should be avoided.[33] The Act provides that no one can refuse to answer questions in care proceedings on the ground that doing so might incriminate him or her or a spouse of an offence (s.98(1)). Further, answers given in such proceedings are not admissible in evidence against the person making them or a spouse in later criminal proceedings, other than for perjury (s.98(2)). As a result, there should no longer be any reason for delaying care proceedings until the completion of any criminal trial of the alleged perpetrator.

Orders pending appeals

The new Act effects considerable improvements in the appeal structure.

Any one with party status in the original proceedings may appeal against the making of a care or supervision order, including an interim order, or the varying or discharging of such an order, or against the court's refusal to make such an order. Local authorities have full rights of appeal.

Decisions by a magistrates' court are appealable to the High Court (s.94(1)). Appeal against decisions in care or supervision proceedings heard in the county court or High Court will go to the Court of Appeal (County Courts Act 1984 s.77(1); Supreme Court Act 1981 s.16).

The Act also introduces for the first time 'orders pending appeals' (s.40). The intention is to maintain the 'immediate status quo' to 'provide continued protection for the child or to prevent interruption in the continuity of his care until the appeal is heard' (*Guidance*, vol. 1, para. 3.61).

The court may order that a child who is subject to an interim care order remains in care until the determination of any appeal against a refusal to make a care order (s.40(1)). Similar powers apply in relation to supervision orders (s.40(2)), and to orders for discharge of care and supervision orders (s.40(3)). The court may include directions as it sees fit (on such questions as contact or even where the child shall live). The *Guidance* rightly observes (vol. 1, para. 3.62) that 'these are the only circumstances, except in relation to contact, in which the court on its own initiative can involve itself by giving directions in management of the welfare of the child in compulsory care'.

An order made under s.40 is only to have effect for such period, not exceeding the appeal period, as may be specified in the order (s.40(4)).

The orders made under s.40 may be extended by an appeal court where an appeal is lodged against a decision of another court with respect to an order pending appeal. However, orders can only have effect until the date the appeal is determined, or where no appeal is made, the period during which it could be made expires. (s.40(5)).

If the court makes a residence order in care or supervision proceedings, as it can because they are family proceedings (s.8(4)), it can postpone the coming into effect of the order or impose temporary requirements pending an appeal under s.11(7). This is a way of effecting a phased return. Masson (1990, p. 88) points out that s.40(3) can also be used to achieve the phased return of a child on the discharge of a care order. The court, she points out, could continue the care order but direct increasing contact with a view to home placement and grant leave to the parents to reapply for discharge after three months.

It must be stressed that orders pending appeals are 'orders' and, therefore governed by s.1(5). The court will need persuading that an order, which may be unsettling for the child, is better for him or her than no order at all.

Discharge and variation of care and supervision orders

Under the old law the grounds for discharging care and supervision orders were unclear. The *Chertsey Justices* case[34] held that the court was not compelled to discharge a care order when the primary condition on which it was made no longer existed. There was no provision, short of resorting to wardship,[35] to effect a phased return. Further, on an application to vary a supervision order, a care order could be made without further proof of the grounds for care proceedings.

Section 39 does not tackle the question of phased returns (but see above). It does, however, address these other issues. The test to be applied in discharge proceedings is the welfare test in s.1 and the checklist in s.1(3) applies. In the past courts[36] tend to have been influenced more by considerations of the fitness of the parent to resume care and control than by the need of the child (Adcock and White, 1980). The emphasis, it is now clear, is on the child's welfare.

There is no longer any power to vary a care order. This is 'in line with the principle that management of compulsory care is the local authority's responsibility' (*Guidance*, vol. 1, para. 3.54). However, when an application to discharge a care order is made, the court may substitute a supervision order (s.39(4). The grounds in s.31(2) do not have to be proved over again (s.39(6)) but the tests in s.1 will have to be satisfied. But, to vary a supervision order to a care order (most likely where there has been non-compliance with the supervision order), it will be necessary to prove again the minimum conditions in s.31(2). It is right that it should be more difficult to upgrade than to downgrade, but this may mean that local authorities will play safe and apply at the outset for the more intrusive order.

Those who can apply for the discharge of a care order are:

(*i*) any person with parental responsibility
(*ii*) the child him or herself (who does not have to be *Gillick*-competent)
(*iii*) the local authority designated by the order.

Note the parent without parental responsibility (the unmarried father) cannot apply for discharge under s.39(1) and anyone else without parental responsibility (a grandparent, a relative, someone with a residence order before the care order was made) is similarly disabled. But, with leave, a residence order could be applied for (s.10) and, if granted, this would discharge the care order (s.91(1)). Where a child applies s/he will be represented by a guardian ad litem. It may be assumed that a young child who wished to apply (see above) might be dissuaded by the guardian ad litem.

Local authorities are required by the Review of Children's Cases Regulations 1991[37] to consider at least at every statutory review of a child in care whether to apply for discharge of the care order. As part of each review the child has to be informed of steps s/he may take, which include applying for discharge of the order, applying for a contact order or variation of an existing contact order or for leave to apply for a residence order. The local authority should also work in suitable cases towards bringing a care order to an end through rehabilitation of the child under s.23(6). The authority should work towards this by advising, assisting and befriending him or her under s.24 (see below) and, if appropriate,by encouraging increased contact.

Those who can apply for the variation or discharge of a supervision order are:

(*i*) any person with parental responsibility;
(*ii*) the child;
(*iii*) the supervisor (s.39(2)).

The comments on (*i*) and (*ii*) above apply also here. The supervisor must consider whether or not to apply for variation or discharge 'where it is not wholly complied with or he considers that the order may no longer be necessary' (*Guidance*, vol. 1, para. 3.58). When considering an application, s/he must bear in mind the court's likely view in the light of s.1 and, in particular, the checklist in s.1(3).

A person with whom the child is living (a 'responsible person', above) can apply for a variation of a supervision order insofar as it affects him or her (s.39(3)).

Where an application for discharge of a care order or supervision order or to substitute a supervision order for a care order has been disposed of, no further application of this kind may be made within six months without leave of the court (s.91(15)). This does not apply to interim orders (s.91(16)) or to applications to vary a supervision order.

Independent visitors

Schedule 2, para. 17, places a duty on a local authority to appoint an independent visitor for any child they are looking after if they believe that it would be in the child's best interest and certain conditions are satisfied. The need for such an appointment arises where communication between the child and his or her parent (or person with parental responsibility) has been infrequent, or where s/he has not visited or been visited by his parents (or person with parental responsibility) for the last 12 months. Under the old law, the appointment of visitors was restricted to children accommodated in CHEs and to children in compulsory care. The Act extends the requirement to all children being looked after by a local authority.

The Definition of Independent Visitors (Children) Regulations 1991[38] prescribe the circumstances in which a person appointed as an independent visitor is to be regarded as independent of the local authority appointing him/her. Certain local authority members, employers and their spouses are not to be regarded as independent (r.2(a)). Where the child is accommodated by some organisation other than a local authority, certain persons connected with that organisation (members, patrons, trustees, employees whether paid or not and spouses of any such person) are not to be regarded as independent (r.2(b)).

The Review of Children's Cases Regulations 1991 places a duty on a local authority to consider at reviews whether an independent visitor should be appointed in respect of a child looked after by them (r.5). The wishes of the child are of particular importance (*Guidance*, vol. 3, para. 7.10). A visitor should not be appointed if the child objects and the authority is satisfied that s/he has sufficient understanding to make an informed decision. It may be possible to appoint a relative in a few cases (*Guidance*, vol. 3, para. 7.17).

The functions of the independent visitor comprise visiting, advising and befriending the child (Sch. 2, para. 17(2)). The visitor should contribute to the welfare of the child, including promoting the child's developmental, social, emotional, educational and religious needs. It will also include, unless there is clear evidence to act differently, supporting the care plan for the child and his or her carers (*Guidance*, vol. 3, para. 7.34). The *Guidance* stresses (vol. 3, para. 7.47) that skilled advocacy is not one of the visitor's roles. So, even where the child is dissatisfied, his or her views are ignored or s/he is being abused by carers, all the visitor can do is draw these concerns to the attention of the social worker or a more senior officer in the SSD (*Guidance*, vol. 3, para. 7.48). Although the *Guidance* adds that in certain cases it may be appropriate to refer the matter to a voluntary organisation which specialises in advocacy (para. 7.48), the stance adopted here may be thought to be rather too local authority-centred. In situations like those described here one would look to something rather more assertive by the independent visitor.

After-care

The Act (s.24) strengthens local authorities' functions in relation to the preparation for leaving care and the after-care of children cared for away from their families.

Local authorities have a duty to advise, assist and befriend all children they are looking after with a view to providing their long-term welfare, and not just their welfare during childhood. They have a duty to advise and befriend young people under 21 who, after the age of sixteen, were looked after by a local authority or accommodated by or on behalf of a voluntary organisation, who request help and satisfy the conditions in s.24(5) (see s.24(2), (4)). There is also a power to advise and befriend young people accommodated in registered children's homes, by health and local education authorities, in any residential care home, nursing home or mental nursing home or who were privately fostered (s.24(2)).

All young people who qualify to be advised and befriended can also be given assistance (s.24(6) and, in exceptional circumstances, this may be in cash (s.24(7)). The *Guidance* (vol. 3, para. 9.99) stresses this is not to 'duplicate the social security system'. And payments are not part of income or capital for the purpose of calculating entitlement to social security benefits (*Guidance*, vol. 3, para. 9.102). Financial assistance may also be given to enable a young person who was looked after by a local authority after age sixteen to be accommodated near their place of work or training etc. and to meet the costs of training (s.24(8)). Grants for education or training may continue beyond age 21 (s.24(9)). To facilitate the carrying out of these duties, local authorities are under a duty to pass information to other local authorities about people they have been advising and befriending (s.24(11), and voluntary organisations, health authorities, local education authorities and those who run registered homes have a duty to inform local authorities about children who leave their care (s.24 (12)). Where care is by a health authority or LEA or in a residential care home, the powers and duties only apply if the child was accommodated for more than three consecutive months, which may start before the child reached the age of 16 (s.24(13), (3)).

The Courts and Legal Services Act 1990 inserted two more subsections into s.24. Local authorities must establish a procedure for considering representations, including complaints, made to them by persons qualifying for advice and assistance about the discharge of their functions under s.24 (s.24(14) and s.24 (15)). This enables the Secretary of State to make regulations governing the way local authorities consider these representations (s.24(15). The latter has been done by the Representations Procedure (Children) Regulations 1991[39] (see below).

There is a full guidance on after care in chapter 9 of *Guidance and Regulations*, volume 3. Attention should be drawn to the principles underlying preparation for leaving care (para. 9.18), the need for SSD to prepare a written statement of its philosophy and practice on the preparation of young people for leaving care and the provision of after-care support (para. 9.20). An easy-to-read guide for young people is recommended (para. 9.25). There is further guidance on financial assistance (paras 9.69 – 9.74). The primary responsibility of the housing department for housing needs is discussed (paras 9.80 – 9.86). This is particularly important to recognise (but see also above) for young people who have left care are overrepresented amongst the homeless (para. 9.84).

Representations and complaints

The establishment of procedures for dealing with representations and complaints was proposed by the Government White Paper in 1987 (para. 31). With similar procedures in the National Health Service and Community Care Act 1990 (s.50), the intention is that the two should be compatible. Common structures for handling representations should be possible (*Guidance*, vol. 3, para. 10.2; but cf. Stace and Tunstill, 1990).

Section 26(3) requires the responsible authority (local authority, voluntary organisation or registered children's home) to establish a procedure for considering any representations (including any complaint) made to it by:

'(a) any child who is being looked after by [it] or who is not being looked after by [it] but is in need;
(b) a parent of his;
(c) any person ... [with] parental responsibility for him;
(d) any local authority foster parent;
(e) such other person as the authority consider has a sufficient interest in the child's welfare to warrant his representations being considered [for example, a relative, a guardian ad litem, a teacher] ... about the discharge by the authority of any of its functions under ... Part (III) in relations to the child.'

The Act 'requires that responsible authorities establish a procedure which provides an accessible and effective means of representation or complaint where problems cannot be otherwise resolved' (*Guidance*, vol. 3, para. 10.3). The *Guidance* envisages that the procedure will be used 'primarily for handling complaints' (*idem*). It will be noted that the first person listed is the child. The *Guidance*, recognising this, directs authorities to check with the child that a complaint submitted on his or her behalf reflects his or her views and s/he wishes the complaint to be made (para. 10.7).

Section 26(4) requires the procedure to contain an independent element. At least one person who is not a member or employee of the authority must take part in the consideration and any discussions held by the authority about the action to be taken in the light of the considerations (see also Representations Procedure (Children) Regulations 1991 r.5, 6, 8). There is nothing in the Regulations which prohibits the independent person involved in the first stage consideration of a case from being a member of the panel which considers the action to take. But the *Guidance* (vol. 3, para. 10.33) indicates that 'the responsible authority will wish to consider to what extent the panel can take a fresh look at the case if the same independent person is involved'.

The *Guidance* gives advice on choosing independent persons: consult community groups, draw on voluntary groups, other agencies and independent professionals (para. 10.33). A consortium or reciprocal arrangements with other authorities is a way of facilitating the availability of independent persons. Regulation 2(1) states who is excluded from acting as an independent person (persons who are either members or officers of the authority). The *Guidance* (para. 10.35) recommends the exclusion also of spouses and cohabitants.

What may be complained about? In short, matters relating to local authority support for families and their children under part III of the Act: complaints about day care, services to support children within the family home, accommodation of a child, after-care (see above) and decisions relating to the placement of a child or the handling of a child's case. Foster parents are not entitled to use the procedure except in connection with decisions about the 'usual fostering limit'. The *Guidance* indicates that local authorities may wish to consider allowing foster parents to make complaints about other matters too (para. 10.9). Representations about matters which affect a group of children may also be considered (*idem*). Representations or complaints about child care matters which fall outside part III are not covered by this procedure, but by the Complaints Procedure Directions. However, 'dissatisfaction about a local authority's management or handling of a child's case, even where related to a court order, may be appropriate to the procedure' (para. 10.10). The inclusion of a child's name on a child protection register (a decision which is difficult to challenge in court: see above) is not carried out under any statutory provision, but the *Guidance* advises (para. 10.10) that 'it would be good practice to provide, with the agreement of the Area Child Protection Committee, an appropriate procedure to handle complaints about inter-agency case conferences and their recommendations'.

The Regulations provide for a two-stage procedure with an independent element at each stage. Regulation 5 requires that an independent person be involved from the outset of the considerations. Regulation 8 requires that a panel be convened including at least one independent person, where a first stage consideration has not satisfied the complainant.

The authority has discretion to decide how exactly to implement the Regulations. Minimum requirements of the Act and Regulations are:

(*i*) to designate an officer to assist in the co-ordination of all aspects of the consideration of complaints (r.3(1));

(*ii*) to publicise the procedure (s.26(8));

(*iii*) to ensure that members of staff and independent persons are familiar with the procedure (r.3(2));

(*iv*) to acknowledge all complaints received by sending an explanation of the procedure and to offer assistance and guidance on it or advice on where assistance and guidance may be obtained (r.4(1));

(*v*) to accept and record any oral complaints in writing, agreeing them with the complainant (r.4(2));

(*vi*) to appoint an independent person to consider the complaint with the authority (r.5);

(*vii*) to consider the complaint with the independent person and respond within 28 days of receipt of the complaint (r.6);

(*viii*) to address their response to the person from whom the complaint was received; and, also, where different, to the person on whose behalf the complaint was made and to other persons who appear to have a sufficient interest or are otherwise involved or affected. The response should advise the complainant what further options are open should s/he remain dissatisfied (r.8(1));

(*ix*) to make arrangements so that where a complainant remains dissatisfied and requests (within 28 days) that the complaint be reviewed, a panel is constituted by the authority to meet within 28 days of the receipt of the complainant's request (r.8(2), (4)). The complainant may be accompanied by another person of his or her choice to speak on his or her behalf (r.8 (6));

(*x*) to ensure that the panel's recommendation is recorded in writing within 24 hours of the completion of their deliberations (r.9(1)) and is sent to the authority, the complainant and the first stage independent person, and to anyone acting on the complainant's behalf (r.9(1));

(*xi*) to decide on their response to the recommendation of a panel after consideration with an independent person from the panel (s.26(7)(a), r.9(4)) and make their decision known in writing to the person who requested that the complaint be considered by the panel, and, where different, the person on whose behalf the request was made, the first stage independent person (if different) and any other persons as appear to have a sufficient interest or are otherwise involved or affected. Notification should be given within 28 days of the recommendation. The letter should explain the authority's decision, the reasons for it and any action taken or which it is proposed to take (s.27(7)(b)). It does not have to follow the recommendations of the panel;

(*xii*) to keep a record of all complaints received and the outcome in each case and identify separately those cases where the time limits imposed by the directions have been breached (r.10(1));

(*xiii*) to provide an annual report on the operation of the procedure (r.10(3)).

A complaints procedure is not a substitute for good practice. It clearly should constitute part of good practice. The Act calls for a change in culture which encourages clients to express views about services and for these comments to be used as opportunities to improve services, relationships and, ultimately, the image of SSDs. Only if that culture genuinely changes will the representations procedure become genuinely meaningful (see also Kelly and Beck, 1990). Concern about the effectiveness of complaints procedure has been voiced in the light of the pindown enquiry (see Lindsay, 1991). If, as he fears, serious allegations are ruled outside the remit of complaints procedures, as, it has to be conceded, has happened (he cites Acorn Grove in Birmingham and Melanie Klein in Greenwich), then there is a real danger that the new procedures will no more protect children's rights than was the case previously. After all, it cannot be denied that 'pindown' and other recent revealed abuses were against the law, but they happened and nothing was done to rectify the abuse for a very long time.

Notes

1. *R* v. *Newham BC ex parte P* [1990] 1 FLR 404.
2. SI No. 893.
3. *A* v. *Liverpool CC* [1982] AC 363; *W.* v. *Hertfordshire CC* [1985] AC 791.
4. (1988), para. 16.37.
5. *Council of Civil Service Unions* v. *Minister for Civil Defence* [1985] AC 374, 410; *R* v. *Derbyshire C.C ex parte* T [1990] 1 FLR 237, 243–4.
6. See *Associated Provincial Picture Houses* v. *Wednesbury Corporation* [1948] 1 KB 223.
7. *R* v. *Bedfordshire CC ex parte C* [1987] 1 FLR 239.
8. *R* v. *Bolton MBC ex parte B* [1985] FLR 343 (local authority misunderstood meaning of a statutory provision).
9. *B* v. *W* [1979] 3 All ER 83 (failure to reveal crucial document).
10. *D* v. *XCCC (No.2)* [1985] FLR 279.
11. Local Government Act 1973, part III.
12. The main articles relied on are 6, 8, and 13.
13. A good example is the *Gaskin* case [1990] 1 FLR 167.
14. *A* v. *Liverpool CC* [1982] AC 363.
15. Cases 9276/81, 9580/81, 9749/82, 9840/82 and 10496/83.

16. Health and Social Services and Social Security Adjudications Act 1983, Schedule 1 inserting Part 1A into the Child Care Act 1980 (sections 12A – 12G).
17. *M* v. *Berkshire CC* [1985] FLR 257; *Re Y* [1988] 1 FLR 299.
18. First stated as such in *M* v. *M* [1973] 2 All ER 81. A more recent statement is *Re S* [1990] 2 FLR 166.
19. That is in the context of wardship. In reality wardship is a species of the High Court's inherent jurisdiction.
20. The unmarried father is a parent.
21. The making of a care order with respect to a child subject to a residence order discharges that order (s.91(2)).
22. SI (1991) No. 891.
23. This gives effect to the *Gillick* decision (*Gillick* v. *West Norfolk and Wisbech Area Health Authority* [1986] AC 112).
24. This may lead to the necessity to conduct a fairly full hearing, contrary to directions under the old law (*R* v. *Birmingham City Juvenile Court* [1988] 1 All ER 683).
25. The *Birmingham* case (note 24). But, as suggested in that note, the new test suggests more evidence will have to be heard than previously.
26. *R.* v. *Croydon Juvenile Court ex parte N* [1987] 1 FLR 252.
27. *R* v. *Birmingham Juvenile Court ex parte P and S* [1984] 1 All ER 393.
28. See *Gillick* v. *West Norfolk and Wisbech Area Health Authority*, note 23.
29. *Re R* [1991] 4 All ER 177.
30. As in *R* v. *Hampshire C.C ex parte K* [1990] 1 FLR 330.
31. *R* v. *Exeter Juvenile Court ex parte H*; *R* v. *Waltham Forest Juvenile Court ex parte B* [1988] 2 FLR 214; *R* v. *Inner London Juvenile Court ex parte G* [1988] 2 FLR 58.
32. Not a problem where the defendant was intending to plead guilty as charged and see HOC No. 88/1972 and HOC No. 84/1982.
33. See *R* v. *Exeter Juvenile Court*, op cit, note 31.
34. *R* v. *Chertsey Justices ex parte E* [1987] 2 FLR 415.
35. *Re J* [1984] FLR 43.
36. *Re W* [1981] 2 FLR 360.
37. SI 1991 No. 895.
38. SI 1991 No. 892.
39. SI 1991 No. 894.

References

Adcock, M. and White, R. (1980) 'Care Orders or the Assumption of Parental Rights – The Long Term Effects', *Journal of Social Welfare Law*, 257.
Bean, A. (1987) 'Interim Care Orders', *Law Society Gazette*, 84, 1382.

Berridge, D. and Cleaver, H. (1987) *Foster Home Breakdown*, Oxford, Blackwell.

Cleveland (1988) *Report of the Inquiry into Child Abuse in Cleveland 1987* (The Butler-Sloss Report), Cm. 412, London, HMSO.

Department of Health and Social Security (1985) *Review of Child Care Law*, London, HMSO.

Department of Health and Social Security (1987) *The Law on Child Care and Family Services*, Cm. 62, London, HMSO.

Department of Health (1989) *An Introduction to the Children Act 1989*, London, HMSO.

Department of Health (1991) *Guidance and Regulations*, vol. 1, London, HMSO.

Department of Health (1991) *Guidance and Regulations*, vol. 3, London, HMSO.

Eekelaar, J. (1991) 'Parental Responsibility: State of Nature or Nature of the State?', *Journal of Social Welfare and Family Law*, 37.

Eekelaar, J. and Dingwall, R. (1990) *The Reform of Child Care Law*, London, Routledge.

Freeman, M. (1982) 'The Legal Battlefield of Care', *Current Legal Problems*, 35, 117.

House of Commons (1984) *Second Report from Social Services Committee*, HC 360, London, HMSO.

Jones, P. (1984) 'Interim Care Orders', *Justice of the Peace*, 148, 246.

Kelly, D. and Beck, J. (1990) 'Will Systems Change the Culture?', *Community Care*, 829, 17.

Law Commission (1988) *Guardianship and Custody*, Law Com. 172, London, HMSO.

Lindsay, M. (1991) 'Complaints Procedures and their Limitations in the Light of the "Pindown" Inquiry', *Journal of Social Welfare and Family Law*, 432.

Maidment, S. (1981) 'The Fragmentation of Parental Rights and Children in Care', *Journal of Social Welfare Law*, 21.

Masson, J. (1990) *The Children Act 1989 Text and Commentary*, Sweet and Maxwell.

Millham, S. *et al.* (1986) *Lost in Care: The Problems of Maintaining Links between Children in Care and their Families*, Aldershot, Gower.

Rowe, J. *et al.* (1984) *Long Term Foster Care*, London, Batsford.

Stace, S. and Tunstill, J. (1990) 'Running on Different Tracks?', *Community Care*, 843, 16.

7

The Public Care System – III

In this chapter some of the consequences of the new threshold for coercive intervention in section 31(2) are considered and examined. This involves a discussion of the problem of school refusing or truancy and the new education supervision order, delinquency after the end of the criminal care order and, for convenience at this place, also the question of secure accommodation, and the new restrictions on the local authority's use of wardship.

The final section of the chapter considers the role of the guardian ad litem.

The education supervision order

It is no longer possible to seek a care or supervision order on educational grounds alone. The specific ground in the 1969 Act, allowing a care order to be sought if the child was not receiving proper education, is repealed.[1] There remains a residual situation where a care order might still be sought: where non-attendance at school is attributable to the parents' quality of care and the child is likely to suffer significant harm. In the leading case under the old law,[2] the father had an implacable objection to comprehensive schools and refused to allow his son to attend one (and, as a result any available school). A care order was upheld by the Court of Appeal. There seems no reason why on similar facts a care order should not still be made. More significantly, the end of the care order is also the end of the so-called 'Leeds system' (Berg *et al.*, 1983; Grimshaw and Pratt, 1985), where extensive use was made of the court's power to adjourn as a means of trying to get truanting juveniles back to school. The practice was 'irregular' and 'unlawful' (Bevan, 1989, p. 678), but also, many argued, effective. Instead, there is the new education supervision order. Section 36 empowers a local education authority to apply for an education supervision order. A court may only make such an order if satisfied that the child is of compulsory school age and is 'not being properly educated' (s.36(3)). A child is being 'properly educated' only if s/he is receiving 'full-time education suitable to...age, ability and aptitude and any special educational needs' (s.36(4)). There is an 'assumption' that non-compliance with a school attendance order, and non-attendance at a school where s/he is registered (within the meaning of the Education Act 1944 s.39) are prima facie evidence that there is not proper education (s.36(5)).

An education supervision order may not be made with respect to a child who is in the care of a local authority (s.36(6)).

Alternatively, the LEA may institute proceedings under s.39 of the Education Act 1944 whereby the parents of the child may be prosecuted. This may be necessary where parents demonstrate hostility to intervention by means of an education supervision order.

If proceedings are brought under s.36 of the Act they are 'family proceedings' (s.8(4)(a)). Since the question relates to the 'upbringing' of a child, the child's welfare is paramount (s.1(1)) and the matters in the checklist (s.1(3)) must be considered. A welfare report may be called for (s.7). The court is not to make an education supervision order unless it considers that doing so would be better for the child than making no order at all (s.1(5)).

The *Guidance* (vol. 7, para. 3.7) advises that the 'effective use of an education supervision order requires commitment, time and skills'. It urges that 'consistent policies are followed within authorities' (*idem*). It seems unlikely that there will be consistency between authorities, though if the advice is followed and policies are made public, there may be concern if major differences are revealed. The *Guidance* suggests that an ESO could help

'where parents find it difficult to exercise a proper influence over their child, and where the child has developed a pattern of poor attendance. It could give the backing of the court to the supervising officer and could complement the efforts of the supervising officer to resolve the child's problems by working with the parents to bring them to accept their statutory responsibilities.' (vol. 7, para. 3.9).

Before applying for an order, the LEA is required to consult the Social Services Committee of the appropriate local authority (s.36(8)). In practice such consultation will be with a professional officer of the SSD authorised to act as an agent under the usual delegation arrangements. The duty is to consult: it does not follow that a policy must be agreed. The consultation process must be speedy for delay will be detrimental to the child. The outcome of the consultation process 'should be confirmed in writing and should indicate whether or not the social services department are involved with the child and/or the family, and if there are any known reasons why an education supervision order would not be appropriate' (para. 3.10).

If proceedings are brought under s.39 of the Education Act 1944, the court may direct the LEA to apply for an ESO. In such circumstances the LEA will need to consult the SSD to determine whether it is necessary to make an ESO to safeguard the child's welfare. When the court directs the LEA to apply for an ESO the LEA must determine whether there are any reasons why it would not be appropriate to make such an application. If the LEA intends not to follow the direction of the court, it must present a report outlining its reasons to the court within 8 weeks of the direction being given (s.40(3), (3A) and (3B) of the 1944 Act, as amended by the Children Act).

Before considering an application for an ESO, all reasonable efforts should have been made to resolve the problem without going to court. The *Guidance* draws attention to the rights parents forfeit if an ESO is made (para. 3.19). In particular, they lose the right to have their child educated in accordance with their wishes.[3] Clearly, it is important that this be drawn to their attention before an order is sought. They should also be made aware of their legal duty to comply with directions made under the order, and of the penalties to which they may be liable if they persistently fail to comply with directions (Sch. 3, para. 18). The child and the family should also be told that if the child persistently fails to comply with directions, the SSD is required to investigate the circumstances (Sch. 3, para. 19). These sanctions look, and are, weak, but whether the child and the family should be told this is another matter.

The Act does not specify the most appropriate supervising officer. The choice lies between an education social worker and an education welfare officer (if suitably qualified). The *Guidance* stipulates (para. 3.13) that LEAs should ensure they provide capable supervising officers. It adds (para. 3.14) that the 'religious, cultural, racial and linguistic background of the child and the family may also influence the choice of supervising officer'.

An application for an ESO must be accompanied by a report. The applicant should be alert to the matters in the statutory checklist (s.1(3)). The *Guidance* (para. 3.15) lists five matters which the report should address. In brief, these are:

(*i*) the child's attendance record (in particular for the twelve weeks prior to court action);

(*ii*) relevant details of the child's circumstances, including age, sex, background and any particular needs including special educational ones;

(*iii*) an assessment of the causes of the child's poor attendance and an indication of the attitudes of the child, parents, schools and other agencies towards this;

(*iv*) a description of the work undertaken and its results, the reasons for the application, including an assessment of any likely educational disadvantage if the order is not made (this is important to clear the hurdle in (s.1(5));

(*v*) the programme of work intended and why it is believed it will help resolve the problem.

A report from the school assessing educational progress is, says the *Guidance* (para. 3(6)), also 'helpful'. I believe it is essential.

The effect of an ESO is set out in Schedule 3, part III. The duty of the supervising officer is to 'advise, assist and befriend and give directions' to the child and the child's parents. The objective is to ensure that the child receives efficient, full-time education suitable to his or her age, ability, aptitude and any special educational needs. 'The aim is to establish and strengthen parental responsibility, and to enable the parents to discharge their responsibility towards the child' (*Guidance*, para. 3.20). 'The supervising officer should always have in mind the need to establish, reinforce and maintain parental authority and should aim to support parents in communicating effectively with the child' (para. 3.22). Before giving directions the wishes and feelings of the child and the parents should, so far is reasonably practicable, be ascertained, including, in particular, their wishes as to the place at which the child should be educated (Sch. 3, para. 12(2)). Two points should be borne in mind. Section 36 of the Education Act 1944 gives parents the right to educate their children 'otherwise' than a school, provided they can satisfy the LEA that the children are being properly educated, and section 56 of the Act empowers LEAs in 'extraordinary' circumstances, with the approval of the Secretary of State, to take the initiative in arranging education otherwise than at school for children of compulsory school age. Secondly, where an ESO is made, parents forfeit a number of rights in relation to their children's education, including that in s.76 of the 1944 Act that pupils are to be educated in accordance with the wishes of their parents and in sections 6 and 7 of the Education Act 1980 on parental preference and appeals against admission directions (Sch. 3, para. 13(2)(b)). But the *Guidance* (para. 3.30) acknowledges that a change of school could be of benefit to the child and 'the parents' temporary loss of rights... need not prevent a change of educational provision should it be necessary. Nor should the loss of parents' rights prevent discussion with them about the arrangements for the education of their child'. The order will normally last for one year, but may be extended for up to three years (Sch. 3, para. 15).

As indicated, the supervisor may make directions. These should be reasonable (it is a defence where parents are prosecuted to show they were unreasonable: Sch. 3, para. 18(2)(b)). Directions may include a requirement that the parents and the child attend meetings with the supervisor or with teachers at school to discuss the child's progress. They need to be made 'with care' (para. 3.33). The supervisor should exercise authority 'with tact' (*idem*).

Where a direction is not complied with, the supervisor must consider 'what further steps to take' (Sch. 3, para. 12(1)(b)). Where a child 'persistently fails to comply' with a direction, the LEA is to notify the appropriate local authority (Sch. 3, para. 19(1)). A parent who persistently fails to comply with a direction is guilty of an offence, and, on conviction, liable to a fine (not exceeding level 3 on the standard scale) (Sch. 3, para. 18). The local authority, when notified, may consider seeking a care order (and see *Guidance*, para. 3.37), but should only do so if the minimum conditions appear to be satisfied. It may be difficult to establish that a child close to the school-leaving age is suffering 'significant harm' by not attending school, even if it can be shown that this failure is attributable to the quality of parental care or the child's being beyond parental control. The prosecution of parents is no real deterrent and anyway achieves very little.[4] It is somewhat surprising that the Act which creates the concept of a 'responsible person' in relation to supervision orders generally (see above) and imposes obligations on that person does not carry over this concept or its consequences to the education supervision order. As a result, the sanctions look weak. If enforcement of the education supervision order is not really possible, the new order looks doomed to fail. We are told (*Guidance*, para. 3.46) that education supervision orders provide a 'new means of ensuring that school age children benefit from an effective education' (para. 3.46). It seems difficult to believe that they will have this effect.[5]

The end of the criminal care order

The abolition of the criminal care order (s.90(1) and (2)) (Harris, 1991) is only part of the Act's package on juvenile delinquency. There is a new duty on local authorities to encourage children within their area not to commit offences (Sch. 2, para. 7(b)). There is also a duty on them to take reasonable steps to reduce the need to bring criminal proceedings against children (Sch. 2, para. 7(a)(ii)). These duties are laid on local authorities as a whole, but in practice the SSD is likely to assume the lead. The *Guidance* concedes (vol. 1, para. 6.3) that it is not expected that local authorities or other agencies will be able to prevent juvenile crime altogether. Advice on juvenile crime prevention is contained in an inter-departmental circular LAC (90)5 'Crime Prevention – the Success of the Partnership Approach'. This stresses:

(*i*) the importance of establishing an inter-agency crime prevention committee;

(*ii*) the role in this committee of community leaders and representatives of the voluntary sector;

(*iii*) the need for the committee to draw up a strategy for crime prevention;

(*iv*) the designation of an individual or agency to co-ordinate these efforts;

(*v*) the importance of obtaining information on the number and pattern of offenders and offences;

(*vi*) the help the media can give to publicise crime prevention initiatives;

(*vii*) the need to ensure that these committees, once set up, continue;

(*viii*) the need to identify sources of funding, in particular from non-public organisations.

There is also a Home Office circular 59/1990, 'The Cautioning of Offenders', which stresses the importance of inter-agency participation in relation to the cautioning of offenders. The purpose of a caution is to deal quickly with a minor offender, to divert him or her from the courts and to lessen the chances of reoffending. The Circular points out that it is useful, if the cautioned person has particular problems, for him or her to be referred, on a voluntary basis, to other agencies which can provide guidance, support and involvement in the community.

The Children and Young Persons Act 1969 contained two routes into care for the juvenile offender. A care (or supervision) order could be made under s.1(2)(f) where an offence (other than homicide) was committed and the child was in need of care or control. The court could also make a care order under s.7(7)(a) of that Act or s.15(1) on discharging a supervision order under s.7(7)(b). The latter, though intended as a residual route became the dominant one. The Criminal Justice Act 1982 ended the distinction between s.7(7) care orders and s.1(2)(f) care orders by requiring the same 'care or control' test to be applied in criminal as in civil hearings. The majority of applications nevertheless used the s.7 route. In Harris's research (1991), 91 per cent of the care orders were made under the s.7(7)(a) criminal jurisdiction.

The Act abolishes the 'offence' condition for a care order. This is swept away with all the conditions. It may still be possible to make a care order where a child commits a criminal offence, but only where the minimum conditions in s.31(2) are proved. This may be possible in particular where the criminal activity is itself dangerous (involvement in violent activities or drug-taking are examples). The power of the court to make care orders under s.7(7)(a) and s.15(1) of the 1969 Act are also abolished.

Instead, there is a new power to attach a 'residence requirement', requiring the juvenile to live for a specified period of time in local authority accommodation, to a criminal supervision order. This new sentence can only be imposed where a further serious offence, punishable by imprisonment for someone over twenty-one, is committed by someone already subject to a supervision order with a requirement under s.12A(3) of the 1969 Act or a residence requirement. The court must also be satisfied that the behaviour which constituted the offence was due, to a significant extent, to the circumstances in which the juvenile was living (unless the previous order imposed a residence requirement). This case apart, the court must obtain a social enquiry report to satisfy itself that this condition has been met, but, whether this is provided by the probation service or the social services department, it is difficult to see how this can be demonstrated. The *Guidance* (vol. 1, para. 6.26) stresses that any 'cause and effect between the juvenile's circumstances and his offending must be based on clear, demonstrable evidence'. A primary objective of a residence requirement is to offer an opportunity for the juvenile and his or her family to 'address the specific difficulties' which gave rise to the offending (*idem*). So, the *Guidance* (*idem*) urges: 'Any assessment...that concludes that there is a significant link between the juvenile's current living circumstances and his offences should be accompanied by a clear action plan about the work to be done to resolve the difficulties.'

The intention behind the new residence requirement is 'to put another step on the escalator of criminal penalties...to prevent [young offenders] from reaching the point on the escalator which amounts to custody...Being required to live in a residential accommodation will not involve the total deprivation of liberty that would be involved in being placed in a custodial institution' (David Mellor, Standing Committee B, cols 502–3).

The motives of the Government are apparent enough but the use of care as punishment stigmatises the whole care system. There could be a reluctance to recommend supervision powers because of their triggering effect. There is also the danger that care provision will become saturated with offenders to the detriment of children who need care. On the other hand, it is possible that the new residence requirement may be perceived as too lenient, with the result that those who, in the past, might otherwise have been committed to care will be pushed up the tariff to a custodial sentence.

It is not clear whether the residence requirement can be made on an offender who is already being looked after by a local authority, either as a result of accommodation being provided under s.20 or by reason of a care order. There is nothing in the Act to prevent this, but it may look incongruous and could lead to such children being pushed up the tariff. If it does, it will have the effect of discriminating against the very disadvantaged children who will continue to make up the bulk of the 'care'population.

Secure accommodation

Less than half of those placed in secure accommodation are in care because they have committed a crime, yet not until the passing of the Criminal Justice Act in 1982 was the placing of a child in secure accommodation by a local authority subject to judicial control. Since 1983 local authorities have been prevented from placing children in their care in secure accommodation unless statutory criteria have applied, and, moreover, have been required to seek the authority of the court to continue such placements beyond a period of 72 hours. Hitherto, children in a variety of other settings have not had this protection. The Act extends statutory controls to children accommodated by health, including National Health Service Trusts, and local education authorities, or accommodated in residential care, nursing or mental nursing homes.

'Restricting the liberty of children is a serious step which must be taken only when there is no appropriate alternative. It must be a "last resort" in the sense that all else must first have been comprehensively considered and rejected – never because no other placement was available at the relevant time, because of inadequacies in staffing, because the child is simply being a nuisance or runs away from his accommodation and is not likely to suffer significant harm in doing so, and never as a form of punishment' (*Guidance*, vol. 4, para. 8.5.; also vol. 1, para. 5.1).

The criteria which must be met before a child may have his or her liberty restricted are, as laid down by s.25 of the Act, essentially as before. They are:

(a) 'he has a history of absconding and is likely to abscond from any other description of accommodation; and if he absconds, he is likely to suffer significant harm; or
(b) if he is kept in any other description of accommodation he is likely to injure himself or other persons.'

Once the criteria cease to apply, s/he can no longer be kept in secure accommodation. There is a well-founded suspicion that children are being kept in such accommodation despite this, and for too long. The percentage of those in secure accommodation for more than six months rose from 20 per cent to 26 per cent between 1984 and 1990 (NACRO, 1991).

The Children (Secure Accommodation) Regulations 1991[6] r.10 allows a child to be kept in secure accommodation without the authority of a court for seventy-two hours, whether or not consecutive, in any period of twenty-eight consecutive days. The maximum initial period for which a court may authorise a child to be kept in secure accommodation is three months (r.11). But it may 'from time to time' authorise further periods not exceeding six months at any one time' (r.12). The maximum period for which a court may authorise a child who has been remanded to local authority accommodation under s.23 of the Children and Young Persons Act 1969 to be kept in secure accommodation is 'the period of the remand' (r.13(1)), and is not to exceed twenty-eight days on any one occasion without further court authorisation (r.13(2)). In addition to the criteria in s.25 and the Regulations, the overriding principles of the Act must be kept in mind. Section 1(5) requires that the court is not to make an order unless this would be better for the child than making no order and section 1(1) requires that the court's welfare must be the court's paramount consideration. Further, proceedings under section 25 have been specified under the Rules of Court[7] as requiring the appointment of a guardian ad litem except where the court does not consider this necessary to protect the welfare of the child.

No child under the age of thirteen may be placed in secure accommodation in a community home without the prior approval of the Secretary of State to the placement (r.4). This replaces the previous minimum age of ten years. The *Guidance* (vol. 4, para. 8.24) advises that a local authority wishing to restrict the liberty of a child under thirteen should first discuss the case with the Social Services Inspectorate. Two classes of child may not have their liberty restricted in any circumstances. They are: (i) people aged sixteen or over but under twenty-one provided with accommodation in a community home under s.20(5) of the Act (above); and (ii) children subject to a child assessment order under s.43 of the Act (below).

Regulation 6 exempts two groups of children from the application of the criteria in s.25(1)(a) and (b), and provides different criteria. These are children detained under the Police and Criminal Evidence Act 1984 s.38(6)[8] and certain children remanded to local authority accommodation under s.23 of the Children and Young Persons Act 1969.[9] Such children may not be placed, and, if placed, may not be kept in secure accommodation:

'unless it appears that any accommodation other than that provided for the purpose of restricting liberty is inappropriate because:

(a) the child is likely to abscond from such other accommoda-
     tion, or
(b) the child is likely to injure himself or other people if he is
     kept in any such other accommodation.'

All children remanded to local authority accommodation and
placed in secure accommodation will have time so spent deducted
from any eventual custodial sentence.[10]

'Secure accommodation' and the 'restriction of liberty' are not
defined as such by the Act or the Regulations, which, in the light of
the Staffordshire 'pin-down' experience (Levy and Kahan, 1991)
and the Utting report (1991) may be concern for alarm. The
Guidance (vol. 4, para. 8.10) says these are interpretational matters
and, therefore, ultimately for the courts to decide. In *R* v. *North-*
ampton Juvenile Court ex parte LB of Hammersmith and Fulham,[11] it
was held that a 'behaviour modification unit' in a hospital where the
regime was designed to restrict liberty was secure accommodation.
The *Guidance* (para. 8.10) adds:

> 'It is important to recognise that any practice or measure which
> prevents a child from leaving a room or building of his own free
> will may be deemed by the court to constitute "restriction of
> liberty". For example, while it is clear that the locking of a child
> in a room, or part of a building, to prevent him leaving
> voluntarily is caught by the statutory definition, other practices
> which place restrictions on freedom of mobility (for example,
> creating a human barrier) are not so clear cut.'

The *Guidance* then buck-passes by suggesting the views of the
authority's legal department be sought as to the legality of the
practice and adds 'the views of the Social Services Inspectorate
might also be sought' (*idem*).

Regulation 8 requires that applications to the court under s.25 are
to be made only by the local authority which is looking after that
child. According to the *Guidance* (vol. 4, para. 8.38) an application
could be made on behalf of the local authority looking after a child
by the local authority managing the secure accommodation in
which s/he is accommodated, where these are different. The
Children (Secure Accommodation) (No.2) Regulations 1991[12] also
enables health authorities, including National Health Service
Trusts, and local education authorities, and those carrying on
residential care homes, nursing homes and mental nursing homes

to apply under s.25 for authority to restrict the liberty of a child they are providing with accommodation. But, if such a child is 'looked after' by a local authority (within the meaning of s.22(1), above), responsibility for making the application remains with the authority (see *Guidance*, vol. 7, para. 5.4).

The court to which applications are to be made are the juvenile (youth) or magistrates' court, as appropriate, where the child is the subject of criminal proceedings (i.e remand to local authority accommodation). In all other cases applications are to be made to the family proceedings court, unless the matter arises in the context of a case already before the County or High Court (when applications should be made to that court).[13]

The court cannot exercise its powers to restrict liberty under s.25 if the child is not legally represented in court, unless, having been informed of his or her right to apply for legal aid and having had the opportunity to do so, he refused or failed to apply (s.25(6)).[14] As indicated above, the court is required to appoint a guardian ad litem unless of the opinion that it is unnecessary to do so to safeguard the child's interests. It is difficult to see how this proviso could ever be satisfied. A secure accommodation order should never be made where a child is not represented by a guardian ad litem.

Section 94 makes provision for appeals to the High Court. Where the appeal is against an authorisation, a child's placement may continue during consideration of the appeal. Where a court has refused to authorise restriction of liberty, and the local authority looking after the child (or other authority or person as appropriate) is appealing, the child must not be retained or placed in secure accommodation during consideration of the appeal (and see *Guidance*, vol. 4, para. 8.49).

In the past there was some doubt, and considerable controversy, over the powers of the wardship court to place or keep children in secure accommodation.[15] Under the Act wardship will no longer be available as a route into secure accommodation for a child looked after by a local authority, and, 'in the exceptional circumstances of an application being made to the High Court to exercise its inherent jurisdiction to give directions as to the placement of a child in secure accommodation, such applications will be subject to the full provisions of section 25 of the Act and the associated Secure Accommodation Regulations' (*Guidance*, vol. 4, para. 8.52).

Regulation 15 requires local authorities with children in secure accommodation to review each case within one month of the start of the placement, and thereafter at intervals not exceeding three months. Each authority is required to appoint at least three persons to undertake such reviews, one of whom must not be employed by the local authority looking after the child or by the local authority managing the secure accommodation in which s/he is accommodated. This independent element in the review process is new. Regulation 16(1) requires the persons appointed to satisfy themselves that the criteria for keeping the child in secure accommodation continue to apply and such a placement continues to be necessary and whether or not any other description of accommodation would be appropriate. The wishes and feelings of the child, any parent, any person with parental responsibility and any other person who has had care of the child, the child's independent visitor if there is one, and the local authority managing the secure accommodation if different should be ascertained and taken into account, as far as is practicable (r.16(2)). These parties must, if practicable, all be informed of the outcome of the review, and the reasons for it. (r.16(3)). If the conclusion of the reviewing panel is that the criteria for restricting liberty no longer apply, the placement is no longer necessary or other accommodation is appropriate, the child's placement must be reviewed 'immediately' (*Guidance*, vol. 4, para. 8.56).

Regulation 17 directs the keeping of records. These must be made available for inspection by the Secretary of State.

Restrictions on the use of wardship jurisdiction

The need to have recourse to the inherent jurisdiction of the High Court ('wardship') has been considerably reduced by the Act, in particular by the 'open-door' policy, the flexible range of orders, the introduction of orders pending appeals (s.40) and the extension of care to concerns about the future (above). Nevertheless, it seems the Government's decision to restrict wardship came late in the day.[16]

The Act restricts the local authority's recourse to wardship in four ways.

First, the High Court's powers to commit a child to care in s.7 of the Family Law Reform Act 1969 are abolished (s.100(1)).

Secondly, the inherent jurisdiction[17] of the High Court cannot be exercised to require a child to be placed in care, supervised by a local authority, or accommodated by or on behalf of a local authority (s.100(2)(a),(b)).

Thirdly, if the local authority wishes to apply to the court for an order under inherent jurisdiction it must obtain leave (s.100(3)) and satisfy conditions in s.100(4). The court must be satisfied that the result could not be achieved by the local authority applying for an order other than by exercise of the court's inherent jurisdiction, and there is 'reasonable cause' to believe that the child will suffer significant harm if the jurisdiction is not exercised. It is likely that the local authority will have to satisfy the same test as for care, even though it does not wish to acquire parental responsibility. There was a strong case for arguing that a lower standard might have applied where intervention was sought on a single issue of upbringing. This would not have undermined the general philosophy of the Act (Mackay, 1989), and may well have served the interests of children better (Eekelaar, 1989). But this line has not been taken.

The inherent jurisdiction of the High Court will remain available to local authorities, but in circumstances yet to be defined. It is possible that leave will be granted liberally, though this would be against the spirit of the Act. It would not, however, be altogether surprising for the judges may feel their wings have been clipped by the new restrictions and try to resist. Matters which could well legitimately fall within the High Court's inherent jurisdiction include the sterilisation of the mentally handicapped,[18] and the equally morally sensitive issue of the defective neonate, when what amounts to euthanasia is being questioned.[19] On this, it is worth contrasting two leading cases. In the so-called 'Baby Alexandra'[20] case in 1981, the Court of Appeal ruled that a life-saving operation to remove an intestinal blockage on a Down's Syndrome baby should be performed. It upheld the right of life where it could not be shown that such life was demonstrably awful. In this case, it seems that the criteria for leave would easily be satisfied: if the court's inherent jurisdiction were not exercised a child in the position of Alexandra would die. But in *Re C*,[21] the child was 'terminally ill even before she was born'.[22] The Court of Appeal agreed with the trial judge, who had held that life-prolonging treatment should be withheld. It is difficult to see how the 'significant harm' criterion would be met in such a case, though, it must be conceded, that much would depend on how 'harm' was interpreted. It would be unfortunate if decisions like that in *Re C* were now to be taken without the public scrutiny of a judicial hearing. The public interest requires this, or some other method of, accountable review. Lord Mackay acknowledged that there were 'difficult borderline cases where at present wardship...would offer a remedy' (1989, p.507).

This is clearly one. The restraint of molestation,[23] to prevent someone discovering a child's whereabouts[24] and to restrain harmful publicity about a child[25] are three further examples. Others, such as the unruly seventeen-year-old,[26] who is outside the remit of care, but was formerly susceptible to wardship, should cause less concern. The invocation of wardship in such a case seems a totally inappropriate use of welfare legislation.

The fourth restriction on a local authority's recourse to the High Court's inherent jurisdiction prevents the High Court from exercising its inherent jurisdiction 'for the purpose of conferring on any local authority power to determine any question . . . in connection with any aspect of parental responsibility for a child' (s.100(2)(d)). This provision is far from clear. Prima facie, it would seem to push or encourage local authorities into applying for care orders (they cannot use prohibited steps or specific issue orders)[27] when they do not want full parental responsibility, but merely seek the court's guidance on a particular matter. A good illustration is the recent case of *Re B*,[28] a pregnant twelve-year-old living with her grandparents. Her mother objected to an abortion. The girl, said to be of 'normal intelligence and understanding', wanted her pregnancy terminated. The local authority was brought in by the GP, wardship proceedings were initiated and a termination was authorised. Under the Act, the grandparents could apply for a residence order, but would then share parental responsibility with the mother,[29] and the further dispute would have to be resolved – all, of course, within a short time limit. A specific issue order would not be available to them.[30] If the GP were now to bring in the local authority, the only option open to it would be to commence care proceedings and to seek to acquire in the process more parental responsibility than it would want or require. For an Act which prides itself on its flexibility, this is a strange consequence. Furthermore, if the girl were already in care, since the local authority would have parental responsibility (s.33(3) and above), it could not invoke the inherent jurisdiction. If, therefore, there was a disagreement between the local authority and the girl's parents, the matter could not be referred to a court for resolution. If the girl is being 'accommodated' (s.20), the local authority may do what is reasonable to safeguard her welfare (s.3(5) above), but whether consenting to an abortion comes within the 'reasonableness' criterion must be doubted.

These restrictions are controversial, though they are consistent with the pro-family ideology of the Act (above). It is right that State intervention into the lives of families should be circumscribed, and not left to depend on a judge's interpretation of welfare. But the fear is that some cases of abuse will slip through the net, cases which might be easier to substantiate in wardship than in care proceedings.[31] It may be significant also that, in a number of recent cases of 'organised' abuse, other forms of abuse have emerged in the course of the wardship hearings.[32] The decision to restrict wardship has been taken precipitately. Given the interpretational problems in the Act (especially in relation to s.31(2), above), there was a strong case for retaining the safety net of wardship in more than the vestigial form envisaged by s.100. Its facility to respond to novel social and moral problems may well be missed.

The use of wardship against local authorities[33] was halted by the House of Lords in *A* v. *Liverpool CC*[34] and *Re W.*[35] Wardship cannot even be used where it would anticipate an authority's exercise of statutory powers.[36] Nor can it be used as a means of reviewing improper or unlawful action by a local authority.[37] Judicial review would have to be used instead. The Cleveland report (1988, para. 16.65) was moved by the perceived injustice of this and recommended that *A* v. *Liverpool CC* be reconsidered. But this suggestion has not been taken up. Instead, symmetry has been restored by restricting the local authority's recourse to wardship. It may be one of the Act's ironies that, in strengthening the position of the parents, the logical step of restoring to them the challenge of local authority decision-making by wardship has not been taken.

There are no restrictions on the use of wardship in non-local authority cases. 'Private' wardship will accordingly continue, unless and until its role is reassessed.[38] It may remain useful where it is desired to achieve more than is possible using s.8 orders or where the applicant wants to avoid applying for leave or where it has been refused. It may be especially valuable where it is desired to retain continuing judicial surveillance of a child's life for, with wardship, parental responsibility will vest in the court and all major issues relating to a child's upbringing will have to be referred back to the court for its decision.

The guardian ad litem

The concept of separate representation of children by a guardian ad litem can be traced back to the Children Act 1975 and from there to the Maria Colwell case in 1973–4 (*Secretary of State for Social Services*, 1974). Under the 1989 Act the role of the guardian ad litem is enhanced. There is a presumption in favour of appointing a guardian ad litem in a wider range of proceedings than previously. They are appointed earlier in the proceedings and, in addition to representing the interests of the child and advising the court on social work matters, they now are charged with assuming a primary role in case management. They have a 'proactive' (*Guidance*, vol. 7, para. 2.2) role as regards the conduct of proceedings, including timetabling and offering advice to the courts on the range of orders available. Concern about the independence of the guardian ad litem service has often been voiced (for example, Levin 1984; *Cleveland*, 1988). Despite this, the duty to provide the Guardian ad litem and Reporting Officers service continues to rest with the local authority. Research into the service has, however, suggested that guardians have been able to maintain independence, though it was noted that 'many did appear to approach their cases like local authority social workers' (Masson and Shaw, 1988, p.181). The courts, however, have been quick to assert the independence of guardians and have quashed a 'benchmark' set by one local authority for the number of hours to be spent on each case.[39] The court stated that the independence of guardians ad litem carrying out their duties under the Act should not be compromised by any restriction in the way they carried out those duties.

The language of s.41(1) is more positive than its predecessor (s.32A(1) of the Children and Young Persons Act 1969).

'For the purpose of any specified proceedings, the court shall appoint a guardian ad litem for the child concerned unless satisfied that it is not necessary to do so in order to safeguard his interests.'

There is no longer any need for the court to order separate representation before it appoints a guardian ad litem. It is anticipated that guardians will be appointed in almost every case. 'The courts are unlikely to find many cases in which it would be inappropriate to appoint a guardian ad litem' (Lord Chancellor, *Hansard*, HL vol. 503, col. 408). The range of proceedings in which a guardian can be appointed is wider than previously. In particular they will be involved in proceedings under part V of the Act. There will thus clearly be a need for 'duty' guardians who will be involved in particular with applications for emergency protection orders out of hours (s.44 and below). (See also *Guidance*, vol. 7, para. 2.70.)

The proceedings 'specified' (see s.41(6) and Rule (2) of the Family Proceedings Rules and the Family Proceedings Courts (Children Act 1989) Rules 1991) are:

(*i*) an application for a care order or supervision order (s.31);

(*ii*) where the court has made an s.37 direction or considering whether to make an interim care order (s.38(1));

(*iii*) an application for the discharge of a care order or the variation or discharge of a supervision order (s.39);

(*iv*) an application to substitute a supervision order for a care order (s.39(4));

(*v*) where the court is considering whether to make a residence order with respect to a child who is the subject of a care order (s.8);

(*vi*) with respect to contact between a child who is the subject of a care order and any other person (s.34);

(*vii*) under part V, i.e. applications for a child assessment order (s.43), an emergency protection order (s.44), the extension of an emergency protection order and a child assessment order (s.45);

(*viii*) appeals arising from the making, or the refusal to make, a care order, supervision order, order for contact under s.34 or residence order (with respect to a child who is the subject of a care order);

(*ix*) appeals arising from the variation or discharge (or refusal of an application to vary or discharge) any of the orders listed in (viii);

(*x*) appeals arising from the refusal to substitute a supervision order for a care order;

(*xi*) appeals arising from the making or refusal to make an order under Part V;

(*xii*) proceedings under s.25 for a secure accommodation order;

(*xiii*) applications under s.33(7) for the leave of court to the proposed change of surname for a child who is the subject of a care order, or the proposed removal of such a child from the UK;

(*xiv*) applications under Sch.2, para. 19(1) for the arranging or assistance in arranging for a child in care of the local authority to live outside England and Wales.

(*xv*) applications under Sch.3, para. 6(3) for the extension, or further extension, of a supervision order originally made under s.31.;

(*xvi*) appeals under (xii – xv).

In addition guardians ad litem and reporting officers will continue to be required in adoption proceedings, as set out in the rules made under the Adoption Act 1976 s.65 (as amended to take into account the Children Act). (As to which see Monro and Forrester, 1991.)

The appointment of the guardian ad litem is dealt with in r.10 of the Family Proceedings Rules and the Family Proceedings Courts (Children Act 1989) Rules 1991. The GAL must not be a member, officer or servant of a local authority (or authorised person) which is a party to the proceedings, unless employed solely as a member of a panel (r.10(7)(a)), or be, or have been, a member, officer or servant of a local authority or voluntary organisation directly concerned in arrangements relating to the care, accommodation or welfare of the child during the previous five years (r.10(7)(b)) or be a serving probation officer, except that a probation officer who has not in that capacity been previously concerned with the child or his or her family and who is part-time may, when not engaged in his duties as a probation officer, act as a guardian (r.10(7)(c)).

S/he is to be appointed 'as soon as practicable after the commencement of specified proceedings' by the justices' clerk or the court unless they consider 'such an appointment is not necessary to safeguard the interests of the child' (r.10(1)). If one is not appointed in this way a party may at any stage in specified proceedings apply for an appointment (r.10(2)). Such an application is to be granted unless it is considered that it is not necessary to safeguard the interests of the child, 'in which case reasons shall be given' and noted (r.10(3)).

The duties of the GAL are set out in Rule 11. The GAL must keep in mind the presumption in s.1(2) of the Act that delay is likely to prejudice the welfare of the child (see also *Guidance*, vol. 7, para. 2.5) and the checklist in s.1(3) (see above). The duties are:

(*i*)   to appoint a solicitor to represent the child and give such advice to the child as is appropriate having regard to his or her understanding and instruct the solicitor on all matters relevant to the interests of the child.

(*ii*) to attend all directions appointments in, and hearings of, proceedings and advise orally or in writing, on:

    (a) whether the child is of sufficient understanding for any purpose including the child's refusal to submit to a medical or psychiatric examination or other assessment that the court has the power to require, direct or order;

    (b) the wishes of the child in respect of any matter relevant to the proceedings, including his attendance at court;

    (c) the appropriate forum for the proceedings;

    (d) the appropriate timing of the proceedings;

    (e) the options available to the court and the suitability of each such option;

    (f) any other matter on which advice is sought by the court or justices' clerk (r.11(4),(5)).

(*iii*) to notify any person whose joinder as a party to the proceedings would be likely, in the guardian's opinion, to safeguard the interests of the child and inform the court or justices' clerk of such a notification, of persons s/he attempted to notify, and of anyone s/he believes may wish to be joined (r.11(6)).

(*iv*) to file a written report advising on the interests of the child not less than seven days before the date fixed for the final hearing of the proceedings. The court or justices' clerk is, as soon as practicable, to serve a copy of this on parties (r.11(7)).

(*v*) to serve and accept service of documents on behalf of the child and, where the child has sufficient understanding, to advise the child of the contents of the documents (r.11(8)).

(*vi*) to make such investigations as may be necessary for him to carry out his or her duties, in particular interviewing, inspection of records and obtaining professional assistance (r.11(9)).

Where it appears to the GAL that the child is instructing a solicitor directly or intends to conduct proceedings him or herself (and is so capable), s/he is to inform the court and perform all duties other than the appointment of solicitor and such other duties as the court or justices' clerk may direct (r.11(3)). The position of the solicitor is considered in Rule 12. S/he is to represent the child in accordance with the guardian's instructions unless the solicitor considers 'having taken into account the views of the guardian ad litem and any direction of the court under rule 11(3), that the child wishes to give instructions which conflict with those of the guardian ad litem and that he is able, having regard to his understanding, to give such instructions on his own behalf, in which case s/he shall conduct the proceedings in accordance with the instructions received from the child' (r.12(1)(a)); or where no guardian ad litem has been appointed and the child has sufficient understanding to instruct a solicitor and wishes to do so, in accordance with the instructions received from the child (r.12(1)(b)); or in default of instructions from a guardian or a child, 'in the furtherance of the best interests of the child' (r.12(1)(c)). The GAL may ask the court to terminate the solicitor's appointment (r.12(4)). There are clearly going to be cases where guardians and solicitors do not agree. In particular a situation is envisaged where the guardian does not think the child is of sufficient understanding and the solicitor thinks s/he is. Cases of alleged sexual abuse where a solicitor wishes to take a girl's instructions which conflict with what the guardian believes to be in her best interests may cause acute difficulties. Some excellent advice on the resolution of these problems may be found in Morris (1986).

The courts have held that, while a case is pending, the local authority must consult the guardian before making a significant change in the child's placement.[40] The guardian cannot, however, make the child a ward of court.[41] It was held under the old law that if a child were warded this ended the guardian's appointment, but this will no longer automatically be the effect of a transfer of the case to the High Court.[42]

The management arrangements for the panels of guardians ad litem and reporting officers are set out in The Guardians ad Litem and Reporting Officers (Panels) Regulations 1991[43] and in volume 7 of the *Guidance* (ch.2). Every local authority must establish a panel (r.2). In making appointments local authorities are to have regard to the 'different racial groups' to which children in the area who may become the subject of specified proceedings belong (r.4(6)). *Guidance* (vol. 7, para. 2.42) advises that 'wherever possible, the particular characteristics of the child and the identities of the parties to the proceedings will determine the choice' of the guardian. It also advises (para. 2.43) that panel membership should, where possible, comprise self-employed social workers, employees of a local authority, employees of a voluntary organisation and probation officers (and see above). It is expected that most guardians will be qualified in social work and have several years of relevant expertise working with children (para. 2.51). The

Regulations emphasise the training of panel members (r.11 and *Guidance*, vol. 7, paras 2.86–2.88).

The right of the guardian ad litem to have access to local authority records and the records of authorised persons is laid down by s.42, as amended by the Courts and Legal Services Act 1990.[44] The right of access does not extend to records held by health authorities, but health records included in the local authority records form part of that local authority's records. The Act does not alter the position as regards adoption applications and guardians and reporting officers in such proceedings continue to have right of access to adoption agency records.

This provision (s.42) was inserted for two reasons. First, the guardian should have all the relevant information and it is not sufficient to rely on the local authority's duty to disclose it. Secondly, local authority records could not be open to all the parties because they may be protected by privilege and wide disclosure could interfere with social work on a case (Solicitor General, *Hansard*, HC vol. 158, col. 626). But, recently, the courts have decided that there is no absolute rule against disclosure of social work records to parties. It might be necessary, the Court of Appeal said, to volunteer disclosure for the benefit of a child.[45] 'The strict approach developed in 1970[46] ... must be relaxed in the light of current legislation and modern opinion about greater openness in society',[47] said Butler-Sloss LJ. In the *Hampshire* decision,[48] a case of alleged sexual abuse of a seven-year-old with Sotos Syndrome, the local authority was said to have a high duty in law to be open in disclosure of all relevant material affecting a child, in this case conflicting paediatric reports. Courts could now direct such disclosure and, consonant with 'partnership', good practice would dictate it. But these judicial pronouncements nevertheless remain authoritative and significant.

The position of the Official Solicitor is not directly affected by s.41. But there will be fewer wardships and guardians ad litem will be able to be appointed for proceedings in the county court and High Court, and, if a case is started in the Family Proceedings Court and is transferred to a higher court, the guardian will be able to continue.[49] The Lord Chancellor has directed[50] that the Official Solicitor shall, if the Court so appoints, act as guardian ad litem and have all the powers and duties of a guardian ad litem. The Court is to do this when the child does not have a guardian ad litem and the court considers there are 'exceptional circumstances which make it desirable in the interests of the welfare of the child' that the Official

Solicitor, rather than a panel member, be appointed guardian ad litem having regard to:

(*i*)   any foreign element in the case which would be likely to require the guardian to make enquiries, or to take other action, outside the jurisdiction of the Court;

(*ii*)   the likely burden on the guardian ad litem where s/he is to represent several children in the proceedings;

(*iii*) the existence of proceedings relating to the child in any other Division of the High Court in which the Official Solicitor is representing the child;

(*iv*)   any other circumstances the Court considers relevant.

In addition, where the Court requests, the Official Solicitor is to instruct counsel as amicus curiae where, in the opinion of the Court, 'an issue of general public importance has arisen or is likely to arise'. The *Guidance* (vol. 7, para. 2.73) draws attention to the 'great expertise' of the Official Solicitor and his access to specialist knowledge. It recommends that Panel Managers establish 'liaison links between their Panel and the Official Solicitor so that Panel guardians... have access to such specialists if the need arises'.

Notes

1. The Education Act 1944 is also amended, so that courts may no longer direct that care proceedings be taken with regard to a child whose parents have been prosecuted under s.39 of that Act.
2. *Re S* [1978] QB 120.
3. Education Act 1944 s.76; Education Act 1980 s.6.
4. Also it is not a continuing offence (*Enfield LBC* v. *F and F* [1987] 2 FLR 126).
5. A more optimistic prognosis is Grenville (1988).
6. See Rule 2(2) of the Family Proceedings Rules and the Family Proceedings Courts (Children Act 1989) Rules.
7. Family Proceedings (Amendment) Rules 1991, SI No. 2113.
8. These children are brought within the scope of these arrangements for the first time.
9. Charged with, or convicted of, an offence imprisonable, in the case of a person aged 21 or over, for 14 years or more, or charged with, or convicted of, an offence of violence, or previously convicted of an offence of violence.

10. Criminal Justice Act 1988 s.130. See also LAC (88)23.
11. [1985] FLR 13.
12. SI 1991 No. 2034.
13. See s.92(2) of the Children Act 1989, as amended by the Criminal Justice Act 1991, s.60(3). For an explanation see *Guidance*, vol. 7, para. 5.5.
14. See s.99 adding subsection (3B) to the Legal Aid Act 1988.
15. See *M* v. *Lambeth LBC (No.3)* [1986] 2 FLR 136 and Maidment (1987).
16. Though it was mooted in the Law Commission's Working Paper (1987).
17. Of which wardship is merely a species. In the future it will be more common to talk of 'inherent jurisdiction'.
18. *Re B* [1988] AC 189.
19. See Freeman (1983), pp. 259–63.
20. *Re B* [1981] 1 WLR 1421.
21. *Re C* [1990] 1 FLR 152.
22. Ibid, p. 254.
23. *Re B* [1975] Fam 26.
24. *Re JT* [1986] 2 FLR 107.
25. *Re L* [1988] 1 All ER 418; *Re C* (No 2) [1990] 1 FLR 263; *Re N. and N* [1990] 1 FLR 149.
26. *Re SW* [1986] 1 FLR 24.
27. See s.9(5)(b).
28. *Re B* [1991] 2 FLR 426.
29. See s.12(2).
30. See s.9(5)(a).
31. For example, *Re P* [1987] 2 FLR 467 (suspected child sexual abuse which it was difficult to prove).
32. See *Social Work Today*, 23(5), 12 (26 September 1991).
33. Also the NSPCC (see *NSPCC* v. *H and H* [1989] 2 FLR 131) and adoption agencies (see *Re W*. [1990] 2 FLR 470.)
34. *A.* v. *Liverpool CC* [1982] AC 363.
35. *Re W* [1985] AC 791.
36. *W.* v. *Nottinghamshire CC* [1986] 1 FLR 565, *W* v. *Shropshire CC* [1986] 1 FLR 359.
37. *Re DM* [1986] 2 FLR 122, *Re RM and LM* [1986] 2 FLR 205; *R* v. *Bedfordshire CC ex parte C*; *R* v. *Hertfordshire CC ex parte B* [1987] 1 FLR 239.
38. The Law Commission is considering this.
39. *R* v. *Cornwall CC ex parte G*, *The Independent*, 20 November 1991 (also in *The Times*, 20 November 1991, and *The Guardian*, 27 November 1991). See now [1992] 1 FLR 270.
40. SI 1991 2051.
41. *R* v. *N. Yorkshire CC ex parte M* [1989] 1 All ER 143.
42. *A* v. *Berkshire CC* [1989] 1 FLR 273; *Re T* [1989] 1 All ER 297.
43. *Re B* [1989] 1 FLR 268.
44. Sch. 16, para. 18(2).

45. *Re M* [1990] 2 FLR 36. See also *B* v. *M* [1990] 2 FLR 46 (a welfare report can disclosed for purposes other than for which it came into existence).
46. In *Re O* [1970] 1 All ER 1088.
47. See *Re M* [1990] 2 FLR 36, p. 43.
48. *R* v. *Hampshire CC ex parte K* [1990] 1 FLR 330.
49. *Cf Re B* [1989] 1 FLR 268.
50. See [1991] 2 FLR 471.

References

Berg, I. *et al.* (1983) 'The Effect of Two Varieties of the Adjournment Procedure on Truancy', *British Journal of Criminology*, 23, 150.

Bevan, H. (1989) *Child Law*, London, Butterworths.

Cleveland Report (1988), *Report of the Inquiry into Child Abuse in Cleveland*, London, HMSO, Cd. 412.

Department of Health (1991) *Guidance and Regulations*, vol. 1, London, HMSO.

Department of Health (1991) *Guidance and Regulations*, vol. 4, London, HMSO.

Department of Health (1991) *Guidance and Regulations*, vol. 7, London, HMSO.

Freeman, M. (1983) *The Rights and Wrongs of Children*, London, Frances Pinter.

Grenville, M. (1988) 'Compulsory School Attendance and the Child's Wishes', *Journal of Social Welfare Law*, 4.

Grimshaw, R. and Pratt, J. (1984) 'Delayed Justice in the Juvenile Court', *Journal of Social Welfare Law*, 104.

Law Commission (1987) *Wards of Court*, London, HMSO.

Levin, J. (1984) 'Guardians Ad Litem in the Juvenile Court', *Family Law*, 14, 296.

Mackay, Lord (1989) 'Joseph Jackson Memorial Lecture', *New Law Journal*, 139, 505.

Maidment, S. (1987) 'Secure Accommodation and Wards', *New Law Journal*, 137, 92.

Masson, J. and Shaw, M. (1988) 'The Work of Guardians Ad Litem', *Journal of Social Welfare Law*, 164.

Monro, P. and Forrester, L. (1991) *Guardian ad Litem*, Bristol, Family Law.

Morris, M. (1986) 'The Guardian Ad Litem and the Child's Solicitor', *Legal Action*, 142.

NACRO (1991) *Juvenile Offenders and the Use of Local Authority Secure Accomodation in England*, NACRO.

Secretary of State for Social Services (1974) *Report of Committee of Inquiry into the Care and Supervision of Maria Colwell*, London, HMSO.

8

Protecting Children at Risk

The law on protecting children at risk has been fundamentally recast by the Act. The over- and inappropriately-used, place of safety order is abolished, and, in its stead, is substituted the new emergency protection order and the innovative and controversial child assessment order. The law regarding police protection is also reformed. Part V of the Act also recognises the importance for the first time of 'safe houses'.

Background to the reforms

The place of safety order can be traced back to 1872[1] but it barely caught the imagination until the 1980s. There was a dramatic increase in the use of such orders in the wake of the Colwell case.[2] Anxieties began to mount that they were being abused. Packman's research (1986, pp. 53–4) suggested that far from the place of safety order being used as an 'emergency measure for the very young child in physical danger', it was increasingly used where the issue was that of "'control" over unsatisfactory parents and over the unruly child'. There were civil liberties concerns too. These were most graphically illustrated, after the Children Act was passed, by the 'dawn raids' in the Orkneys in 1991.[3] The first 'official' criticism came from the *Short* report (1984). The *Beckford* report (1985) was also critical: of the length of orders, of the grounds, of the absence of any appeal or review procedure and of the inappropriate use of the order. Those (Dingwall, 1986; Parton, 1986) who criticised this report for wishing to turn social workers into a 'family police, operating in a vastly more coercive fashion' (Dingwall, 1986, p. 503) did not pick up the implications of this critique.

The legal effects, in particular, whether social workers in possession of one could have the child medically examined, also caused concern.[4] This surfaced in the Carlile case and led the report to recommend a developmental assessment for a child under five. The 'prime virtue' of this, as seen in the *Carlile* report (1987, p.154), was that 'it would partake of none of the coercive nature of a removal and detention of a child from the child's parents and home'. The applicant would merely have to satisfy the magistrate that s/he believed that the health, safety or welfare of the child might be at risk, coupled with a single refusal to produce the child on request for such examination. This is the germ that has grown into the child assessment order. By the time of the *Cleveland* report (1988), the White Paper (1987) had recommended the replacement of place of safety orders by emergency protection orders. The Cleveland report welcomed the proposed change.[5] It was in Cleveland that the final nail in the coffin of the place of safety order was hammered.[6] Though described in the report (para. 16.5) as a 'discretionary judicial act' it was clear to many observers that it had become a routinised act of rubber-stamping and that it trampled on the rights of parents and children.[7] Neither the White Paper nor the *Cleveland* report envisaged, however, the possibility of an EPO being contested. It was clear that it was the concerns engendered in Cleveland which led to a change of opinion by the Government and to the provision in the Act which provides for an EPO to be challenged after 72 hours.[8]

The Bill when published provided for emergency protection orders, but not for child assessment orders. Virginia Bottomley, who was to become Minister of Health after the Children Act was passed, had in 1988 introduced a Medical Examination of Children at Risk Bill,[9] but the *Cleveland* report had not favoured this, believing that the existence of two orders would confuse the issue for social workers. *Cleveland*, it seemed, had prevailed over *Carlile*. The Lord Chancellor, in particular, was opposed to the concept of the child assessment order: 'a major interference in family life', he called it (HL vol. 503, col. 316). But there were those, the NSPCC in particular (Harding, 1989; Wilson, 1989), who continued to press for the child assessment order. In the House of Lords Lord Mottistone moved an amendment. The Government's response was to expand the grounds for an EPO to the situation where access to a child was being unreasonably refused. But critics rightly observed that this did not address the concern for which the child assessment order had been proposed and, more fundamentally, it reintroduced into the emergency protection order some of the very drawbacks of the place of safety order, in particular that it could lead to the removal of children in situations short of a genuine emergency. Eventually, a compromise was effected: there would be a new child assessment order and the emergency protection order would be expanded in the way just described.[10] The CAO was originally envisaged as lasting for up to twenty-eight days. It was reduced to fourteen days and, finally, once it was realised that a child could be removed on a lesser order (the CAO) for a larger period of time than on the stiffer order (the EPO), to seven days (one less than provided for by an EPO). As David Mellor put it (HC vol. 158, col. 593): 'By reducing the period from twenty-eight days to seven days, we have shown a marked concern that the order should not be excessive'. But, as Parton astutely observes (1991, p. 189):

'the Government, having decided on a CAO, had to compromise between the contradictory criteria that such an assessment should fulfil. While the criteria for the social assessment suggested three months,[11] the criteria of the judicial tariff system suggested less than eight days. It was the latter which eventually took precedence.'

Whether at seven days the CAO is operable was doubted (see e.g. David Hinchcliffe, HC vol. 158, col. 605). Concern was also voiced over the intensity of the assessment, given it would have to be compressed into seven days.

And so arrived, after the only real controversy on the passage of the Act, both the child assessment order and the emergency protection order, the latter expanded beyond its original scope to cope with the very problem that the child assessment order is designed to tackle. The two orders must now be examined. First, though, attention must be given to the local authority's investigative duties which, though placed after protective powers in the Act, clearly should precede any use of the two orders. Indeed, it is difficult to see how a local authority can convince a court that it needs an EPO or CAO without first having conducted an investigation.

The local authority's investigative duties

In a number of countries there is mandatory reporting of child abuse (Christopherson, 1989; Maidment, 1978). The *Review of Child*

Care Law decided against introducing this in England (1985, para. 12(4)). Under the Children and Young Persons Act 1969 (s.2(1)) local authorities were under a legal duty to make enquiries on receiving information suggesting that there were grounds for bringing care proceedings unless satisfied that this was unnecessary. (Lawson, 1980). The Act recasts this investigative duty. It is now broader and there is a more positive obligation to conduct enquiries.

Under s.47 the duty to make, or cause to be made, the enquiries which they consider necessary applies where the authority is informed that there is a child in their area who is subject to an EPO or in police protection, or they have reasonable cause to suspect that there is a child in their area who is suffering, or is likely to suffer, significant harm. These enquiries are to enable them to decide whether they should take any action to safeguard or promote the child's welfare. This investigative duty also applies where they have obtained an EPO (s.47(2)). The local authority clearly has a discretion but the enquiries must, in particular, be directed towards establishing whether they should make any application to the court or exercise any other of their powers (in particular those in part III of the Act, above), and, in the case of a child with respect to whom an EPO has been made and who is not in accommodation, whether it would be in the child's best interests for him or her to be in such accommodation (s.47(3)). There is, however, no right as such to take over the child's accommodation. They are also to consider, in the case of a child in police protection, whether it would be in the child's best interests for it to ask for an application to be made by the designated officer (see below) on its behalf for an EPO (s.47(3)(c)). The local authority's discretion is also circumscribed by s.47(4) (obtain access orders unless it has sufficient information) and s.47(5) (consult the LEA in relation to education matters).

In making their enquiries under s.47(1), the local authority must take such steps as are reasonably practicable (unless they are satisfied that they already have sufficient information) to obtain access to the child, or to ensure that access is obtained to him or her on their behalf by a 'person authorised' by them for the purpose. These enquiries are with a view to enabling the authority to determine what action, if any, to take with respect to the child (s.47(4)). Where investigations are frustrated by an unreasonable refusal of access, there may be grounds for an EPO under s.44(1)(b) (below). Where, in the course of enquiries, the local authority or person authorised by them is refused access or denied information as to the child's whereabouts, the local authority must apply for an EPO, CAO, care order or supervision order 'unless satisfied that his welfare can be satisfactorily safeguarded without their doing so' (s.47(6)). This provision bears the imprint of the *Carlile* report (1987) which blamed social workers for not knowing about, and failing to use, powers[12] to gain access to Kimberley Carlile, which, had they been used, might have prevented her death.

Where, having concluded their enquiries, the local authority decides not to seek any of the above orders, they must consider whether there should be a later review of the child's circumstances and, if so, must fix a date on which the review is to begin (s.47(7)). Where they conclude that they should take action to safeguard or promote the child's welfare, they shall take that action, so far as it is both within their power and reasonably practicable for them to do so (s.47(8)). This emphasises the positive duties of local authorities and the need to act swiftly. The *Guidance* (vol. 1, para. 4.86) adds that 'as a matter of good practice, where action involves an application for an order and the application is refused, the authority should consider whether and when to review the case'. The action envisaged by s.47(8) is not limited to the initiation of court proceedings. 'Action' could mean providing day care under s.18, or accommodation (with consent) under s.20, or using any other of its Part III powers.

Section 47 also provides a statutory version of 'Working Together'. Influenced by the *Beckford* (1985) and *Cleveland* (1988) reports, s.47(9) – (11) attempts to promote inter-agency co-operation. It is the duty of:

other local authorities;
any local education authority;
any local housing authority;
any health authority;
any NHS trust;[13]
and any other person authorised by the Secretary of State[14]

to assist the local authority with their enquiries, in particular by providing relevant information and advice if called upon by the authority to do so (s.47(9), (11)). The list omits the police, but 'police refusal to co-operate on any matter would be indefensible' (David Mellor, Standing Committee B, col. 342) (and see Metropolitan Police and Bexley London Borough, 1987 and Byrne and Bloxham, 1986 on one example of police–social services co-operation). It also omits the probation service, but probation officers are officers of the court and 'are already under a duty to assist in these matters' (David Mellor, *idem*). These rationalisations can hardly be described as satisfactory, particularly given the obstructive attitudes taken by some police forces in the past. There is no obligation to assist a local authority where doing so would be 'unreasonable in all the circumstances of the case' (s.47(10)). It is, however, presumably 'reasonable' to pass on information where this will amount to a breach of confidence. *Working Together* (1991, para. 3.10) advises that 'arrangements for the protection of children from abuse ... can only be successful if the professional staff concerned do all they can to work in partnership and share and exchange relevant information, in particular with social services departments (or the NSPCC) and the police'. It directs: 'Those in receipt of information from professional colleagues in this context must treat it as having been given in confidence. They must not disclsose such information for any other purpose without consulting the person who provided it.' It continues (para. 3.11):

'Ethical and statutory codes concerned with confidentiality and data protection are not intended to prevent the exchange of information between different professional staff who have a responsibility for it ensuring the protection of children.'

The General Medical Council in November 1987 expressed the view that the interests of the child are 'paramount' and override the general rule of professional confidence. Indeed the view is postulated that 'not only is it permissible for the doctor to disclose information to a third party but it is the duty of the doctor to do so'. The United Kingdom Central Council for Nursing, Midwifery and Health Visiting, in its paper on confidentiality (April 1987), is more guarded, but advises that practitioners should consult with others and be prepared to justify decisions to pass on or withhold confidential information. 'There will often be ramifications and these are best explored before a final decision as to whether to withhold or disclose information is made'. Arguably more guarded still is the Code of Ethics for Social Work, adopted by BASW in 1986: information should be divulged 'only with the consent of the client (or informant) except where there is clear evidence of serious danger to the client, worker, other persons or the community or in other circumstances judged exceptional, on the basis of professional consideration and consultation (see further Stevenson, 1989).

Child assessment orders

The child assessment order (introduced by s.43) is designed for the situation whence there is fear for a child's health, development or safety, but no hard evidence. A child has been failing to attend a day nursery or family centre. A neighbour has reported hearing a child's screams. A child has not been seen for some time and there are suspicious circumstances. According to the *Guidance* (vol. 1. para. 4.9) a CAO will usually be most appropriate where the harm is 'long-term and cumulative rather than sudden and severe': sexual abuse can fall into this category. Under s.47(4) (above) there is a duty to take such steps as are reasonably practicable to obtain access to the child. If this is refused, there is ground for a CAO. There is also, however, ground for an EPO under s.44(1)(b) and (c) (below). *Guidance* (vol. 1, para. 4.4) stresses that the CAO is 'emphatically not for emergencies'.

An application by a local authority should always be preceded by an investigation under s.47 (above). *Working Together* (1991, para. 5.14.5) directs

'Since the application is only to cover non-emergency situations, there will be no justification for the investigation to be merely superficial. The court considering applications will expect to be given details of the investigation and how it arose, including in particular details of the applicant's attempt to be satisfied as to the welfare of the child by arrangements with the people caring for the child. If the court is not satisfied that all reasonable efforts were made to persuade those caring for the child to co-operate and that these efforts were resisted, the application is likely to founder on the grounds that s.43(1)(c) is not satisfied.'

Only a local authority or 'authorised person' may apply for a CAO. The court has to be satisfied on each of the following three conditions:

— that the applicant has reasonable cause to suspect that the child is suffering, or is likely to suffer, significant harm;
— that an assessment of the state of the child's health and development, or of the way he has been treated, is required to enable the applicant to determine whether or not the child is suffering, or is likely to suffer, significant harm;

— that it is unlikely that such assessment will be made or be satisfactory in the absence of a CAO.

Proceedings under part V are not 'family proceedings'. Accordingly, the court must either make or refuse to make the order applied for and cannot make any other kind of order. There is one exception to this: it can make an EPO instead of a CAO (s.43(3)). The court must have regard to the overriding principle that the child's welfare is paramount (s.1(1)) and to the presumption of no order in s.1(5).

The 'court' means a full court conducting a hearing on notice and not 'a magistrate sitting at home in his pyjamas' (Stuart Bell, *Hansard*, HC vol 158, col. 594). The applicant must take such steps as are reasonably practicable to ensure that prior notice of the application is given to the parents, anyone else with parental responsibility or who is caring for the child, any person allowed to have contact with the child by virtue of an order under s.34, and the child (s.43(11)). The child will usually be represented by a guardian ad litem. The application may be challenged. There is a right of appeal against the making of, or the court's refusal to make, a CAO. Under s.91(14) and (15) the court may prevent a further application being made by particular persons (including the local authority) without the court's leave, or refuse to allow a further application for a CAO within six months without leave.

The court can allow up to seven days for the assessment. The order must specify the date by which the assessment is to begin (s.43(5)). Concern was expressed in Parliament as to how an 'assessment' could be done in seven days. Indeed, the Lord Chancellor, noting that 'a developmental assessment is likely to involve a series of examinations, meetings or interviews over an unspecified or even indefinite period of time, and ... may involve various professional persons' (HL vol. 504, col. 433), was dubious as to whether it could be conducted in eight days (only the EPO was then under consideration). The *Guidance* (vol. 1, para. 4.12), alert to this problem, recommends the applicant 'should make the necessary arrangements in advance of the application, so that it would usually be possible to complete within such a period an initial multi-disciplinary assessment of the child's medical, intellectual, emotional, social and behavioural needs'. This, says the *Guidance* (*idem*), 'should be sufficient to establish whether the child is suffering, or likely to suffer, significant harm and, if so, what further action is required'. Whether this is misplaced optimism will emerge from practice. Certainly, it seems to suppose an ideal unlikely to be achieved in reality. A child assessment order does not confer parental responsibility on the applicant. It has two effects. First, there is a requirement that any person who is in a position to do so produces the child (s.43(6)(a)). This person is likely to be the parent but the provision is not so limited. A person caring for the child is in a position to produce him or her. That person may argue that s/he lacks the authority to do so, but under s.3(5) has permission to do what is reasonable to safeguard or promote the child's welfare. The parent cannot object because s/he cannot exercise parental responsibility in conflict with a court order (s.2(8)). Secondly, it authorises the carrying out of the assessment in accordance with the terms of the order (s.43(7)). If the relevant person fails to produce the child, the applicant will have grounds for seeking an EPO under s.44(1)(b) (enquiries being frustrated by access being unreasonably refused).

A child of sufficient understanding to make an informed decision may refuse to submit to a medical or psychiatric examination or other assessment (s.43(8)). This provision (and the others[15] like it) implements the House of Lords' decision in *Gillick* v. *West Norfolk and Wisbech Area Health Authority*.[16] In the words of Lord Scarman, the parental right 'yields to the child's right to make his own decisions when he reaches a sufficient understanding and intelligence to be capable of making up his mind on the matter requiring decision'.[17] It is one of the duties of the guardian ad litem to advise the court whether the child is of sufficient understanding for any purpose including in particular the question of refusal to submit to a medical or psychiatric examination (see Family Proceedings Rules 1991 and Family Proceedings Courts (Children Act 1989) Rules 1991, r.11(4)(a) (and above)). The *Guidance* (vol. 1, para. 4.13) notes that in performing this duty the guardian 'may need to seek the assistance of professionals in other disciplines', particularly 'where a child suffers from a handicap which impairs his ability to communicate'. It advises that offering the child advice may result in the child withdrawing opposition, but adds 'all professionals should take particular care to avoid coercing the child into agreement even where there is a belief that the refusal to comply is itself the product of coercion by a parent, relative or friend'.

Whether the *Guidance* really grasps the nettle here may be doubted. To talk of 'handicap' in its narrow sense and 'coercion' oversimplifies the intellectual and emotional conflicts that may be involved. It would be unrealistic to pretend otherwise than that the main problem area will be the case of the adolescent girl believed to have been sexually abused by her father, stepfather or other close relative. She will have been traumatised by the abuse, perhaps over many years. It is well-known that the effect of this experience, which may go back many years, may make the girl incapable of making a rationally autonomous decision about whether she wishes to expose her father. She may be intellectually capable of a level of decision-making that satisfies the test in the *Gillick* decision, but at the same time be so emotionally dependent and confused as to be incapable of weighing up the considerations. Each case will have to be resolved individually. No rule can be laid down. But it should be borne in mind that we all make mistakes. If we are to take rights seriously (Freeman,1992), one of the rights we must accord to persons, and this includes children, is the right to make wrong decisions (Dworkin, 1978). We should only interfere with the decision of a child of competence when the decision she wishes to take is irreparably harmful or in some way is likely to thwart her life choices. (Richards, 1980). In practice, it will be difficult to reconcile these conflicts. However, if we believe in treating children's rights seriously, and this is an ideal embodied in the Act, their decisions must be given equal concern and respect. How this problem is resolved will tell us much about the attitude of the courts and social workers to children's rights and, in particular, to their right to autonomy. The Act, it has to be said, gives very much less attention to the implications of a child's autonomy than it does to that of her parents.

Section 43 (9) provides for keeping the child away from home for the purposes of the assessment. This may only be done in accordance with the court's directions, where it is necessary for the assessment and for the period or periods specified in the order. Presumably, the court must be satisfied that it is necessary. This is implied, though not spelt out (but see the *Guidance*, vol. 1, 4.15). The *Guidance (idem)* is helpful on the question. Stressing that it is a 'reserve position', it cautions against overnight stays. 'The assessment should be conducted with as little trauma for the child and parents as possible ... The need for an overnight stay might arise if the child were thought to have special needs or characteristics which necessitated overnight observation ... In exceptional circumstances, either for medical or social work reasons, an overnight stay might facilitate the completion of the assessment. Examples might include where the child has eating difficulties, seriously disturbed sleep patterns or other symptoms that would require 24 hour continuous observation and monitoring'. If the court directs that the child may be kept away from home, it must also give directions about the contact the child is to have with other persons during this period (s.43(10)). Section 34 is not applicable, but its philosophy of a presumption of reasonable contact is. The court may direct, and should certainly consider the arrangements for, parents (or others) being allowed to stay with the child overnight. The contact question should be governed by the paramountcy principle in s.1(1), but as a direction, not an order, it is not subjected to the presumption in s.1(5). The child's wishes and feelings are not a matter to which the Act directs attention in this context, but they ought to be considered (see also *Guidance*, vol. 1, para. 4.16).

That in certain circumstances a child may be removed from home on a CAO does not mean that a CAO is a variant of an EPO. The purpose of the two orders is quite different. However, as indicated above, the court is required not to make a CAO if satisfied that there are grounds for an EPO (s.43(4)). The *Guidance* explains (vol.1, para. 4.17) that this power 'has been given to the court to guard against expressed fears that some applicants might opt for the less serious order when in reality the full powers of the EPO are required'. The *Guidance* warns (*idem*) against a 'failure to act decisively to an optimistic view' of the effect of a CAO, and the serious consequences this may have for the child.

What is the applicant to do if the person responsible for the child fails to produce him or her for the assessment in accordance with the order? Fear that this may happen is one good reason why a court hearing an application for a CAO might make an EPO under s.43(4). But if a CAO has been made and not complied with, a number of courses of action are open. First, there may be the possibility of negotiation. It is possible that the order has not been understood or there may be another satisfactory explanation for the non-production. But, secondly, where there is deliberate and conscious obstruction, it may be necessary to resort to other measures. These are (i) an EPO (if s.44(1)(b) is satisfied and see below); (ii) the use of police powers under s.46 (below), but there are no powers of search under the Act, though in extreme circumstances powers under s.17 of the Police and Criminal Evidence Act 1984 may be used (below), (iii) an application for an interim care order or interim supervision order (above). The *Guidance* (vol. 1, para. 4.19) notes that 'a person who has been abusing a child may be prepared to go to extreme lengths to prevent the child being seen or assessed', so that the potential significance of the non-production of the child should not be underestimated.

If the child is kept away from home for the assessment and what is revealed is so serious that the child cannot be allowed to return home, an EPO will have to be sought. The assessment, whether with removal or not, may reveal a concern for the child's health and development which can be met by the provision of services under part III of the Act, including the provision of accommodation under s.20. If further assessment is required, (and with a maximum period of seven days which cannot be extended) this may be common, it may be possible for this to be achieved on a voluntary basis with the parents. If not, and the minimum conditions can be satisfied, the possibility of seeking an interim care or supervision order will need to be explored. It is likely that many parents, seeing this as the alternative and being convinced of the value of further assessment, may agree to allow this voluntarily. It should be stressed that only one parent need consent (s.2(7) empowers one parent to act alone).

It is easy to be sceptical about the value of child assessment orders and, in practice, the threat to acquire one may become more common than the use of the order itself. But some are in no doubt as to their value. Perhaps, the clearest statement is to be found in literature of the NSPCC (the main protagonist of the CAO). It argues (Harding, 1989; Wilson, 1989) that the benefits of a CAO are:

(*i*)   parental responsibility is retained by the parents so that there is the least possible stress within the family;

(*ii*)   the child can be seen by the family doctor in a familiar environment, thus protecting the child from stress and worry;[18]

(*iii*) the parents are likely to cooperate so that the social work relationship with the family will not be damaged; and

(*iv*)   the child is protected in serious situations, short of emergencies.

Emergency protection orders

The EPO replaces the place of safety order. The purpose of the order is to enable the child in a genuine emergency to be removed from the place where s/he is, or retained where s/he currently is (for example, a hospital), if and only if this is what is necessary to provide immediate short-term protection.

The main characteristics of the EPO are:

(*i*) the court has to be satisfied that the child is likely to suffer significant harm or cannot be seen in circumstances where the child might be suffering significant harm (s.44(1));

(*ii*) the person obtaining the order obtains also parental responsibility for the child (s.44(4(c));

(*iii*) the order lasts for a maximum eight days with one possible extension of 7 days (s.45(1), s.45(5), s.45(6));

(*iv*) certain persons, including the child and a parent, may apply for discharge after 72 hours (s.45(8),(9));

(*v*) an EPO can be made by a single justice;

(*vi*) applications can be *ex parte* (i.e. in the absence of other interested parties) and, with the leave of the clerk of the court, may be made orally;

(*vii*) the application must name the child, or where this is not possible, must describe him/her as clearly as possible (s.44(14));

(*viii*) the court may make directions as to contact with the child and/or medical or psychiatric examination or assessment. A *Gillick*-competent child may refuse to submit (s.44(6),(7)).

The *Guidance* (vol. 1, para. 4.30) stresses that an application for an EPO is 'an extremely serious step' and should not be regarded as a 'routine response to allegations of child abuse or a routine first step to initiating care proceedings'. On the other hand, s.47(6) must be borne in mind. A local authority must apply for an EPO (or CAO, care order or supervision order) if, while investigating, they are denied access to the child or information as to whereabouts, unless satisfied that the child's welfare can be satisfactorily safeguarded without their doing so.

The local authority should always explore alternatives to seeking an EPO. Where the issue is child abuse, one solution is to remove the alleged abuser from the home. The Law Commission (1989) is currently exploring the possibility of a new public law remedy to achieve this. In the meanwhile, the local authority should consider the possibility of using Schedule 2, para. 5 which permits the provision of housing or cash assistance to an abuser to enable him to leave (and see above). It should also advise the non-abusing parent on the value of using private law remedies to oust the abuser albeit temporarily.[19] Ouster injunctions usually last for a maximum of three months,[20] but can be made 'until further order'.[21]

As was the case with place of safety orders, any person can apply for an EPO. In the normal case the applicant will be a local authority or the NSPCC, but 'in dire circumstances' (*Guidance*, vol. 1, para. 4.32) a neighbour or a relative or schoolteacher may need to protect a child at risk. The police may also apply but should be able to use the procedure under s.46. Rules of Court require the applicant to notify the local authority, amongst others, of the application, at which point the local authority's investigative duties under s.47 come into operation (see above). The Emergency Protection Order (Transfer of Responsibilities) Regulations 1991[22] allow the authority to take over the order (and the powers and responsibility attendant on it) if they consider that it would be in the child's best interests (r.2(c)). In forming the opinion (see r.3) the local authority is to consult the applicant and have regard to the ascertainable wishes and feelings of the child, the child's needs, the likely effect of any change in the child's circumstances, age, sex and family background, the circumstances which gave rise to the application, any directions of a court and other orders, the relationship, if any, of the applicant to the child and any plans the applicant may have in respect of the child. Many of these considerations are closely modelled on s.1(3) (the checklist, above). Applications by the NSPCC are not exempt from these Regulations. The *Guidance* (vol. 1, para. 4.33) anticipates that 'the process of local dialogue and consultation between the NSPCC and the authority will mean that the transfer powers are rarely exercised without the latter's consent'.

The grounds for an EPO are set out in s.44(1). Note the words 'if, but only if' in the preamble and remember s.1(1) and s.1(5) govern applications for EPOs.

Under s.44(1)(a) the *court* must be satisfied that there is reasonable cause to believe that the child is likely to suffer significant harm

    (*i*) 'if he is not removed to accommodation provided by or on behalf of the applicant; or

    (*ii*) if he does not remain in the place in which he is then being accommodated.'

It is the court that must be satisfied (on a balance of probabilities), not the applicant. *Guidance* (vol. 1, para. 4.42) advises that this paragraph is 'for cases where the child has been seen, or seeing him may not be relevant, for example where a baby has just been born into a family with a long history of violent behaviour to young children'. The authority may be carrying out enquiries under s.47 or be responding to a direction under s.37. It should be noted that the test concentrates on the *future*. Past or present significant harm are, therefore, only relevant to the extent that they indicate the likelihood of significant harm in the near future. Since there is a presumption of no order (s.1(5)), the applicant will have to convince the court that urgent action is essential and there is no alternative to an EPO. It is important that alternatives (for example, the provision of accommodation under s.20) be explored. If the parents are co-operative, an application for an EPO may be unnecessary. It should be borne in mind that the use of s.20, followed, if necessary, by the application for an interim care order will give the parents an opportunity to prepare a case.

Section 44(1)(b) provides for an application by a local authority where enquiries are being made with respect to a child under s.47(1)(b) and those enquiries are being frustrated by access to the child being unreasonably refused, and they have reasonable cause to believe that access to the child is required as a matter of urgency. The ground only applies to *local authorities*.

Section 44(1)(c) provides for an application in the same circumstances by an *authorised person* (see s.44(2) and s.31(9)) who has been making enquiries. The authorised person (in effect the NSPCC) must additionally satisfy the court as to their reasonable cause for suspicion.

The *Guidance* (vol. 1, para. 4.38) explains the circumstances in which s.44(1)(b) and (c) are to be used. These 'frustrated access' grounds are 'for use in an emergency (where access is required as a matter of urgency) where enquiries cannot be completed because the child cannot be seen but there is enough cause to suspect the child is suffering or likely to suffer significant harm'. An EPO on one of these grounds is to be distinguished from a CAO, for use where there is a need for further investigation but no immediate danger.

'The hypothesis of the grounds at s.44(1)(b) and (c) is that this combination of factors is evidence of an emergency or the likelihood of an emergency' (*Guidance*, vol. 1, para. 4.39). The court will have to decide whether the refusal of access is unreasonable. This will depend on all the circumstances (when was the request made? are the parents prepared to take their child to a doctor?). A person seeking access must produce evidence of his or her authority if asked to do so (s.44(3)): good practice would dictate that this be done without the necessity of being asked.

The court can require a person with information about a child's whereabouts to disclose that information where this is not available to the applicant (s.48(1)). Self-incrimination does not justify a person's refusal to comply (s.48(2)). Failure to comply with the order is contempt of court and may amount to an offence under s.44(15). The court can also authorise entry to premises to search for the child (s.48(3)) or other children (s.48(4)). The *Guidance* advises (vol. 1, para. 4.52) that applicants should ask for this authority as a matter of course. If, on searching the premises, a second child is found and the applicant believes there are sufficient grounds for making an EPO, the order authorising the search for the second child may be treated as an EPO (s.48(5)). It is a criminal offence intentionally to obstruct an authorised person exercising powers under s.48(3) or (4). If this does occur (or it is anticipated), the court can issue a warrant authorising any constable to assist the authorised person in entering and searching the named premises (s.48(9)). The authorised person may accompany the police officer if s/he wishes, although the court may direct otherwise (s.48(10)(b)). Any warrant which the court issues to the constable may direct that, if s/he chooses, the constable may be accompanied by a doctor, nurse or health visitor (s.48(11)). The *Guidance* (vol. 1, para. 4.56) advises that it would be good practice always to request such a direction. The warrant will authorise the constable to use reasonable force if necessary to assist the applicant in the exercise of his or her powers to enter and search the premises for the child (s.48(9)).

Guidance (vol. 1, para. 4.57) advises that when making an application for an EPO, the applicant should consider whether at the same time s/he needs to apply for a warrant for a police officer to come with, if s/he is requesting authorisation to enter and search premises. It adds: 'if any difficulties in gaining entry are foreseen, or if the applicant believes that he is likely to be threatened, intimidated or physically prevented from carrying out this part of the order, the possibility of simultaneously obtaining a warrant should always be considered'. The *Guidance* (*idem*) makes reference also to s.17(1)(e) of the Police and Criminal Evidence Act 1984, for use in 'dire emergencies' and s.25(3)(e) of that Act, allowing arrest without warrant to protect a child.

Anyone can apply for an EPO under s.44(1)(a). A local authority can apply under s.44(1)(a) and (b); an authorised person (currently only the NSPCC) under s.44(1)(a) and (e). The application will usually be heard *ex parte*. Rules of Court provide for *inter partes* hearings (a full hearing), but in most emergency situations this will be impracticable. The *Cleveland* report (1988, para. 16,15) did recommend that, where a court is available, the application, including *ex parte* applications, should be made to a court. The *Guidance* (vol. 1, para. 4.46) cautions that putting the parents on notice might in some cases place the child in greater danger. It does not add, however, that where the parent is given notice and is present at the hearing, an application for discharge cannot be made after 72 hours (s.45(11)). It will be interesting to see whether the courts interpret 'present' literally or restrictively. Parents may be 'present' physically without any understanding of what is involved. It would surely be wrong if this precluded an application for discharge. A parent may also be 'present' without notice (one day is prescribed) and will, accordingly, have the right to challenge the order after 72 hours.

Because most applications will be heard *ex parte*, Rules of Court require the applicant (not the court) to serve a copy of the application and the order within 48 hours on the parties to the proceedings, any person who is not a party but has actual care of the child and the local authority in whose area the child is normally resident if that authority is not the applicant. If service takes place at the end of the 48 hour period, the parent only has 24 hours to challenge the order. Nevertheless, the *Guidance* (vol. 1, para. 4.47) stresses the need to inform parents of their rights and responsibilities under the order. The EPO itself comes with an explanatory note. The *Guidance (idem)* wisely advises authorities to consider making this available in other relevant languages.

The effects of an EPO are:

(*i*) any person who is in a position to do so must comply with any request to produce the child to the applicant (s.44(4)(a));

(*ii*) the authorisation of the removal of the child and the prevention of the removal of the child from any place in which s/he was accommodated at the time of the order (s.44(4)(b)). The child is entitled to an explanation, appropriate to age and understanding. The older child, his/her solicitor or GAL will receive a copy of the application and the order;

(*iii*) gives the applicant parental responsibility (s.44(4)(c)), but only to take such action as is reasonably required to safeguard or promote the welfare of the child (s.44(5)). So, for example, if the abuser has gone, the authority to remove the child ceases.

(*iv*) the applicant must allow the child reasonable contact with parents, persons with parental responsibility, any person with whom the child was living immediately before the order or in whose favour a contact order is in force or any person acting on behalf of any of those persons (for example, a solicitor) (s.44(13)). What is 'reasonable' is up to the applicant. There is no appeal to a court;

(*v*)   the court may make directives about assessments, examinations and contact (s.44(6) – (9)). A *Gillick*-competent child may refuse to submit to the examination or assessment (s.44(7)). (See the discussion above.)

Consistent with the philosophy of the Act, that a child should not be kept away from parental care for longer than necessary, the applicant is required to return the child, or allow him to be removed, where it appears to be safe to do so, even though the EPO is still in force (s.44(10)). The EPO remains in force (until it expires). The child is to be returned to the care of the person from whose care s/he was removed. Where this is not reasonably practicable s/he must be returned to his or her parent, any person with parental responsibility or such other person as the applicant, with the agreement of the court, considers appropriate (s.44(11)). If circumstances change, the applicant may again exercise power under the EPO at any time while it remains in force if it appears to him or her that it is necessary to do so (s.44(12)). The possibility that this may happen should be made clear to parents where a child has been returned and the EPO has not yet expired.

An EPO may be granted for up to 8 days (s.45(1)). When the eighth day is a public holiday or a Sunday, the court may specify a period for the order which has the effect of extending it to noon on the first later day which is not such a holiday or a Sunday (s.45(2)). Where the child is in police protection (below), and the designated officer applies for an EPO, the period of 8 days of any EPO starts from the date the child was taken into police protection, and not from the date of the EPO application (s.45(3)). An EPO may be extended once only (s.45(6)), and for a period of up to seven days, including public holidays and Sundays. The Rules of Court require an application for an extension to be made on notice in a full *inter partes* hearing by any person who has parental responsibility for the child as a result of an EPO (i.e. only a local authority or authorised person) and is entitled to apply for a care order (s.45(4)). The court may only extend the period of the order if it has reasonable cause to believe that the child is likely to suffer significant harm (s.45(5)). The *Guidance* (vol. 1, para. 4.66) advises that 'if there has been a genuine emergency and the authority believe care proceedings should follow it should normally be possible to proceed to satisfy the court as to the grounds for an interim order within the first period. If an extension is sought the court will want to be satisfied as to the reasons for the delay'. But what this overlooks is that under the Rules of Court three days' notice must be given before the application for the interim order is heard, two days needs to be allowed for the post, so that the decision to apply for an interim order will need to be taken before three days of the EPO have elapsed, before the authority even knows whether the parents are applying for a discharge. If *Working Together* (1991, para. 6.11) is followed, the decision to apply for an interim order will be discussed in the presence of the parents who will be told of the intended application and of their right to apply for discharge of the EPO. They can be forgiven for finding this difficult to understand!

There is no right of appeal against:

(a) the making of, or refusal to make, an EPO;
(b) the extension of, or refusal to extend, an EPO;
(c) the discharge, or refusal to discharge, an EPO;
(d) the giving, or refusal to give, any direction in connection with an EPO (s.45(10)).[23]

Orders, as have been seen, last for a maximum of fifteen days. An Application for discharge may be heard after seventy-two hours (below). Directions may be varied on application (s.44(9)).

Applications for discharge can be made immediately but cannot be heard by the court before the expiry of seventy-two hours beginning with the making of the order. They can be made by the child (there is no restriction on age or competence), a parent, any person with parental responsibility, and any person with whom s/he was living immediately before the making of the order (s.45(8)). An application to discharge is not allowed where the person who would otherwise be entitled to apply was given notice of the hearing at which the order was made and was present (see above). It may well be better for parents not to be present in order to have the opportunity to challenge the order after seventy-two hours. But there is a danger of the courts being clogged up with applications for discharge (an *inter partes* hearing could be lengthy). They, it may be expected, would prefer the original application to be on notice with the parent present.

Where an EPO has been extended, an application for discharge cannot be made (s.45(11)(b)). The parent's opportunity for challenge is limited to the *inter partes* hearing at which the extension was sought and granted.

The *Guidance* (vol. 1, para. 4.69) points out that the seventy-two hour provision will enable 'confusion' to be sorted out and give parents etc. time to prepare their case should they wish to challenge the order. But 'it is not intended that seventy-two hours will become the effective time limit by which the authority must complete its assessment if it is to contest an application to discharge the order'. It envisages that if an authority advises the court that an assessment has not been completed that 'unless the circumstances have so changed as to allay any concerns the authority may have had for the safety of the child it is unlikely that the court will agree to discharge the emergency protection order'. This may mean that few discharges will be made. How often will an assessment have been completed within seventy-two hours? On the other hand, as indicated above, there are suggestions in the *Guidance* that an application for an interim order ought to have been considered before the expiry of seventy-two hours.

Police protection

The police have an important role in child protection (*Working Together*, 1991, paras. 4.11–4.17).

Where a constable has reasonable cause to believe that a child would be otherwise likely to suffer significant harm s/he may remove the child to 'suitable accommodation' (not as before a 'place of safety') and keep him or her there. Alternatively, s/he may take such steps as are reasonable to ensure that the child's removal from hospital, or other place in which s/he is being accommodated, is prevented (s.46(1)). When these powers are exercised, the child is said to be in 'police protection' (s.46(2)). No child can be kept in police protection for more than 72 hours (s.46(6)).

As soon as is reasonably practicable after taking a child into police protection, the constable must (s.46(3)):

(a)   inform the local authority in whose area the child was found of the steps that have been and are proposed to be taken with respect to the child and the reasons for taking them;

(b)   give details to the authority within whose area the child is ordinarily resident of the place where the child is being accommodated;

(c) inform the child (if s/he appears capable of understanding) of the steps that have been taken, the reasons for taking them, and of further steps that may be taken;

(d) take such steps as are reasonably practicable to discover the wishes and feelings of the child;

(e) where the child was taken into police protection other than to accommodation provided on behalf of a local authority or to a refuge, ensure that s/he is moved to such accommodation;

(f) take such steps as are reasonably practicable to give information to the child's parents, every other person who is not a parent but has parental responsibility and any other person with whom the child was living immediately before being taken into police protection. The information is the steps taken and to be taken and the reasons for them (s.46(4)).

The constable must also 'secure' that the case is inquired into by a 'designated officer' (s.46(3)(e)). S/he has a number of responsibilities in addition to inquiring into the case. S/he may apply on behalf of the local authority in whose area the child is ordinarily resident for an EPO to be made in respect of the child (s.46(7)). The application can be made whether the authority know of it or agree to its being made (s.46(8)) though clearly good practice dictates that this should never happen. The duration of the EPO is limited by s.45(3), so that the period of police protection and the EPO cannot together exceed 8 days. The police cannot apply for an extension nor can they commence care proceedings. The local authority can apply for an EPO while the child is in police protection. It is probable that the courts will reject the strategem of a parent (for example) applying for an EPO in order to end police protection.[24]

While the child is in police protection neither the constable nor the designated officer acquire parental responsibility (s.46(9)(a)). But the designated officer must nevertheless do what is reasonable in all the circumstances of the case to safeguard or promote the child's welfare, bearing in mind the short period of time that police protection will last (s.46(9)(b)).[25] Does this include seeking medical treatment or an assessment for the child? The answer is not clear but a distinction can, it is thought, be drawn between emergency treatment and assessment. As far as the former is concerned, this should come under the umbrella of reasonable safeguarding of the child's welfare (though without parental responsibility the police cannot consent to treatment). If assessment is required (for example, to investigate whether sexual abuse has taken place), an EPO should be sought (the police cannot apply for a CAO). The question clearly was not considered by Parliament. Such a contentious issue as to whether a *Gillick*-competent child could refuse to submit to treatment is left open. Common law principles (the *Gillick* decision and *Re R*[26]) would be applicable.

The designated officer must also allow the child's parents, persons with parental responsibility, any person with whom the child was living immediately before being taken into police protection, any person with contact under s.34 and any person acting on behalf of any of those persons to have such contact, if any, with the child as, in the designated officer's opinion, is both reasonable and in the child's best interests (s.46(10)). *Guidance* advises (vol. 1, para. 4.76) that the feelings and wishes of the child should be fully considered, though the Act surprisingly omits this. What is 'reasonable' must take account of a number of factors (the length of the protection, the reason why the child is in protection, the child's age, the child's wishes and feelings).

Refuges for children at risk

The problem of young 'runaways' is now well-documented (Newman, 1990). Section 51 enables 'safe houses' legally to provide care for children who are absent from home or local authority accommodation without permission. The Secretary of State is empowered to issue certificates to voluntary homes, registered homes (s.51(1)), and foster parents (s.51(2)) which will exempt them from offences (see s.51(7)) of harbouring etc. children for whom they are providing a refuge.

The Regulations as to the issue and withdrawal of certificates are in the Refuges for Children at Risk (Children's Homes and Foster Placements) Regulations 1991.[27] The child must appear to be at risk of harm before s/he is accepted into the refuge and when s/he is in the refuge he must be at risk of harm if s/he were not staying at the refuge (r.3). The police must be notified of every admission within twenty-four hours, with a view to the parent or other specified person being notified that the child is in a refuge and provided with a telephone contact number, but not the address, of the project. The police should also be notified when the child leaves. Where a child remains in the refuge for more than fourteen concecutive days, or more than twenty-one days, in any period of three months, the protection from prosecution will apply, but the certificate can be withdrawn altogether from the refuge, since it will not be being used in accordance with the basis upon which the certificate was granted (*Guidance*, vol. 4, para. 9.9).

The protection from prosecution extends to the organisation and to those persons providing the home (including the foster parent), but those involved in outreach work are not protected (*Guidance*, vol. 4, para. 9.10).

A certificate can be withdrawn at any time (r.4). We are told that certificates will not be 'issued lightly' (*Guidance*, vol. 4, para. 9.13: see also David Mellor, *Hansard*, H.C. vol. 158, col. 609). Both SSDs and the police will have had the opportunity to express a view on whether a certificate should be issued. There is no right of appeal against refusal or withdrawal of a certificate. We can expect guidance to the police on the legal framework within which refuges will have to operate.

Notes

1. The Infant Life Protection Act of that year.
2. Data have not been collected in a consistent way, leading to different views as to the increase.
3. These have now been roundly condemned by the Secretary of State.
4. The legal position was described as 'somewhat opaque' by Hayes and Bevan (1988, p.44). A DHSS *Circular* (88)2 did not inject a lot of clarity.
5. See *Cleveland* report (1988) para. 16.14.
6. Critics of Cleveland were quick to round on the use of place of safety orders and the effects of them. See, in particular, Bell (1988). See also Freeman (1989, p. 106).
7. But Lyon and de Cruz (1988, p.377) are more sceptical.
8. As had been recommended in both the *Beckford* and *Carlile* reports.
9. She described the concept as 'rather like paying a parking ticket'. The parents 'must either produce the child for a medical within the required time of three days or appear in the juvenile court, or before a magistrate, to explain their objections' (*Hansard*, HC vol.158, col. 691).
10. Amazingly, this was *never* debated.
11. See The Department of Health *Guidance on Protecting Children* (1988). See also D. Mellor, Standing Committee B, col. 317.
12. Under Children and Young Persons Act 1933, s.40.
13. Added by Courts and Legal Services Act 1990, Sch. 16, para. 20.
14. As yet none have been authorised.

15. See s.44(6), 38(6).
16. *Gillick* v. *West Norfolk and Wisbech Area Health Authority* [1986] AC 112 (see above).
17. Ibid., p. 186.
18. This is possible but, as indicated, the child may be removed for assessment (s.43(9)).
19. See Domestic Violence and Matrimonial Proceedings Act 1976 s.1 (where the parents are not married) and Domestic Proceedings and Magistrates' Courts Act 1978 s.16 and Matrimonial Homes Act 1983 s.1 (where they are).
20. See *Practice Note* [1978] 2 All ER 1056.
21. *Galan* v. *Galan* [1985] FLR 905; *Spencer v Camacho* [1983] 4 FLR 662.
22. SI (1991) No. 1414.
23. As substituted by the Courts and Legal Services Act 1990, Sch. 16, para. 19.
24. See *Nottingham CC* v. *Q* [1981] Fam. 94, where a similar ploy was described as an abuse of the process of the court.
25. See also s.3 (5), above.
26. [1991] 4 All ER 177.
27. SI (1991) No. 1507.

References

Beckford Report (1985) *A Child in Trust: Report of the Panel of Inquiry investigating the Circumstances surrounding the Death of Jasmine Beckford*, L.B. of Brent.
Bell, S. (1988) *When Salem Came to the 'Boro*, London, Pan.
Byrne, K. and Bloxham, R. (1986) 'When Sensitivity is on Trial', *Social Services Insight*, 20 (20–27 April).
Carlile Report (1987) *A Child in Mind: Protection of Children in Responsible Society: Report of Commission of Inquiry into the Circumstances Surrounding the Death of Kimberley Carlile*, London, L. B. of Greenwich.
Christopherson, J. (1989) in O. Stevenson (ed.) *Child Abuse*, Brighton, Wheatsheaf.
Cleveland Report (1988) *Report of Inquiry into Child Abuse in Cleveland* (Butler-Sloss), London, HMSO, Cm. 412.
Department of Health (1988) *Diagnosis of Child Sexual Abuse – Guidance for Doctors*. London, HMSO.
Department of Health (1991) *Guidance and Regulations*, vol. 1, London, HMSO.
Department of Health (1991) *Guidance and Regulations*, vol. 4, London, HMSO.
Dingwall, R. (1986) 'The Jasmine Beckford Affair', *Modern Law Review*, 49, 488.
Dworkin, R. (1978) *Taking Rights Seriously*, London, Duckworth.

Freeman, M. (1989) 'Cleveland, Butler-Sloss and Beyond', *Current Legal Problems*, 42, 85.
Freeman, M. (1992) 'In the Child's Best Interests?', *Current Legal Problems*, 45, 173.
Harding, J. (1989) 'A Child Assessment Order: To Be or Not To Be?', *Community Care*, 758, 6.
Hayes, M. and Bevan, V. (1988) *Child Care Law*, Bristol, Jordans.
Law Commission (1989) *Domestic Violence*, London, HMSO.
Lawson, A. (1980) 'Taking a Decision to Remove the Child from the Family', *Journal of Social Welfare Law*, 141.
Lyon, C. and De Cruz, P. (1988) 'Child Sexual Abuse and the Cleveland Report', *Family Law*, 18, 370.
Maidment, S. (1978) 'Some Legal Problems Arising out of the Reporting of Child Abuse', *Current Legal Problems*, 31, 149.
Metropolitan Police and Bexley London Borough (1987) *Child Sexual Abuse: Joint Investigation Project Final Report*, London, HMSO.
Newman, C. (1990) *Young Runaways*, London, Church of England Society.
Packman, J. (1986) *Who Needs Care?*, Oxford, Blackwell.
Parton, N. (1986) 'The Beckford Report: A Critical Appraisal', *British Journal of Social Work*, 16, 511.
Parton, N. (1991) *Governing The Family: Child Care, Child Protection and the State*, Basingstoke, Macmillan.
Richards, D. (1980) 'The Individual, the Family and the Constitution', *New York University Law Review*, 55,1.
Wilson, A. (1989) 'Should We Have a Child Assessment Order? The Case For', *Childright*, 55, 12.
Working Together (1991), *A Guide to Arrangements for Inter-Agency Co-operation for the Protection of Children from Abuse*, London, HMSO.

9

The Legal Regulation of Substitute Care

In this chapter the various forms of substitute care are discussed. Much of the law is a re-enactment with amendments of previous legislation (as to which see Freeman and Lyon, 1984), though there are some significant reforms, notably in the law relating to child-minding. The new law should be looked at in conjunction with important new Regulations in particular the Children's Homes Regulations 1991,[1] the Children (Private Arrangements for Fostering) Regulations 1991,[2] the Disqualification for Caring for Children Regulations 1991[3] and three sets of Regulations on Child Care and Day Care.[4]

Community homes

Part VI of the Act, together with Schedule 4, and the Children's Homes Regulations deal with the provision, organisation, management and cessation of community homes. These should be read in conjunction with the *Guidance* (vol. 4, ch. 1). The recent Utting report (1991) is useful supplementary guidance.

All local authorities must provide community homes for children who are looked after by them and for the welfare of other children who are not looked after by them (s. 53(1)). But the arrangements they make are those they 'consider appropriate'. They may do so alone or jointly with one or more other local authorities. They must ensure that different types of accommodation are available, which are suitable for different purposes and the requirements of different types of children (s.53(2)). Attention should be drawn to the helpful statement in the *Guidance* (vol. 4, para. 1.(7)):

'Children no longer spend a large proportion of their childhood growing up in residential care. Increasingly, homes have adjusted to meet the particular needs of children during a phase of their career in care and have adopted various approaches to the care of children. For example, some homes work with children to prepare for a definite goal in a task centred manner; other homes attempt to reproduce family life and support children into adulthood; certain homes attempt to create a therapeutic milieu and work with children psychologically damaged by abuse; still other homes are geared to addressing a child's unacceptable behaviour by means of a systematic behavioural regime.'

The *Guidance (idem)* hopes that 'an increasing variety of imaginative and positive approaches to the residential care of children will develop'.

Community homes include homes provided and maintained by local authorities and those provided by voluntary organisations (s.53(3)). Where a local authority and a voluntary organisation agree that, in accordance with an instrument of management, the management, equipment and maintenance of a home shall be the responsibility of the local authority or a voluntary organisation, the home will be a community home. Where the managerial function is provided by a local authority, the home is designated as a 'controlled community home'. (s.53(4)). Where that function is carried out by a voluntary organisation, the local authority is to designate the home as an 'assisted community home' (s.53(5)).[5] By being 'designated', the controls over voluntary homes in part VII and Schedule 5 are avoided (below).

Schedule 4 contains the details on the management and conduct of community homes.[6] Paragraphs 1 and 2 permit the Secretary of State to make instruments of management for homes which are controlled or assisted community homes. Paragraph 3 deals with managerial functions. These are to be performed by the managers of the homes as agents of the 'responsible body' (the authority or organisation). Annual accounts have to be submitted to the responsible body. The employment of staff at a home is a 'matter reserved' for the decision of the responsible body (Sch. 4, para. 3(8)). It is important to remember this in the light of the recent pin-down (Levy and Kahan, 1991) and *Beck* scandals. The Children's Homes Regulations 1991 r.5 stipulate that the responsible authority (defined in r.2(1)) is to ensure that the number of staff at each children's home and their experience and qualifications are adequate to ensure that the welfare of children accommodated there is safeguarded and promoted at all times.

The Children's Homes Regulations 1991 replace the Community Homes Regulations 1972.

Regulation 4 requires the responsible authority to compile and maintain a statement of the purpose and functions of the home. The particulars to be included in the statement are listed in Part 1 of Schedule 1 to the Regulations. 'The overall purpose of the statement is to describe what the home sets out to do for children and the manner in which care is provided' (*Guidance*, vol. 4, para. 1.18). It should convey some idea of the 'feel' of the home. A yardstick for a home's success is the extent to which it meets its stated aims. The Uttting report (1991, para. 3.24) has recommended that individual homes include programmes of health education and health care in the statements of objectives.

Regulation 5 provides that homes should be adequately staffed (see above). *Guidance* indicates (vol. 4, para. 1.29) that it is not appropriate to specify one set of staff ratios for the differing kinds of children catered for. In the light of recent experience (for example Beck and 'regression therapy') the comment that homes should not attempt to use methods of care beyond the competence, experience and qualifications of the staff (para. 1.30) is particularly pertinent. Guidance on the vetting of staff is given.[7] Responsible authorities are required to notify the Secretary of State of conduct suggesting that a person may not be suitable for work with children (r.19(2)(b); see also *Guidance*, vol. 4, para. 1.167(b)). The composition of staff should reflect the racial, cultural and linguistic background of the children being cared for. The Race Relations Act 1976 (s.5(2)(d)) allows the recruitment of staff from a particular racial background where there is a genuine occupational qualification. This test is satisfied.

Regulation 6 requires suitable and properly equipped and furnished accommodation to be provided for each child in a home including disabled children accommodated in children's homes. Regulation 7 requires the responsible authority to ensure the provision of sufficient washing, bathing and toilet facilities, adequate heating, lighting, decoration, maintenance etc., facilities for children to meet privately with parents and others (e.g. a guardian ad litem), laundering facilities and access to a pay telephone. There is guidance on the location of the home (paras 1.58–1.61). 'If possible a home should be indistinguishable from an ordinary family residence in outward appearance and siting' (para. 1.59).

There is guidance also on structure and layout of the home (paras 1.62–1.70).

Regulation 8 forbids any form of corporal punishment. Guidance adds (vol. 4, para. 1.91) that this includes 'any intentional application of force as punishment including slapping, throwing missiles and rough handling [and] punching or pushing in the heat of the moment in response to violence from young people'. But it does not prevent a person 'taking necessary physical action, where any other course of action would be likely to fail, to avert an immediate danger of personal injury to the child or another person, or to avoid immediate danger to property'. 'Holding' a distressed child is not excluded. This Regulation must be welcomed but it makes up only partially for the reluctance to incorporate a ban on corporal punishment by all, including parents, in the Act itself (Newell, 1989).

Any deprivation of food and drink is also prohibited. The *Guidance* (vol. 4, para. 1.91) adds it is 'inappropriate to force a child to eat foods which he dislikes'. Other prohibited control devices are restrictions on visits to or by the child or any restriction on or delay in communications by telephone or post with a parent, a person with parental responsibility, relatives or friends, an appointed visitor, an assigned social worker, a guardian ad litem of the child and any solicitor acting for the child or whom the child wishes to instruct. Also not allowed are any requirement that a child wear distinctive or inappropriate clothes; the use or withholding of medication or medical or dental treatment (so that 'drugging' is ruled out – the end it is to be hoped, of a disgraceful practice); the intentional deprivation of sleep; the imposition of fines, except by way of reparation; and any intimate physical examination of the child. The use of accommodation physically to restrict the liberty of any child is also prohibited, except in premises approved by the Secretary of State for use as secure accommodation and under criteria set down in s.25 and the Children (Secure Accommodation) Regulations 1991 (see above). The *Guidance* qualifies this (vol. 4, para. 1.91) by laying down that 'locking external doors and windows at night time, in line with normal domestic security, is not excluded'. *Guidance* nevertheless recognises that 'some form of sanction' is necessary where there are instances of behaviour that would be unacceptable in any family or group environment (para. 1.90). But it urges that 'formal disciplinary measures should be used sparingly and in most cases only after repeated use of informal measures has proved ineffective'.

Regulation 10 requires those responsible for homes to assist with the making of, and giving effect to, arrangements with respect to the continued education, training and employment of young people over school age accommodated in the homes.

Regulation 11 requires that each child is, as far as is practicable, to have an opportunity to attend such religious services and receive such instructions as are appropriate to the religious persuasion to which the child may belong. The regulation also requires that the child be provided with facilities for religious observance, for example special diets and clothing. *Guidance* observes (para. 1.124) that the child should feel that every possible consideration is being given to respect for his or her religion.

Regulation 12 requires that children in homes should be provided with food in adequate quantities properly prepared, wholesome and nutritious, and for some reasonable choice to be provided so far as is practicable. Special dietary needs due to health, religious persuasion, racial origin or cultural background must be met. *Guidance* (para. 1.136) emphasises the significance of shopping as an 'important life skill' and urges that children, wherever possible, be involved in the food purchasing process, particularly where this would help them prepare for independent living.

Regulation 13 requires responsible authorities to enable each child to purchase clothes according to his or her needs, so far as is practicable. *Guidance* (vol. 4, para. 143) rules out bulk buying and special purchasing arrangements, spelling the end, if it still existed anywhere, of the 'voucher' system. The special needs of children, for example Muslim girls, are discussed in the *Guidance* (paras 1.146–1.147).

Under Regulation 8 of the Arrangements for Placement of Children (General) Regulations 1991[8] (and above), a written case record on each child must be established by the authority responsible for the placement of the child. This applies in respect of every child accommodated in any home governed by the Children's Homes Regulations.[9] In addition, Regulation 15 of the Children's Homes Regulations requires that the responsible authority should arrange that an individual case record is maintained in each children's home on each child in the home. As the *Guidance* puts it (vol. 4, para. 1.154) 'it becomes the child's "memory" in lieu of parents' recollections'. The case record is an essential tool for those responsible for planning for the child. *Guidance* (para. 1.160) directs that records should not include 'gratuitous value judgments' and 'stigmatising descriptive terms such as "delinquent", "maladjusted" or "uncontrollable" which carry the risk of "labelling" the child'. The Regulation requires that records be retained for at least 75 years from the birth of the child or, if less, for 15 years after the child's death. The guardian ad litem is to have access to the records (Regulation 16).

There is also an obligation to maintain other records listed in Schedule 3 of the Regulations, as regards such matters as workers, accidents, menus, disciplinary measures imposed and a daily log of events occurring in the home (r.17). Regulation 19 requires that certain significant events must be notified by the responsible authority to the children's parents. These include serious accidents, serious illnesses and conduct by a member of staff suggesting that s/he is not a suitable person to be employed in work involving children. There is guidance on this in the *Guidance* (vol. 4, para. 1.167).

Regulation 22 requires monthly visits to all homes by those responsible (or their representatives) and written reports of such visits. The Secretary of State is empowered by Regulation 23 to direct that a child being looked after by a local authority should be accommodated in a controlled or assisted community home when no places in the home are available to the authority looking after the child.[10]

Regulations 24–30 and Schedules 4 and 5 govern applications for registration (see also *Guidance*, vol. 4, paras 1. 172-1.174). Regulation 31 makes provisions regarding particulars to be notified on the establishment of a voluntary home (listed in Schedule 7) and annual returns.

Regulations 32–34 govern the duties of local authorities under s.62 and s.64(4) (below) to satisfy themselves as to the welfare of children in voluntary and private children's homes in their areas (see further below).

The Regulations do not address the question of child abuse in children's homes. There is, however, full guidance in volume 4 of the *Guidance* (paras 1.179–1.192). *Working Together* (1991, para. 5.20) should also be consulted. Abuse in homes would be more likely to come to light if there were systematic inspection of community homes, and this has been recommended (Utting, 1991, paras 4.34–4.47). The remaining statutory provisions dealing with community homes require little comment. Section 54 permits the Secretary of State to direct that premises cease to be used as a community home.[11] This may be done where the premises are 'unsuitable' or where the home is not being conducted in accordance with the regulations or is 'otherwise unsatisfactory'. A community home, where there was evidence of abuse by staff, might well come into this category. Section 55 provides for certain disputes relating to controlled or assisted community homes to be determined by the Secretary of State.[12] Upon determination of the dispute the Secretary of State can give such directions as s/he thinks fit to the authority or organisation concerned. The Secretary of State's authority does not extend to disputes about religious instruction provided in a home, where the trust deed contains a term granting an ecclesiastical authority the power to decide any disputes (s.55(5)). Section 56 requires voluntary organisations providing controlled or assisted community homes to give two years' notice before they stop providing a home.[13] The lengthy notice and heavy financial burdens involved (see s.58) may constitute a strong disincentive to voluntary discontinuance when their implications are realised, and may result in the voluntary organisation having to transfer all or part of the premises or property owned by the home to the local authority. Section 57 permits local authorities to withdraw the designation of a community home as 'controlled' or 'assisted' and requires them to give two years' notice of their intention to do so.[14] Section 58 requires proprietors of controlled or assisted homes which close to repay any increase in the value of the premises which is attributable to the expenditure of public money to the 'responsible authority' or the Secretary of State.[15]

Voluntary homes

Part VII and Schedule 5 of the Act are concerned with the regulation of voluntary homes and the statutory obligations of voluntary organisations towards children looked after by them.

The powers of voluntary organisations to provide accommodation for children are set out in s.59. This imposes equivalent obligations on voluntary organisations as are imposed on local authorities by s.23. This was discussed above and reference should be made to this. Section 59 gave the Secretary of State power to make regulations on fostering, placements generally, and on reviews and complaints and these have been made. The Arrangements for Placement of Children (General) Regulations 1991,[16] discussed above, apply to placements by a voluntary organisation as they do to placements by a local authority (r.2(b)). So do the Foster Placement (Children) Regulations 1991,[17] also discussed above (r.2(1)(b)), and the Review of Children's Cases Regulations 1991,[18] discussed above (r.1(2)(b)). The Representations Procedure (Children) Regulations 1991[19] has, as envisaged, extended the representations and complaints procedure to voluntary organisations (r.11). The details of this, in relation to local authorities, were considered above. The extension to voluntary organisations necessitates some minor amendments but these are of no substance. The details can be found in Regulation 11 of the Representations Procedure (Children) Regulations 1991.

A voluntary organisation (as, indeed, a local authority)[20] may *inter alia* place a child in a voluntary home (s.59(1)(b)). A voluntary home is defined (s.60(3)) as

'any home or other institution providing care and accommodation for children which is carried on by a voluntary organisation but does not include –

(a) a nursing home, mental nursing home or residential care home;

(b) a school;

(c) any health service hospital;[21]

(d) any community home;

(e) any home or other institution provided, equipped and maintained by the Secretary of State;

(f) any home which is exempted by regulations made for the purposes of this section by the Secretary of State.'

No voluntary home shall be carried on unless it is registered (s.60(1)). The detailed requirements on registration procedures are in Schedule 5, part 1. An application must be made in prescribed form by those intending to carry on the home. The Secretary of State may grant it or refuse to do so or grant it subject to conditions (para. 1). Where s/he takes either of the latter two courses, s/he must give written notice to the applicant including the reasons for the decision (para. 2). S/he has power to cancel the registration of a home not conducted in accordance with the Children's Homes Regulations 1991 (considered above). S/he may also vary the conditions subject to which a home is run or impose additional conditions (para. 1). In all these situations, the person carrying on the home must be informed of his or her right to make representations to the Secretary of State within fourteen days of receipt of notice (para. 3). If the Secretary of State decides to adopt the proposal, s/he is to serve written notice of the decision on any person on whom s/he was required to serve notice of the proposal. This must explain the right of appeal (para.4), which lies to a Registered Homes Tribunal (para.5). Appeals must be brought within 28 days. The Tribunal has power to confirm the decision or direct that it shall not have effect, vary any condition to which the appeal relates or direct that it shall cease to have effect, or propose any condition itself (para. 5).

It is the duty of the person in charge of a voluntary home to provide the Secretary of State within 3 months of the establishment of the home, particulars laid down by Schedule 7 of the Children's Homes Regulations 1991 under Regulation 31 of those Regulations (para. 6). These particulars must be sent in annually. Failure to provide particulars, without reasonable excuse, is an offence (para. 6(5)).

The conduct of voluntary homes is governed by the Children's Homes Regulations 1991 (see above). The use of accommodation for the purpose of restricting the liberty of children in voluntary homes is prohibited by The Children (Secure Accommodation) Regulations 1991[22] r.18(1)). There was vociferous opposition in the House of Lords to the use of secure accommodation by voluntary organisations (*Hansard*, HL vol. 503, col. 498 *et seq*). This Regulation accepts that it is wrong.

The Secretary of State has the power to inspect premises where children are being accommodated by or on behalf of a voluntary organisation (s.90(1)(c)). The children may also be inspected (s.80(4)).[23]

Section 61 provides that where a child is accommodated by or on behalf of a voluntary organisation, it is the duty of the organisation to safeguard and promote his or her welfare, to make such use of services and facilities available for children cared for by their own parents as appears to the organisation reasonable and to advise, assist and befriend the child with a view to promoting his or her welfare when s/he ceases to be so accommodated. This is the exact equivalent of the statutory duties imposed on local authorities by s.22(3) and s.24(1) (see the discussion above). Similarly, the organisation is, so far as is reasonably practicable, to ascertain the wishes and feelings of the child, the parents, persons with parental responsibility and any other person whose wishes and feelings the organisation consider to be relevant (s.61(2), the parallel of s.22(4)), and in making decisions is to give due consideration to the child's wishes and feelings, having regard to his age and understanding, to the wishes and feelings of parents, etc. (see the list just mentioned) as they have been able to ascertain, and to the child's religious persuasion, racial origin and cultural and linguistic background (s.61(3), the parallel of s.22(5)) (see generally above). The aim is that children should not be treated differently whether they are being looked after by local authorities or in the voluntary sector. The only difference of note is that the duty to protect the public, allowing a local authority to derogate from its general duties to children, has no counterpart where voluntary organisations are concerned (see s.22(6)–(8)).

Local authorities have a duty to satisfy themselves that voluntary organisations providing accommodation within their area are satisfactorily safeguarding and promoting the welfare of the children (s.62(1)). Where they are not satisfied they must, unless they consider that it would not be in the best interests of the child, take such steps as are reasonably practicable to secure that the care and accommodation of the child is undertaken by a parent, a person with parental responsibility or relative.[24] They must also consider the extent to which, if at all, they should exercise any of their statutory functions (s.62(5)). This does not apply where the child is being accommodated on behalf of a local authority. Where that is so, the local authority's duties are those stipulated in part III, particularly s.22.

In addition, local authorities are required to arrange for children accommodated by voluntary organisations to be visited 'from time to time' in the interests of their welfare (s.62(2)). These visits are governed by the Children's Homes Regulations 1991. The Regulations make it clear that visits must be carried out by an officer of the authority (rr.32, 33, 34). Regulation 32 specifies three circumstances necessitating visits:

(a) where there is information that a child not in the care of or being looked after by a local authority has been placed in a voluntary home – within twenty-eight days of being so informed;

(b) where the organisation makes representations to the authority that there are circumstances which require a visit – within 14 days of receiving such representations;

(c) when informed that the welfare of the child may not be being safeguarded or promoted within seven days of being so informed.

After the first visit, the authority must arrange such further visits as appear to them to be necessary. In any event a further visit must take place within 6 months where the authority is satisfied the child's welfare is being safeguarded and promoted and within twenty-eight days where they are not so satisfied (r.33). The officer must see the child alone, unless exceptionally s/he considers it unnecessary (r.34(1)(a); read all relevant case papers and records (and sign and date them to indicate they have been seen); and make a written report of the visit. The voluntary organisation has to provide suitable accommodation for a visit (r.34(2)).

The authorities' duties are backed up with rights of entry and inspection. Any person authorised by an authority may enter, at any reasonable time, any premises in which children are accommodated, may inspect the premises and the children and may require any person to cooperate by allowing the inspection of records and by providing information when requested (s.62(6). It is not clear whether a warrant is required to enter the premises, but, if necessary, it can be obtained under s.102. 'Reasonable time' is not defined. This could be interpreted to exclude night-time visits (or 'dawn-raids'). Where access is required at such times, the answer lies in seeking an EPO (s.44 and above). Intentional obstruction[25] is an offence (s.62(9)).

A final duty of the local authority is to offer advice and assistance to a young person formerly accommodated by or on behalf of a voluntary organisation (s.24(2)). This duty only arises where they are satisfied that the voluntary organisation does not have the necessary facilities for advising and befriending (s.24(5)(b)).

Registered children's homes

Part VIII and Schedule 6 govern registered children's homes and replace the Children's Homes Act 1982 (as amended), the first legislation to regulate private homes at all (Freeman and Lyon, 1984). The 1982 Act offered the scantiest of regulation and was not implemented. Part VIII and Schedule 6 essentially reproduce the provisions in the 1982 Act, which is repealed.

A 'children's home' is defined in s.63(3) as follows:

'(a) ... a home which provides (or usually provides or is intended to provide) care and accommodation wholly or mainly for more than three children at any one time; but

(b) does not include a home which is exempted by or under any of the following provisions of this Section or by regulations made for the purposes of this subsection by the Secretary of State.'

'Home' includes 'any institution' (s.63(9)). Where a private home caters for three children or less at any one time, it will come under Part IX which provides for private foster homes. There are exemptions: a home in which the child is cared for and accommodated by a parent, a person with parental responsibility or a relative (s.63(4)); a community home, voluntary home, residential care home, nursing home, health service hospital (but not health service trust hospital), home provided, equipped and maintained by the Secretary of State (s.63(5)) and a school[26] (but an independent school may be treated as a children's home where it provides accommodation for not more than fifty children, and is not a home approved by the Secretary of State under s.11(3) of the Education Act 1981 (s.63(6)).

No child may be cared for and provided with accommodation in a children's home unless the home is registered with the local authority (s.63(1)). Voluntary homes have, it has been seen, to be registered with the Secretary of State. A person who carries on a children's home without registering commits an offence unless s/he has a reasonable excuse (s.63(10)). The details of the registration procedure are set out in Schedule 6, part 1 and in the Children's Homes Regulations 1991 (Regulations 25–30). The local authority may limit the number of children to be accommodated (r.26). A home is not to be registered until it has been inspected (r.28(1)) and is to be inspected at least twice a year thereafter (r.28(2),(3)). The conduct of registered children's homes is provided for in the Children's Homes Regulations 1991. The details were discussed in relation to community homes and no further discussion is necessary.

The person carrying on the home has the same duties towards children being accommodated as local authorities and voluntary organisations do (see s.22(3)–(5), s.24(1), s.61, discussed above) (s.64). The duties exist whether the home is registered or not. Section 62 (except s.62(4)) applies to children's homes (s.64(4)), so that local authorities have duties to satisfy themselves that the children's welfare is being safeguarded and to arrange for children to be visited (see above). Under the former Children's Homes Act 1982, there was only a duty to inspect. A concern remains that homes may employ unsuitable persons (Sone, 1991). There is, as with voluntary homes, power conferred on the local authority to provide after-care (s.24(2)). The person carrying on the home must notify the local authority when a child over 16 leaves (s.24(12)).

Persons who are disqualified from fostering a child privately (see s.68 and below) are prohibited from carrying on, or being concerned in the management of, or having any financial interest in, a registered children's home, unless they have disclosed the fact of their disqualification to the local authority and obtained its written consent (s.65(1)).[27] The Act also prohibits the employment of such persons unless the employer has disclosed the disqualification to the authority and obtained its written consent (s.65(2)). Anyone contravening either requirement commits an offence, unless, as regards the offence in s.65(2), s/he proves that he did not know, and had no reasonable grounds for believing that the person whom s/he was employing was disqualified (s.65(5)). If consent is refused (and it is to be expected that it usually will be), an appeal lies to the Registered Homes Tribunal (s.65(3)).

Private fostering arrangements

Part IX and Schedules 7 and 8 regulate private fostering arrangements and replace the Foster Children Act 1980 (Freeman, 1980). There is nothing stopping parents using private foster parents (they can delegate parental responsibility),[28] but there has for some time been concern about the dangers inherent in it (Holman, 1973, 1986; Barclay, 1982; Ogden, 1991). There has been a decline in the number of children being privately fostered, though the true number cannot be calculated (DHSS, 1988). Most are believed to be black, often the children of West African students (Atkinson and Horner, 1990). Under the previous law control centred on notification, rather than registration (as with voluntary and private homes). The Act continues this system. It is, accordingly, the duty of the local authority to satisfy itself that the welfare of children, privately fostered within its area, is being satisfactorily safeguarded and promoted (s.67(1)).

'Foster child' is defined in a rather simpler and less confusing way than under the 1980 Act. A 'privately fostered child'[29] is a child under sixteen, or eighteen if disabled (s.66(4)), who is cared for and provided with accommodation by someone other than a parent, a person who has parental responsibility or a relative (s.66(1)), for at least twenty-eight days (s.66(2),[30] and who does not come within the exemptions contained in Schedule 8. These include children looked after by local authorities, those in premises in which a parent or person with parental responsibility or relative who has assumed responsibility for his or her care is for the time being living, those in children's homes, voluntary homes, schools, hospitals, residential care homes, those detained or subject to guardianship under the Mental Health Act 1983, those placed for adoption or within the definition of 'protected child' under adoption legislation.

The welfare of privately fostered children is addressed in section 67. This states:

'It shall be the duty of every local authority to satisfy themselves that the welfare of children who are privately fostered in their area is being satisfactorily safeguarded and promoted and to secure that such advice is given to those caring for them as appears to the authority to be needed.'

The matters as to which the local authority must satisfy itself are listed in the Children (Private Arrangements for Fostering) Regulations 1991,[31] r.2(2). These include the purpose and duration of the arrangement, standard of care, suitability of the foster parent and the household, arrangements for the child's education and, surprisingly placed last, the ascertainable wishes and feelings of the child (but see also *Guidance*, vol. 8, paras. 1.4.39–1.4.42). The role of local authorities is to satisfy themselves that the arrangements are satisfactory, but they do not approve or register private foster parents. *Guidance* on the question of suitability is given in volume 8 (1991, para. 1.5). If they are not so satisfied, they are to take steps that are reasonably practicable to secure that the child's care and accommodation are undertaken by a parent, a person with parental responsibility or a relative, unless they consider that this would not be in the best interests of the child, and must then consider the extent to which, if at all, they should exercise any of their functions under the Act (s.67(5)). If the child is likely to suffer significant harm, compulsory measures of care can be initiated (s.31, s.44). If the child is 'in need', the local authority have the duties set out in Part III and schedule 2 (and see, in particular, para. 10). A possibility may be the provision of local authority accommodation under s.20. But these problems may be anticipated if proper 'advice' is given, so that this function of a local authority's role (in s.67(1)) should not be underestimated. These Regulations provide also for visits to children (r.3). These are to be 'from time to time as the authority consider necessary' and, in particular, in the first year within one week from its beginning and then at intervals of not more than six weeks and in subsequent years at intervals of not more than three months. If considered (by the local authority officer) appropriate, the child is to be seen alone (r.3(2)).

The key regulatory mechanism is notification. This is now governed by the Children (Private Arrangements for Fostering) Regulations 1991. These provide (r.4) that, except in an emergency, a person who proposes to foster a child by private arrangement and is not yet providing accommodation for that child is required to notify the local authority not less than six weeks and not more than thirteen weeks before s/he receives the child. A person receiving a child in an emergency or who is already caring for and providing accommodation for that child when s/he becomes a foster child must notify the local authority within 48 hours of the fostering arrangements beginning (r.4(2)). This requirement will often apply where the person was registered as a child-minder, for a particular child under eight for the first twenty-eight days of placement, immediately after that twenty-eight days has expired. The content of the notice (which must be in writing) is specified by 4(3) and (4). 'Emergency' is not defined in the Regulations and in practice nearly all placements will be notified as having been emergencies. As Atkinson and Horner (1990, p.19) point out, the assessment of the suitability of the persons and premises is then likely to be 'less objective'. It may also be that the parents cannot be contacted to discuss the matter. They may even be abroad.

If the child moves, the former foster parents must notify their local authority in writing within forty-eight hours, stating the name and address of the person into whose care the child has been moved (r.5(1)). This does not apply where the foster parent intends to resume the fostering arrangement after an interval of not more than twenty-seven days, but if this intention is abandoned or the interval expires, notice must be given to the local authority within forty-eight hours (r.5(3).

Under Regulation 6(4) any parent of a privately fostered child, any other person with parental responsibility, must notify the local authority in whose area the child was fostered of the ending of the fostering arrangement.

Under Regulation 6(1), there is a duty on any person who is, or proposes to be, involved, whether or not directly, in arranging for a child to be fostered privately, to notify the local authority in whose area the child is to be fostered not less than six nor more than thirteen weeks before the commencement of the arrangements.

There is also a new duty (r.6(2)) on any parent, or person with parental responsibility, to notify the local authority in whose area the child is proposed to be privately fostered, if s/he knows about the arrangement (even if s/he is not directly involved), not less than six and not more than thirteen weeks before the fostering arrangement begins. *Guidance* indicates (vol. 8, para. 1.6.16) that this is 'expected to ensure a greater degree of protection to children'.

Guidance adds to the Regulations (see vol. 8, para. 1.6.21) that agencies, 'particularly health visitors and schools, should be encouraged to liaise with social services departments about the existence of private foster children of whom the social services department may be unaware'. Joint planning is emphasised.

Volume 8 of the *Guidance* deals with a number of other matters, of which two only will be singled out. Given the high percentage of black children in the privately fostered population, a very high percentage of whom will be fostered with white families, the *Guidance* has a number of pertinent comments. The Regulations incorporate the question of whether the child's needs arising from his religious persuasion, racial origin and cultural and linguistic background are being met within the general welfare of the child (r.2(2)(c)). It is thus a matter as to which the local authority must satisfy themselves under s.67 of the Act. *Guidance* develops this in paras 1.7.21–1.7.24. It is noted that the practice of placing children in homes of a different race and culture may 'pose a contradiction for local authorities when carrying out their functions under Regulation 2(2)(c)' (para. 1.7.22). 'In such circumstances', *Guidance* advises, 'the local authority should seek to establish the prospective foster parent's understanding of the child's culture and the level of his willingness to do so'. Local authorities are also encouraged to see that the foster parent is advised about the provision of resources and facilities to assist in meeting the 'racial, cultural, religious and linguistic needs of the child. This can be done, for example, by involving the voluntary sector, local religious groups and minority ethnic communities' (para. 1.7.23). *Guidance*, whilst recognising potential problems, does stress that these are 'private arrangements', so that local authorities should not seek 'to prevent them because of potential difficulties, save where other considerations justify the imposition of requirements or a prohibition' (para. 1.7.24). The *Guidance* also alerts practitioners to the problem of female circumcision (in reality genital mutilation) (see paras 1.7.16–1.7.19), which was banned in 1985.[32] There is also a reference to male circumcision (para. 1.7.20) ('simple and straightforward...posing no harm or danger to the health and welfare of the child').[33]

The *Guidance* also addresses the question of corporal punishment (para. 1.5.13). This is not prohibited by the Regulations[34] but the *Guidance* essentially reproduces as advice for private foster parents what the Children's Homes Regulations provides in relation to homes (paras. 1.5.13). It states: 'The social worker should explore the foster parent's views on discipline, including a preparedness to accept that corporal punishment is inappropriate for children who are privately fostered'.

Section 68 of the Act disqualifies certain persons in circumstances prescribed in the Disqualification for Caring for Children Regulations 1991[35] from involvement in private fostering without the consent of the appropriate local authority. A disqualification should only be lifted in the 'most *exceptional* circumstances' (*Guidance*, vol. 8, para. 2.6.). The disqualification also applies where another person in the same household,[36] or an employee,[37] comes within the Regulations (s.68(3)). Where a local authority refuses to consent, it must give reasons (s.68(4)). Schedule 8, para. 8 provides a right of appeal against such a refusal. (See also *Guidance*, vol. 8, para. 2.8.) To foster in contravention of this provision is an offence (s.70(1)(d)), but, if the disqualification does not relate to the foster parent, s/he has a defence if s/he did not know and had no reasonable grounds for believing that the other person was disqualified (s.70(2)). The list of those disqualified is in Regulation 2. Included are parents of children who have been made the subject of care orders, who have lost parental rights by a local authority resolution, scheduled offenders,[38] those who have had children removed from them under adoption legislation and those who have been concerned with a voluntary or registered home which has been removed from the register and who have applied for registration and been refused or who have been prohibited from being a private foster parent, refused registration to be a child minder or provider of day care or had his or her registration cancelled.

Section 69 permits the local authority to prohibit an individual from fostering a child privately on the grounds that s/he is not suitable, the premises are not suitable or it would be prejudicial to the welfare of the child for him or her to be, or continue to be, accommodated by that person in those premises (s.69(2)). The prohibition may be general (s.69(3)(a)), relate to specific premises (s.69(3)(b)), or to a particular child in particular premises (s.69(3)(c)). Where a prohibition is imposed, it may subsequently be cancelled if no longer justified (s.69(4)). This does not require a change of circumstances, as formerly.[39] Where a prohibition is imposed, reasons must be given (s.69(7)). There is a right of appeal (Sch.8, para. 6). For the details see paragraph 8. There is also the power to impose requirements (Sch. 8, para. 6). Prohibitions should become an 'effective framework for promoting and safeguarding the welfare of children' (*Guidance*, vol. 8, para. 1.8.23). Persons on whom a prohibition has been imposed are disqualified from private fostering, and from carrying on or being employed in a children's home, voluntary home, day care or child-minding.

Child-minding and day care for young children

There has for a considerable time been concern about the standard of child-minding facilities (Jackson and Jackson, 1979; Moss, 1987; Moss and Melhuish, 1991). Part X and Schedule 9 repeal the Nurseries and Child-Minders Regulation Act 1948 and introduce a new unified registration system for child-minders and others providing day care for young children to replace the former separate registers for child-minders and nurseries. Hitherto, this has been the least regulated form of substitute care. The registration system has not thought to have been very effective. The Act strengthens controls.

Every local authority is required to keep a register of child-minders and one of people providing day care s.71(1)). A person acts as a child-minder if s/he looks after one or more children under the age of eight for reward for more than two hours in any day (s.71(2), unless that person is a parent, relative, person with parental responsibility or foster parent (s.71 (4)). The same period applies to persons providing day care. Where a person provides day care on different premises, separate registration of the person is required with respect to each premises. The basic distinction between child-minders and other providers of day care is that child-minders care for children on 'domestic premises' (those used wholly or mainly as a private dwelling), and day carers who care for children on non-domestic premises, which can include 'any vehicle' (s.71(12)).

'Nannies' are not child-minders (s.71(5)) and do not have to register when looking after a child wholly or mainly in the home of their employer. Where two employers use the same nanny, s/he[40] will continue to be exempt, provided s/he looks after any of the children wholly or mainly in the home or either of them (s.71(6)). But if more than two employers are involved, registration is required. 'Nanny' is defined as someone employed to look after a child by a parent, person with parental responsibility or a relative who has assumed responsibility for a child's care (s.71(13)).

A local authority may refuse to register a child-minder if they are satisfied that the applicant or any person looking after, or likely to be looking after, any children on any premises on which the applicant is, or is likely to be, child-minding is not fit to look after children under the age of 8 (s.71(7)). This applies also to day carers (s.71(9)). Registration may also be refused, in either case, where any person living or employed, or likely to be living or employed, on the premises to which the application relates, is not fit to be in the 'proximity' of children under eight (s.71(8),(10)). *Guidance* on the meaning of 'fit person' is given in volume 2, paragraph 7.32. An application may also be refused where the authority are satisfied that the premises are not 'fit' to be used for looking after children under eight either because of their condition or the condition of any equipment used on the premises or for any reason connected with their situation, construction or size (s.71(11)) (and see *Guidance*, vol. 2, para. 7.34). Premises which are not safe are clearly not fit. The absence of planning permission or a restrictive covenant against this use might also render premises unfit. *Guidance* on suitability of premises is given in volume 2, paragraph 7.33. The Child Minding and Day Care (Applications for Registration) Regulations 1991[41] lists the information that applicants must provide. These include details about the applicant and, where appropriate, the person whom it is proposed will be in charge, including qualifications and experience, and of the premises in which the children will be looked after. Details of other persons living in (or likely to be in) these premises, and any person assisting (or likely to be assisting) in looking after children must also be given.

Schedule 9 contains a lengthy list of exemptions from the registration requirements. Excluded are schools, children's homes, voluntary homes, community homes, residential care homes, nursing homes, mental nursing homes, hospitals and 'occasional facilities' (Sch. 9, para. 5) defined as facilities where day care is provided for less than six days a year. In the case of such facilities, the authority must be given written notice before the first occasion on which the premises are used. The occasional creche provider is thus exempt (for example at conferences – *Guidance*, vol. 2, para. 7.30).

A person may be disqualified from registering as a child-minder or day care provider in accordance with the Disqualification for Caring For Children Regulations 1991 (the details of which were discussed in the section on private fostering). The Act requires local authorities to impose requirements on registrations of child-minders and providers of day care (ss. 72, 73). Certain conditions must be imposed: these relate to the maximum number of children, or the maximum number within specified age groups; the obligation to maintain premises and equipment and to ensure that safety standards are met; the duty to keep records of children looked after; assistants and persons living on the premises; the requirement to notify the authority of any changes in this respect; and, in the case of day care providers, the number of assistants required to look after the children on the premises (see s.72(2); s.73(3)). Advice is given on staff/child ratios in the *Guidance* (vol. 2, para. 6.50) and has provoked controversy (Deech, 1991). In determining the maximum number of children, the authority is to take account of other children who may be on the relevant premises (s.72(4) and s.73(6)). A local authority may add to these requirements (s.72(5) and s.73(7)) and may also vary or remove them (s.72(6); s.73(8)), but they cannot do anything which is 'incompatible' with obligations laid down in s.72(2) or s.72(3). The authority must give reasons for imposing its requirements (s.77(2)), must act reasonably (see s.72(1), s.73(1)). If it does not do so, judicial review may lie.[42] There are appeals against imposing, removing or varying any requirement (s.77(1)(d)) and refusing to grant any application for the variation or removal of any such requirement (s.77(1)(e)).

Section 74 empowers local authorities to cancel the registration of child-minders and day care providers. Cancellations must be notified in writing (s.74(5)), with reasons (s.77(2)) and can be appealed (s.77(6)). A child-minder's registration may be cancelled if circumstances justify refusing to register that person (s.71(7), (8)) and the care provided is 'seriously inadequate' having regard to the needs of that child or the child-minder has contravened or failed to comply with a requirement imposed under s.72, or failed to pay the annual fee.[43] The meaning of 'seriously inadequate' may need to be tested in litigation. The *Guidance* (vol. 2, para. 7.52) offers the following indicia: signs of uncaring neglect, grossly inappropriate types of activity and play opportunities, failure to recognise and respond sensitively to the child's religious, racial, cultural and linguistic needs (and see Lane, 1992); gross lack of emotional and physical warmth. It adds that in assessing whether there is failure to recognise and respond to religious etc. needs (s.74(6)), authorities 'might consider whether he is being treated less favourably on racial grounds or he is being ridiculed or his dietary needs are not provided for'. It should be noted that the standard 'seriously inadequate' offers the opportunity for intervention at a much lower threshold than 'significant harm' (s.31; s.44). It must be right that children can be removed from child-minders and day care providers more easily than from parents. Even so, it would have been better had the word 'seriously' been omitted.

Section 75 empowers local authorities in cases of emergency to apply to the court: to cancel a person's registration; to vary an imposed requirement; to remove or impose a requirement. An application may be made *ex parte* and has to be supported by a written statement of reasons (s.75(3)). It must 'appear' to the court that the child is suffering, or is likely to suffer, significant harm.[44] The court has discretion to make the order (s.75(1)(b)). Cancellation of registration etc. is effective from the date of the order. It should be stressed that it may also be necessary to protect the carer's own children under parts IV and V of the Act.

Section 76 deals with inspection (see also *Guidance*, vol. 2, ch. 8). Every local authority is now required to carry out inspections of relevant premises at least once a year (s.76(4)). This is a minimum requirement (D. Mellor, Standing Committee B, col. 394). Any person authorised by the authority may enter domestic or non-domestic premises where child-minding or day care is at any time carried on or provided (s.76(1)). S/he may also enter premises in relation to which the authority has reasonable cause to believe that a child is being looked after (s.76(2)). S/he may then inspect the premises, any children being looked after, the arrangements made for the children's welfare (including the extent to which *their* needs are being met) and any records kept in accordance with the legislation (s.76(3)). It is an offence to obstruct intentionally any authorised person (s.76(7)). Where entry is refused a warrant can be obtained under s.102(6). An EPO may also be sought (and may be necessary): a warrant can also be obtained under this (s.48(9)).

It continues to be an offence to provide day care for children under 8 without being registered with respect to the premises on which the care is provided (s.78(1), (2)). Defences of lack of knowledge (s.78(10), (11)) are new. Also new is the enforcement notice procedure. An enforcement notice can be served on anyone who acts as a child-minder without registering (s.78(4)). It is effective for one year (s.78(5)). It is only an offence to carry on unregistered child-minding if an enforcement notice has been served, but the offence is committed even if the minding occurs in another area (s.78(7)). Once a notice has been served, the person concerned may only child-mind if s/he registers in accordance with s.71(1)(a).

Children accommodated by health authorities and local education authorities

The vulnerable position of children living away from their parents in long-stay hospitals and other establishments outside the 'care system' has often been commented upon (Oswin, 1978; Shearer, 1980). The Act for the first time brings the care of such children under the umbrella of children's legislation. Section 85 covers those placed by health authorities or LEAs in NHS (or NHS Trust)[45] hospitals and state-maintained special schools, care homes or schools offering special education. Section 86 covers children in private homes and hospitals who are there to receive treatment, specialised care or education because they are physically or mentally handicapped, chronically ill or have special educational needs.

Where a health authority or NHS Trust, LEA or person carrying on a residential care home, nursing home or mental nursing home accommodates, or intends to accommodate, a child for a consecutive period of at least three months, the accommodating authority or person carrying on the home must notify the authority (s.85(1); s.86(1)). They must also notify the authority when they cease to accommodate the child. On receiving notification, the authority must take such steps as are reasonably practicable to enable it to determine whether the child's welfare is adequately safeguarded and promoted where s/he is being accommodated, and the extent to which, if at all, it should exercise any of its functions under the Act in relation to the child (s.85(4), s.86(3)). Any person carrying on a home who fails, without reasonable excuse, to comply with the notification requirements commits an offence (s.86(4)). A person authorised by the local authority may enter any of the homes listed in s.86 to establish whether there has been compliance with the requirements of the section (s.86(5)). It is an offence intentionally to obstruct such a person (s.86(6)). If entry is refused, a warrant may be obtained (s.102) (see also s.48(9), where an EPO has also been sought).

Independent schools

Independent schools come within the remit of children's legislation for the first time (Fielding, 1991; Fry, 1991). Section 87, passed in the wake of revelations of sex abuse at Crookham Court School and Castle Hill School, imposes two new duties. It is the duty of proprietors of independent schools, which are not either residential care homes or children's homes, to safeguard and promote the welfare of children for whom they provide accommodation (s.87(1), (2)). Schools which cater for less than fifty pupils are not covered by s.87, since they fall within the definition of children's homes or residential care homes. Secondly, it is the duty of local authorities in whose area a school is situated to take reasonable steps to determine whether the duty is being complied with (s.87(3)). Where the local authority is of the opinion that the proprietor or person running the school has failed to comply with s.87(1), it must notify the Secretary of State, who may send a notice of complaint under the Education Act 1944 s.71 (as amended by Schedule 13, para. 9). In a serious case this could (and should) lead to the closure of the school. Where the child is suffering significant harm, s/he may be removed by an EPO. Alternatively, the local authority may accommodate the child with a parent's agreement under s.20 – until the parent is able to collect the child.

Any person authorised by the local authority may, to enable the authority to discharge its duty under s.87, enter at any reasonable time any independent school within their area which provides accommodation (s.87(5)). Inspections are governed by the Inspection of Premises, Schools and Records (Independent Schools) Regulations 1991.[46] This permits the inspection of premises (r.2), children (r.3) (where this includes physical examination, a child of sufficient understanding may withhold consent (r.3(2))),[47] and records (r.4). The records are those containing information concerning the state of health, emotional or developmental well-being or welfare of children including medical treatment, accidents, cases of absconding, details of complaints and details of punishments administered to any child in the school (and not just to pupils of the school, so that punishments given by parents who are members of staff to their own children are included). However, there is no obligation to keep records and the Regulation merely permits an inspection of those that exist. There is further guidance on inspection in *Guidance* (vol. 5, 1991, Annex B and ch. 4). It is an offence intentionally to obstruct anyone exercising these powers (s.87(9)). A warrant may be obtained (s.102) (see also s.48(9) where an EPO has been sought).

There is a useful volume of *Guidance* on Independent Schools (vol. 5). This draws attention to a number of important matters of which the following are a selection.

There is an overlap between the role of HMI and SSDs. If SSDs observe any matters relating to educational provision, which they think unsatisfactory, they should report these matters to the DES (or Welsh Office) (para. 2.5). There is an important section on child protection (paras 3.2.1–3.2.4). A careful if ambivalent line is trod on corporal punishment. This is still permitted at independent schools where the pupil's fees are paid by the parents. The *Guidance* advises (para. 3.9.4) that 'if in exceptional circumstances it is decided to use corporal punishment, it should not be unreasonable (for trivial offences or applied indiscriminately to whole classes) or excessive'. It is 'widely regarded as particularly inappropriate for children with sensory, physical and intellectual impairment and those with emotional and behavioural difficulties' (para. 3.9.5). The Government cannot, however, bring itself to ban corporal punishment in independent schools, despite the fact that it is a breach of the UN Convention of the Rights of the Child (see Arts 19, 37 and 28) (Newell, 1991(b)).

In the light of the establishment of a Boarding School Helpline (Fry, 1991), *Guidance* addresses the question of complaints (paras 3.11.1–3.11.7). Although headed 'Complaints Procedure', no procedure as such is established under the Act. *Guidance*, nevertheless, advises on mechanisms for handling complaints. Formal complaints, it indicates, should be dealt with 'promptly and confidentially' and should always involve someone 'independent of the school, e.g. an officer or member from the LEA or SSD' (para. 3.11.5). There is no objection to keep records of complaints, but 'SSDs will wish to inspect records of complaints routinely during their visits' (para. 3.11.7). But, with nearly 1000 independent boarding schools, these inspections cannot be expected to be more than cursory.

Notes

1. SI (1991) No. 1506
2. SI (1991) No. 2050.
3. SI (1991) No. 2094.

4. Child Minding and Day Care (Applications for Registration) Regulations 1991, S.I. No. 1689; Child Minding and Day Care (Registration and Inspection Fees) Regulations 1991, S.I. No. 2076; Child Minding and Day Care (Applications for Registration and Registration and Inspection Fees) (Amendment) Regulations 1991, SI No. 2129.
5. This re-enacts with minor amendments s.31 of the Child Care Act 1980.
6. Replacing sections 35–9 of the Child Care Act 1980.
7. See also the Joint Circular LAC 88/19 and DES Circ. 12/88.
8. SI (1991) No. 890.
9. And see *Guidance*, vol. 2, paragraphs 2.78 *et seq.*
10. As in the Child Care Act 1980.
11. Re-enacting, with minor drafting amendments, s.40 of the Child Care Act 1980.
12. Re-enacting, with minor drafting amendments, s.42 of the Child Care Act 1980.
13. Re-enacting, with minor drafting amendments, s.43 of the Child Care Act 1980.
14. Re-enacting, with minor drafting amendments, s.43A of the Child Care Act 1980.
15. This enacts, with substantial amendments, s.44 of the Child Care Act 1980. Money received by the Secretary of State is paid into the Consolidated Fund (s.106(2)).
16. SI (1991) No. 890.
17. SI (1991) No. 910.
18. SI (1991) No. 895.
19. SI (1991) No. 894.
20. See s.23(2)(c).
21. But not, it seems, a hospital run under the Health Service Trust. The opportunity for amendment to include this, taken in a number of other provisions in the Act, has not been taken.
22. SI (1991) No. 1505.
23. Re-enacting sections 74 and 75 of the Child Care Act 1980.
24. This calls for intervention at a lower threshold than in other places in the Act where the 'significant harm' test applies.
25. Anything which makes it more difficult for a person to carry out his or her duty is an obstruction (*Rice* v. *Connolly* [1966] 2 QB 414).
26. See also s.87, below. Independent boarding schools which are exempted from registering as children's homes are subject to local authority inspection.
27. Re-enacting, with minor amendments, s.10 of the Children's Homes Act 1982.
28. See s.2(9) of the Act.
29. This is the first legislation to use the word 'private'.
30. This is presumably a single continuous period. However, the *White Paper* (1987, para. 80) seems to have intended periods to be aggregated.
31. SI (1991) No. 2050.

32. Prohibition of Female Circumcision Act 1985.
33. A misguided and offensive contrast is Miller (1990). See also Newell (1991(a)).
34. There were attempts to ban it during the Bill's passage through Parliament, but all were unsuccessful.
35. SI (1991) No. 2094.
36. Not defined. The previous legislation used the word 'premises' (Foster Children Act 1980 s.7(2)). 'Premises' is wider than 'household', which suggests common living arrangements (see *e.g. Hopes* v. *Hopes* [1949] P.227). If so, the Act protects children less than the 1980 Act did.
37. And not, therefore, an independent contractor ('daily' might well be so considered).
38. See Disqualification for Caring for Children Regulations 1991, r.2(l).
39. Under the Foster Children Act 1980, s.10(3).
40. The Act so committed to the masculine pronoun uses 'she' where nannies are referred to, but not for example in the case of child-minders!
41. SI (1991) No. 1689, amended by the Child Minding and Day Care (Applications for Registration and Registration and Inspection Fees) (Amendment) Regulations 1991, SI No. 2129. Fees are dealt with by the Child Minding and Day Care (Registration and Inspection Fees) Regulations 1991, SI No. 2076 (also amended by SI No. 2129). As promised the fees have been kept low, in response to opposition that felt there should not be fees at all.
42. *Associated Provincial Picture Houses* v. *Wednesbury Corporation* [1948] 1KB 223.
43. Day care providers' registrations may be cancelled in comparable situations.
44. *Guidance* (vol. 2, para. 7.53) gets this wrong. It states that 'the court is required to satisfy itself', which is similar to the language under s.44 (EPO) ('be satisfied'). 'It appears to the court' is a lower standard.
45. See National Health Service and Community Care Act 1990, Sch. 9, para. 36(5). Children in adult psychiatric hospitals are not covered.
46. SI (1991) No. 975.
47. This power does not extend to the children of members of staff or children living with such a member of staff as a member of his or her household, unless the child is also attending the school as a pupil (r.3(3)).

References

Atkinson, C. and Horner, A. (1990) 'Private Fostering – Legislation and Practice', *Adoption and Fostering*, 14(3), 17.
Barclay, P. (1982) *Social Workers: Their Role and Tasks*, London, Bedford Square Press.

Deech, R. (1991) Letter to *The Independent*, 25 September.

Department of Health (1987) *The Law on Child Care and Family Services*, London, HMSO.

Department of Health (1991) *Guidance and Regulations*, vol. 2, London, HMSO.

Department of Health (1991) *Guidance and Regulations*, vol. 4, London, HMSO.

Department of Health (1991) *Guidance and Regulations*, vol. 5, London, HMSO.

Department of Health (1991) *Guidance and Regulations*, vol. 8, London, HMSO.

Fielding, N. (1991) 'A Loss of Independence?', *Community Care* 849, 20.

Freeman, M. (1980) *The Child Care and Foster Children Acts 1980*, London, Sweet and Maxwell.

Freeman, M. and Lyon, C. (1984) *The Law of Residential Homes and Day Care Establishments*, London, Sweet and Maxwell.

Fry, A. (1991) 'All Above Board', *Social Work Today*, 22(20), 9.

Holman, R. (1977) *Trading in Children*, London, RKP.

Holman, R. (1986) 'The Twilight Zone', *Community Care*, 626, 18.

Jackson, B. and Jackson, S. (1979) *Child Minder*, London, RKP.

Lane, J. (1991) 'Obstacle Race', *Social Work Today*, 23(23), 25.

Levy, A. and Kahan, B. (1991) *Pindown Experience and The Protection of Children*, Staffs.

Miller, A. (1990) *Banished Knowledge*, London, Virago.

Moss, P. (1987) *Review of Childminding Research*, London, Institute of Education.

Moss, P. and Melhuish, T. (1991) *Current Issues in Day Care for Young Children*, London, HMSO.

Newell, P. (1989) *Children are People Too*, London, Bedford Square Press.

Newell, P. (1991(a)) *UN Convention and Children's Rights in UK*, London, NCB.

Newell, P. (1991(b)) 'A New Age of Respect', *Community Care, 873, 12*

Ogden, J (1991). 'Culture Shocks', *Social Work Today* 22(23), 9.

Oswin, M (1978). *Children Living in Long-Stay Hospitals*, Spastics International Medical Publications, London, Heinemann.

Shearer, A (1980). *Handicapped Children in Residential Care*, London, Bedford Square Press.

Sone, K. (1991). 'Slipping through the Net', *Community Care*, 892, 14.

Utting, W. (1991) *Children in the Public Care*, London, HMSO.

10

Adoption Issues

Adoption law and practice are relatively untouched by the Act but there are changes, some consequential, others more substantive and innovative. Major reform of adoption law is on the drawing board (Department of Health, 1990) and can be expected in the next few years. It will, it is anticipated, continue trends in the Children Act. The import of the Act on adoption must be considered here. Of greatest significance are the abolition of custodianship (Freeman, 1986), the new adoption contact register and the new Adoption Allowance Regulations 1991.[1]

The changes are found in Schedules 10 and 15, the Regulations just referred to and, for further advice, volume 9 of the *Guidance* (1991).

Before the more significant changes are discussed a few of the consequential ones will be listed.

Consequential changes

(a) An adoption order will now vest parental responsibility in the adopter(s).[2]

(b) Words like 'custody' and 'actual custody' are now replaced by the word 'home' (for example, in the new s.72(1A) of the Adoption Act 1976).

(c) Where there are references to a child 'in care' these are now to be understood to refer to a child in care by virtue of a care order: those to being 'looked after' include those being 'accommodated'.

(d) The local authority's social services functions (in s.2 of the 1976 Act) have been amended to take account of the new functions in the 1989 Act.

More major changes

(a) The power under s.34 of the Adoption Act to remove a protected child from unsuitable surroundings to a place of safety is abolished. Use must now be made of the emergency protection order (s.44).

(b) The repeal of sections 14(3) and 15(4) of the 1976 Act means that courts are no longer required not to make an adoption order in favour of a step-parent if the court considered a divorce court custody order would be preferable.[3] The repeal of paragraphs (1) and (4) of s.37 of that Act means courts are no longer required to consider whether custodianship would be better.[4] Custodianship is replaced by the residence order (s.8). Courts are now free to make a residence order whether or not parents have agreed to adoption. *Guidance* (vol. 9, para. 1.14) points out that these measures 'accord with the Children Act's intention of giving the courts a free hand to make whatever orders best serve the interests of the child'.

(c) The protected status of a child will come to an end within two years from the giving of the notice if no adoption order is made.[5]

(d) Children freed for adoption are no longer treated as being 'in the voluntary care' of a local authority. The Act makes provision for arrangements to be made for a child to be accommodated by a local authority or on its behalf.[6] Such arrangements can be terminated at any time. Similarly, a child is no longer 'in the care of' a voluntary organisation. The *Guidance* (vol. 9, para. 1.18) explains that these measures are 'designed in part to enable parents to have confidence in the voluntary nature of "accommodation"'.

(e) The right to apply to free a child for adoption has been restricted. Previously, an application could be made without the consent of a parent or guardian if the child was 'in the care of' an adoption agency. Though not defined, 'care' was taken to include 'voluntary care'. Now an adoption agency will not be able to apply for a freeing order without the consent of a parent or guardian, unless the agency is a local authority in whose care the child is by virtue of a care order.

(f) A step-parent and a spouse (the parent of the child) may apply for an adoption order where the parent is at least eighteen and the step-parent twenty-one. Previously, both had to be at least twenty-one.[7]

The adoption contact register

Since 1975[8] adopted people over the age of eighteen have been able to apply for access to their original birth certificate (Triseliotis, 1984). Those adopted before 12 November 1975 are required to see a counsellor first: those adopted after 11 November 1975 may chose whether or not to see a counsellor before being given the information.

Using the information on a birth certificate some adopted people have been able to trace and make contact with their birth parents and/or other relatives.[9] But it has been difficult to know whether contact would be welcome.

The purpose of the Adoption Contact Register is to put adopted people and their birth parents or other relatives in touch with each other where this is what they both want. The Registrar General is required to set up an Adoption Contact Register.[10] It is in the two parts. Part I will have the name, current address and details relating to the birth of an adopted person who wishes to contact his birth parents or other relatives. Part 2 will contain the name, current address and identifying details of a birth parent or relative who wishes to contact an adopted person. The Registrar General will send to the registered adopted person the name of any relative who has also registered, together with the address the relative has supplied. No information about the adopted person will be given to the relative, except that the Registrar General will inform the relative when his or her details have been passed on to the adopted person. Annex B of volume 9 of the *Guidance and Regulations* contains documentation relating to the Adoption Contact Register.

Adoption allowances

Adoption allowance schemes were introduced in 1982 (Freeman, 1984; Hill, Lambert and Triseliotis, 1989). Previously, local authorities had to submit allowance schemes to the Secretary of State for approval or amendment. Under the new Regulations, an adoption agency, whether a local authority or approved society, will be able to pay an adoption allowance, subject to the provisions in the Regulations. There is considerable evidence that adoption allowances are important in facilitating the adoption of children who would otherwise be unlikely to have the opportunity for permanence and security which adoption can provide (Lambert and Seglow, 1988).

By contrast, long-term fostercare is thought to be insecure and, 'ambiguous' (Triseliotis, 1983). The specific circumstances in which an adoption allowance may fall for consideration are found in Regulation 2. They are:

(i)   the child has established a strong and important relationship with the adopters. This will arise where a child has been living with foster parents who wish to adopt but cannot afford to lose their fostering allowance;

(ii) adoption with siblings or where a child may have shared a home with an unrelated child with whom s/he has developed close ties;

(iii) special needs. The child is mentally or physically disabled or suffering from the effects of emotional or behavioural difficulties and, as a result of the condition, requires a special degree of care which necessitates extra expenditure. This is intended to cover also children who are 'sensorily impaired' (*Guidance*, vol. 9, para. 2.27). Children with emotional or behavioural difficulties may include those who have been abused. *Guidance* advises (para. 2.29) that payment is intended where the child's condition is 'serious and long-term';

(iv) a risk of deterioration in the future of a mentally or physically disabled child or one with emotional or behavioural difficulties where the payment of an allowance is not immediately justified but might become so. The agency may agree in principle to the payment of an allowance and make the payment in the future when satisfied that the child's condition has deteriorated such as to make it necessary;

(v)   a high risk of developing a medical condition, the nature of which would result in higher expenditure for the adopters. Again the agency may agree in principle to payment, but postpone it until the condition develops. There must be 'strong grounds for concern about the child's medical prognosis' (para. 2.31).

The *Guidance* advises (para. 2.34) that 'entitlement to an allowance does not automatically follow if the child's circumstances satisfy one or more of (these) conditions'. An allowance may be paid where the agency has decided that 'adoption by the adopters would be in the child's best interests' and 'after considering the recommendation of the adoption panel, that such adoption is not practicable without payment of an allowance (r.2(1)).

The amount of the allowance is determined by the adoption agency. In determining it, it is to take into account the financial resources available to the adopters, the amount required by the adopters in respect of their reasonable outgoings and commitments and the financial needs and resources of the child (r.3(2)). Mobility and attendance allowance payable in respect of the child are disregarded; so is child benefit where the adopters are in receipt of income support (r.3(3)). The amount must not exceed the amount of the fostering allowance payable if the child were fostered (r.3(4)(b)). It must not include any element of remuneration (r.3(4)(a)). Apparently, some allowances paid under approved schemes have included some element of remuneration. The *Guidance* insists (para.2.58) that this practice must cease. The *Guidance* advises (para. 2.57) that 'care and sensitivity' will have to be exercised in having regard to the standard of living of the family which the child is to join. But it cautions that, though the child will be expected to share this standard, it is not the intention of the adoption allowance provisions to subsidise what might be considered a very high standard of living'.

Regulation 2(3) enables the agency to pay an allowance in accordance with the Regulations to adopters who were receiving an allowance under the previous system and who agree to receive an allowance complying with the Regulations. But such persons are entitled to continue to receive an allowance under the terms and conditions which applied to a revoked scheme if they so wish.

The procedure to be followed is set out by Regulation 4. When an agency makes the decision that adoption is in the child's best interests, *Guidance* recommends (para. 2.63) that, at the same time, the agency should consider whether the child's circumstances are such that an allowance may become payable on placement. When the agency subsequently decides to place the child, the adopters should be advised that an allowance may be payable after the agency has considered the adopter's circumstances in relation to those of the child. The adopters should be given advice and information about the principles underlying adoption allowances, as well as about how the allowance is calculated and review arrangements (see r.6, below). The *Guidance* (para. 2.64) recommends that adopters be given this as part of the agency's written proposals in respect of the adoption under r.12(1) of the Adoption Agencies Regulations 1983.

Unless the adopters do not wish to receive an allowance, the circumstances of the adopters and the child should be assessed, and the adopters notified of the proposed decision. The Regulations are silent as to the time for the adopters to consider the agency's proposals and make any representations. The *Guidance* (para. 2.65) suggests twenty-eight days as a 'guide to good practice'. It also draws to attention (para. 2.66) the Complaints Procedure Directions 1990. After considering any representations, a final decision should be reached and the adopters notified in writing, setting out the information specified in Regulation 5 (including amount, date of first payment, method by which the allowance will be paid, arrangements and procedure for review, responsibilities of the adopters to notify any change of circumstances).

Regulation 6 requires an annual review and a review at any time when there has been a notification of change of circumstances. Agencies are advised to 'demonstrate flexibility' in responding to changes of circumstances and at the annual review (para. 2.73).

It is stressed that there is no requirement or expectation that an agency should visit the adopters once the court order is made (para. 2.76). If there is to be any post-adoption social work, this is 'independent from the administration of adoption allowances; neither is conditional upon the other' (para. 2.75). The *Guidance*, however, accepts that some adopters may welcome an opportunity for contact with the agency 'and agencies may, accordingly, wish to give adopters the option of a home visit' (para.2.77).

Regulation 6(5) provides for circumstances in which an agency shall terminate the allowance. These are:

(*i*) where the child ceases to have a permanent home with the adopters;

(*ii*) where the child ceases full-time education and commences employment or qualifies for placement on a Government training scheme;

(*iii*) where the child qualifies for income support or unemployment benefit in his or her own right;

(*iv*) where the child reaches 18, unless s/he remains in full-time education, in which case it may continue until s/he is 21;

(*v*) where any predetermined period between the agency and the adopters expires (*Guidance*, para. 2.78, gives the example of the child whose birth parent is dying of AIDS where the need for an allowance is necessary to assist contact arrangements with the parent – the period would end with the birth parent's death).

The Regulations do not provide for an adoption allowance to recommence once it has been terminated. *Guidance* (para. 2.79) accordingly recommends suspension rather than termination where there is doubt about whether a child has ceased to have a home with the adopters (for example, where the child is being accommodated by a local authority on other than a respite basis).

Regulation 7 provides that a record of each adoption allowance should be included with the adoption case records set up under Regulation 14(2) of the Adoption Agencies Regulations 1983. The record should be stored in a place of special security for at least seventy-five years. The record relating to the allowance is and must be treated as confidential. There are exceptions in Regulation 15 of the 1983 Regulations.

Notes

1. SI (1991) No. 2030, as amended by Adoption Allowance (Amendment) Regulations 1991, SI No. 2130.
2. Sch. 10, para. 5(2).
3. See *Re D* [1981] 2 FLR 102.
4. See *Re S* [1987] Fam. 98.
5. Sch. 10, para. 18(4), substituting a new s.32(4) into the 1976 Act.
6. Sch.10, para. 6(1), adding a new s.18(2A) to the 1976 Act.
7. Sch.10, para. 4, substituting a new s.14 in the 1976 Act.
8. Children Act 1975 s.26.
9. 33,000 have taken advantage of this provision (perhaps 15 per cent of those entitled).
10. Sch.10, para. 21, inserting a new s.51A into the Adoption Act 1976.

References

Department of Health (1990) *Inter-departmental Review of Adoption Law*, Discussion Paper 1 (*The Nature and Effect of Adoption*), DH London.
Department of Health (1991) *Guidance and Regulations*, vol. 9. London, HMSO.
Freeman, M. (1984) 'Subsidized Adoption' in P. Bean (ed.) *Adoption - Essays in Social Policy, Law and Sociology*, London, Tavistock.
Freeman, M. (1986) *The Law and Practice of Custodianship*, London, Sweet and Maxwell.
Hill, M. Lambert L. and Triseliotis, J. (1989) *Achieving Adoption with Love and Money*, London, National Children's Bureau.

Lambert, L. and Seglow, J. (1988) 'Paying for Permanence: Adoption Allowances in England and Wales 1982–1986', *Adoption and Fostering*, 12(1), 26.

Triseliotis, J. (1983) 'Identity and Security', *Adoption and Fostering*, 7(1), 22.

Triseliotis, J. (1984) 'Obtaining Birth Certificates' in P. Bean (ed.) *Adoption – Essays in Social Policy, Law and Sociology*, London, Tavistock.

11

Children with Disabilities

Provisions in the Act

The Children Act contains a number of specific provisions which
relate to children with disabilities (and see Lyon, 1990 and Russell,
1990):

(*i*)   s.23(8) requires that 'where a local authority provides
        accommodation for a child whom they are looking after
        and who is disabled, they shall, so far as is reasonably
        practicable, secure that the accommodation is not unsuita-
        ble to his particular needs';

(*ii*) Sch.2, para. 2 separates out the requirement on local
        authorities to open and maintain a register of children
        with disabilities in their area;

(*iii*) Sch.2, para. 3 provides that a local authority may assess a
        child's needs for the purpose of the Children Act at the
        same time as any assessment under under other Acts (for
        example, the Education Act 1981).

(*iv*) Sch.2, para. 9 requires local authorities to provide services
        for children with disabilities which are designed to minimise
        the effects of the children's disabilities and give them the
        opportunity to lead lives that are as normal as possible.

The social context of disability

These provisions apart, the Act does not deal with children with
disabilities as such. But the social context of disability is such that
the lives of families with disabled children create problems for local

authorities (and voluntary organisations) over and above those of other children and families in need. 'Disabled children and their families require a range of supportive services, and if these are to be effective, fully used and sensitive to consumer needs, professionals, managers and carers need to review and update them constantly' (Russell, 1989, p.169). They should be aware of the latest research findings and the value of these for planning services. Russell (1989) is an excellent overview of this. In short, the effect on parents of having a disabled child must be recognised: the effect on parental expectations and self-image (Cunningham, 1988), the increased vulnerability. The effect of the disability dimension on all questions including abuse (Measures, 1992) must also be recognised. Disabled children are more likely to experience at least one spell in a one-parent family (Cooke and Bradshaw, 1986). There is a high incidence of depression (Wolkind, 1981). Stress-related problems are common. This is frequently associated with a child's difficult behaviour but the cumulative effects of economic and social disadvantage are also significant (Gath, 1978; Burden, 1980). Indeed, Pahl and Quine (1984) found less stress in two-parent families with adequate income. They also found that some families are so stressed as to be incapable of negotiating personal support. (see also Quine and Pahl, 1985). The Fish committee (1985) found many families from ethnic minority groups felt alienated and rejected. There were frequent misunderstandings arising from very different attitudes to disability in different cultural groups.

There is little research or published criteria for the evaluation of early support services for families with disabled children. But the Honeylands project (Brimblecombe and Russell, 1985) shows the importance of involving consumers not only in the initial development, but also in managing changes and developments in response to new emerging needs. The importance of recognising whole-family needs and of integrating services into a coherent 'package' to avoid duplication and overload is stressed also (and see for confirmation, Cunningham, 1988; and Davis *et al.*, 1988). There is increased recognition also of the need for 'partnership': the importance of demonstrating respect for families, developing trusting relationships with them and recognising the real difficulties.

There is considerable emphasis in this context of the importance of respite care. As to this, Oswin's research (1984) that stressed the need to think of children first and identified an inherent tension in the fact that respite care is frequently directed to parent relief is of major significance. Clearly, respite care must be seen as part of a coherent child care policy. There is a need for preventive services to avoid children slipping into long-term care through escalating use of respite care. The Avon research (Robinson, 1987) warns against assuming respite care is a panacea for all family problems: it pointed to the need for more home-based services. According to Russell (1989, p. 176), parents are more likely to be satisfied with respite care if it is 'clearly linked to a voluntary organisation, school or wider service like Honeylands or Preston Skreens (as to which see Pahl, 1981) in order to put the service in context and to ensure that respite care is a rewarding experience for the child'.

As for children who cannot live with their natural families, there are encouraging pointers for future developments in Leonnard (1988). Initial funding had been provided to 'set up small homely units in the community for those children who will continue to need health care and who had largely been living in long-stay hospitals'. The project offered a vital opportunity to examine the processes by which a policy of 'normalisation' and 'dignity' for a very disadvantaged group of children could be translated into practice. The research identified key factors in providing good residential services: attitudes; planning and involvement of everyone at an early stage and, crucially, that the housing itself was 'unexceptionally homely, comfortable, without being ostentatious, ordinary family houses in ordinary streets'.

Other research has examined the problems of adolescents in the period of transition to adult services. There are, it appears, often alarming gaps in services even in well-resourced health authorities with good children's services (Brimblecombe *et al.*, 1985). Problems such as loneliness, lack of social confidence and poor self-esteem. A number felt their problems sprang from being at home where their needs were not sympathetically met. The Bargh research (1987) identified depresssion, stigma and rejection and stressed the importance of encouraging self-advocacy.

Treating children with disabilities as children – the principles

It is clear that in the past the needs of children and young people with handicaps and their families have been inadequately provided for. The Act offers an opportunity and a framework for change.

The *Guidance* (1991, vol. 6) sets out six principles for work with children with disabilities in the context of the Act (para. 1.6):

(*i*)   the welfare of the child should be safeguarded and promoted by those providing services;

(*ii*) a primary aim should be to promote access for all children to the same range of services;

(*iii*) children with disabilities are children first;

(*iv*) recognition of the importance of parents and families in children's lives;

(*v*)   partnership between parents and local authorities and other agencies;

(*vi*) the views of children and parents should be sought and taken into account.

It stresses (para. 1.8) that treating children as children first is of paramount importance but adds that it is important to recognise that they are also persons with disabilities. There is also, therefore, a need to be aware of other legislation (Chronically Sick and Disabled Persons Act 1970, Education Act 1981, Disabled Persons Act 1986) and of local arrangements dealing with the provision of services for disabled persons.

As children in need

Children with disabilities are specifically included within the statutory definition of 'children in need' (s.17(10)) (above). SSDs are encouraged by s.17 and Schedule 2 to provide day and domiciliary services, guidance and counselling, respite care and a range of other services as a means of supporting children with disabilities within their families. The Act recognises that sometimes a child can only be helped by providing services for other members of his or her family (s.17(3)). According to the *Guidance* (vol. 6, para. 3.3), the definition of children in need and the powers provided in Part III of the Act should be seen as 'an important opportunity not only to ensure that children with disabilities are treated as children first, but also to ensure access to the range of generic and specialist provision available to support children and families in their own homes and their local communities'.

The SSD is not obliged to provide all the needed services itself. Section 17(5)(a) states that every SSD shall facilitate the provision by others (including in particular voluntary organisations) of services which the local authority have power to provide by virtue of sections 17, 18, 20, 23 and 24 of the Act. An SSD may also arrange for others to provide services on their behalf (s.17(5)(b)). The different sectors have distinctive contributions to make (Annex A of *Guidance*, vol. 6 contains a useful list), and a co-ordinated package of services may best serve the needs of the family. Needs may fluctuate throughout the year, reflecting different pressures of family life. Services need to be individually tailored. *Guidance* advises (para. 3.5) that in some instances 'provision of a discrete service (e.g. aids and adaptation to a house or transport in order to use a local after-school club) may assist' the leading of a fulfilling life without further provision of services.

Co-ordinating services

A key to the Act is collaborative working and this is to the fore in work with disabled children. *Guidance* (para. 4.1) urges new organisational links between SSDs and NHS staff. Section 27 requires other SSDs, LEAs, local housing authorities, DHAs and NHS Trusts to comply with a request fom an SSD for assistance in providing services under Part III, so long as it is compatible with their own legal duty or other duties and does not unduly prejudice the discharge of any of their functions (and see above).

There is an obligation to keep a register of children with disabilities (Sch. 2, para. 2). Parents do not have to agree to registration. *Guidance* (para. 4.3) looks towards an understanding of disability 'which encourages parents to agree to registration and which is meaningful in terms of planning services for the child in question and children in general'. The *Guidance* advocates the creation of joint registers between health, education and social services. On confidentiality, LAC (88)17 should be consulted. If the register is computerised the Data Protection Act 1984 applies.

Assessment and planning

There are no assessment procedures laid down in the Act or in Regulations. Assessments will need to be undertaken in the context of Part III and Schedule 2 and bearing in mind the principles underlying the Act (thus taking account of the child's and family's needs and preferences, racial and ethnic origins, culture, religion and any special needs relating to the circumstances of individual families).

Assessments can be combined with those under other legislation (the Education Act 1981; Disabled Persons Act 1986; Chronically Sick and Disabled Persons Act 1970). In many cases children with disabilities will need services to continue into their adulthood. The assessment process accordingly has to take a longer perspective than in the case of other children. *Guidance* requires (para. 5.3) that the outcome of assessment should be 'a holistic and realistic picture of the individual and the family being assessed, which takes into account their strengths and capacities as well as any difficulties and which acknowledges the need to make provision appropriate to the family's cultural background and their expressed views and preferences'. The provision of services involves an initial assessment of need, a continuing process of reassessment and a review of the plan for the child. *Guidance* (para. 5.4) looks to a 'smooth transition when the young person reaches 18 and comes within the NHS and Community Care Act 1990'.

Partnership with parents and children

As discussed in chapter 2, partnership with parents and the child, where s/he is of sufficient understanding, is a key theme in the Act. Research identified the importance of partnership in relation to disabled children before it was articulated clearly in relation to children generally. The *Guidance*, following this theme, emphasises (para. 6.4) the importance of a plan for best service provision forming the basis of an agreement with the child, parent or other carer. Partnership is the guiding principle where the services are to be provided within the home or by the provision of accommodation under voluntary arrangements. The parent's authority and control should be enhanced, not undermined.

Services to children living with their families

A number of such services may be identified:

  (*i*)   the Portage Home Teaching Scheme;
 (*ii*)   Family Centres (Sch. 2, para. 9) (above);
(*iii*)   Befriending Schemes;
 (*iv*)   Day Care Centres (above).

See further *Guidance*, vol. 6, ch. 8.

Accommodation as a service

Where a child with disabilities is provided with accommodation, the Act requires (s.23(8)) that the accommodation should not be unsuitable to the needs of the child. *Guidance* (para. 11.1) gives the example of the provision of suitable adaptations to a foster parent's home. The Act also states that the services provided should minimise the effects of a child's disability (Sch. 2, para. 9).

When a child is looked after by a local authority, they must endeavour to promote contact between the child and parents, relatives and friends and anyone else closely connected (Sch. 2, para. 15). There is a similar duty where the child is living away from family but is not accommodated by the local authority (Sch. 1, para. 10). But this duty is qualified: it must be necessary in the opinion of the local authority to safeguard or promote the child's welfare. The possibility of appointing an independent visitor (Sch. 2, para. 17) should not be overlooked, where the child has not been visited by a parent or person with parental responsibility for over a year. A relative may be appointed (*Guidance*, para. 11.8), but, where there is ongoing contact with a relative, such a relationship can be encouraged (for example, by payment of expenses) without changing the relative's status to that of independent visitor.

Guidance emphasises the value of respite care (para. 11.11 *et seq*). It recognises that some children receive such care in NHS provision, but it also stresses (para. 11.12) that it is 'clear government policy that children with a learning disability should no longer live in long stay mental handicap hospitals'. It advocates 'care in small homely, locally-based units', in line with the research referred to above.

It is important not to ignore the Regulations. The details were discussed in earlier chapters. In this context, attention should be given to Regulation 13 of the Arrangement for Placement of Children (General) Regulations 1991, which allows for a preplanned respite care arrangement involving a series of placements at the same place to be treated as a single placement (above) (see further Lyon, 1990(b)).

Working with education services

The key document is the Circular (Assessments and Statements of Special Educational Needs: Procedures Within The Education, Health and Social Services) (DES 22/89). Paragraph 17 of this notes:

'Where it is thought that a child may need special educational provision, the positive and constructive approach is to focus on his or her needs rather than on disabilities. The feelings and perceptions of the child concerned should be taken into account and older children and young persons should be able to share in discussions on their needs and any proposed provision. The extent to which a learning difficulty hinders a child's development does not depend solely on the nature and severity of the difficulty. Other significant factors include the personal resources and attributes of the child as well as the help and support provided at home and the provision made by the school and LEA and other statutory and voluntary agencies. A child's special educational needs are thus related both to abilities and disabilities and to the nature and extent of the interaction of these with his or her environment.'

The Circular highlights four cases when an SSD or health authority may initiate an assessment of a child's potential special educational needs. They are:

(*i*)   if the child has a medical condition likely to affect future learning ability;

(*ii*) if the child has been admitted in connection with a social condition which is likely to affect future learning ability (such as social deprivation, whether negligence, neglect or child abuse);

(*iii*) if the child is receiving treatment likely to affect future learning ability;

(*iv*) if the child has been admitted to a children's or adolescent psychiatric ward.

Under the Education (Special Educational Needs) Regulations 1983, LEAs must seek educational, medical and psychological advice relating to a child with potential educational needs, together with advice from any other source which they consider desirable in making an assessment under s.5 of the Education Act 1981. Parents have the legal right to see all advice used in drawing up a statement. The LEA has the final responsibility for collating such advice and making any decisions. Where a statement results, copies of all the documents leading to it must be appended, since the information forms part of the statement. When the LEA notifies the parent of their decision to assess a child's special educational needs, a copy of this notification must be sent to an officer nominated for this purpose by the SSD. This is intended to offer the SSD an opportunity to consider whether they know of any problems affecting the child relevant to that authority and the range of services it might offer, and to indicate to the LEA whether the SSD has information relevant to the assessment of the child's special educational needs. Any advice offered will be attached to the statement and can be seen by the parents. *Guidance* (para. 9.7) advises that notification of SSDs by LEAs may be an important opportunity for the SSD to meet with and inform parents of children in need with disabilities 'at a very early stage' and to provide information about available services.

Under s.10 of the Education Act 1981, DHAs must notify parents of children under five of any relevant voluntary organisations which would be likely to help them. Information provided by SSDs could usefully be made available to DHAs to give to parents when making such a referral. DHAs and SSDs will frequently be working together to support particular children and families: collaboration is likely to be the most fruitful approach. (See, further, Russell, 1991.)

The role of the child health services

Children with disabilities should be identified at an early stage through access to effective surveillance programmes. Child health services have a major contribution to make to the early identification of children in need.

Guidance advises (para. 10.3) that SSDs should liaise with their child health services counterpart not only to encourage parents to share in recording their child's development and health care needs, but also to ensure that where children in need are identified parents and child can contribute to decisions on the type of care and support provided to the family.

Child health services have an important role to play in assessment of a child's need in the context of a proposed day care, residential or foster placement.

The transition to adulthood

Section 24(1) of the Act gives SSDs new duties to advise, assist and befriend each child whom they or certain other agencies (see above) look after with a view to promoting, that person's welfare when s/he ceases to be looked after by them. *Guidance* recognises the vulnerability of young people with disabilities at the transition to adult life (para. 16.4). The importance of SSDs working closely with the youth service, schools and colleges is stressed (para. 16.6).

Under the Education Act 1981 there is a requirement that the LEA reassess all pupils with statements at thirteen years and six months. This is to assist the plan for post-school provision. The Disabled Persons Act 1986 s.5 requires LEAs to notify the relevant SSDs at the time of the first annual review of a statement following the child's fourteenth birthday (or at the time of a reassessment after that birthday, whichever is earlier). This notification is required so that the SSD may consider whether the child will require any future services from the SSD after s/he has left school. LEAs have a further duty to notify the SSD between twelve months and eight months before the actual date of ceasing full-time education. Section 5 then requires the SSD to carry out an assessment of the young person's needs, normally three months before s/he leaves school.

SSDs should also consider their duties under the Chronically Sick and Disabled Persons Act 1970 and Disabled Persons Act 1986. *Guidance* points out (para. 16.13) that the ability of a young person with disability to return home, or move into independent living, may depend on the aids and adaptations that are provided to make existing accommodation suitable. It adds: 'When the child has lived away from home for some years, reunification will be particularly difficult to achieve if the home is unsuitable and heavy burdens of care are suddenly imposed on the family.'

Guidance cautions against residential care being regarded as 'a failure' (para. 16.15). It is, rather, a 'positive option, where parents, families and friends have a continuing role'. SSDs are advised to consider, as a matter of urgency, 'how they can work in partnership with their health and education counterparts to develop new patterns of residential services which provide good quality care in the local community' (para. 16.15).

Working in partnership means that young people and their families need clear information on the range of services available. They need access to local support groups and voluntary organisations. Many provide an 'outreach' service that can put individuals in touch with local self-help or self-advocacy groups. There should also be opportunities for working together within the authority's own services.

References

Bargh, J. (1987) *Play Back the Thinking Memories*, London, National Children's Bureau.

Brimblecombe, F. *et al.* (1985) *The Needs of Handicapped Young Adults*, Dept of Child Health, University of Exeter.

Brimblecombe, F. and Russell, P. (1987) *Honeylands: Developing a Service for Families with Handicapped Children*, London, National Children's Bureau.

Burden, R.L. (1980) 'Measuring the Effects of Stress on Mothers of Handicapped Infants', *Child Health, Care and Development*, 6, 111.

Cooke, K. and Bradshaw, J. (1986) 'Child Disablement, Family Dissolution and Reconstitution', *Developmental Medicine and Child Neurology*, 28, 610.

Cunningham, C. (1988) *Early Intervention: Some Results from the Manchester Cohort Study*, Dept of Mental Handicaps, University of Nottingham.

Davis, H. *et al.* (1987) *The Parent Adviser Scheme*, London Hospital Medical College.

Department of Health (1991) *Guidance and Regulations*, vol. 6, London, HMSO.

Fish Committee (1985), *Equal Opportunities for All?* London, ILEA.

Gath, A. (1978) *Down's Syndrome in the Family*, London, Academic Press.

Leonnard, A. (1988) *Out of Hospital*, University of York.

Lyon, C. (1990(a)) *The Implications of the Children Act 1989 for Children and Young People with Severe Learning Difficulties*, Barkingside, Barnado's.

Lyon, C. (1990(b)) *Living Away from Home: The Legal Impact on Young People with Severe Learning Difficulties*, Barnado's NW Division.

Measures, P. (1992) 'Abuse – The Disability Dimension', *Social Work Today*, 23(20), 16.

Oswin, M. (1984) *They Keep Going Away*, Oxford, Blackwell.

Pahl, J. (1981) *Preston Skreens: A Family Support Service for Mentally Handicapped Children*, Canterbury Health Services Research Unit, University of Kent.

Pahl, J. and Quine, L. (1984) *Families with Mentally Handicapped Children: A Study of Stress and a Service Response*, Canterbury Health Services Research Unit, University of Kent.

Quine, L. and Pahl, J. (1985) 'Examining the Causes of Stress in Families with Severely Mentally Handicapped Children', *British Journal of Social Work*, 15, 501.

Robinson, C. (1987) 'Key Issues for Social Workers Placing Children for Family Based Respite Care', *British Journal of Social Work*, 17, 257.

Russell, P. (1989) 'Handicapped Children' in B. Kahan (ed.), *Child Care Research, Policy and Practice*, London, Hodder and Stoughton.

Russell, P. (1990) 'Introducing the Children Act', *British Journal of Special Education*, 17, 35.

Russell, P. (1991) 'The Children Act: A Challenge for All', *British Journal of Special Education*, 18, 115.

Wolkind, S. (1981) 'Depression in Mothers of Young Children', *Archives of Disease in Childhood*, 56, 1.

12

Courts, Reports and Evidence

Courts

The Act does not, to the disappointment of some, create a Family Court as such. But it makes a number of significant changes to the structure and jurisdiction of the courts concerned with the welfare of children.

Most significant is the creation of concurrent jurisdiction in all proceedings under the Act. There remain three tiers of courts: the High Court, the County Court, and the Magistrates' Court. The County Court's business is distributed between Divorce County Courts, Family Hearing Centres and Care Centres.[1] At magistrates' level there is now a Family Proceedings Court, staffed by a Family Court Panel (s.92(1)) The juvenile court's jurisdiction to hear care proceedings has been removed. There is now, for the first time, a right of appeal to the High Court. The Lord Chancellor explained the objectives of these changes as (*i*) to create a flexible system under which cases may, according to their complexity, be heard at the appropriate level of court; (*ii*) to enable all proceedings affecting the child to be heard in the same court at the same time, and (*iii*) to ensure that cases are heard by magistrates and judges who are experienced in, and who have been trained in, family work. (*Hansard*, HL vol. 502, col. 494).

Concurrent jurisdiction among the three tiers of courts to hear all children's proceedings under the Act is created by s.92(7). There are some exceptions. Magistrates cannot hear an application or make an order involving the administration or application of any property belonging to or held in trust for a child or any income of such property (s.92(4)). They also cannot make secured periodical payments and property transfer orders in applications for financial provision for children (Schedule 1, para. 1). There is now concurrent jurisdiction in respect of care proceedings though in most instances these must start in the magistrates' court.

'Start' and 'transfer' provision

It is one of the central objectives of the Act that cases should be managed efficiently. The new 'start' and 'transfer' provisions are designed to assist the achievement of this. The Children (Allocation of Proceedings) Order 1991 provides that as a general rule all public law proceedings are to begin in a magistrates' court (this can be any magistrates' court) (r.3). The exceptions to this are (*i*) where proceedings are brought following a s.37 direction made by the High Court or a county court; and (*ii*) where there is to be consolidation with certain pending public law proceedings. In the first situation such proceedings will be commenced in the court which made the direction where that court is the High Court or a county court care centre or in such county court care centre as the court which made the direction may order. In the second situation, the proceedings should be commenced in the court where the other proceedings are pending.

The order does not specifically provide for the commencement of private law proceedings. They may be commenced in any level of court. However, if a matrimonial cause is pending relating to a child in a particular county court, an applicant who wishes to commence private law proceedings must do so to that court.

Applications to vary, extend or discharge an order under the Children Act or Adoption Act 1976 must be made to the court which made the original order (r.4). But applications for different orders are to be commenced like any other new application. So, for example, if a care order has been made by a county court, an application under s.34 for contact must be made to a magistrates' court.

Article 6 allows magistrates to transfer proceedings between themselves where it is in the interests of the child: (a) because it will avoid delay; (b) for the purposes of consolidation or (c) for some other reason. The receiving court's justices' clerk must consent to the transfer.

Article 7 sets out the criteria for transfer of *public* law proceedings from a magistrates' court to a county court. These are: (a) exceptional gravity, importance or complexity; (b) consolidation with pending proceedings and (c) urgency where no other magistrates' court can take the case. Certain proceedings cannot be transferred (applications for an EPO and associated applications and applications to protect children in an emergency under s.75, above). Applications for secure accommodation orders may only be transferred if such an application is to be consolidated with other family proceedings.

Article 8 provides for the transfer of *private* law proceedings from a magistrates' court to a county court. The only criterion for such a transfer is that a magistrates' court considers that, in the interests of the child, the proceedings can be dealt with more appropriately in a county court. The transfer may be to any divorce centre county court, except where the proceedings are being transferred for reasons of consolidation, in which case they should be sent to where the other proceedings are pending.

Where a magistrates' court has refused a party's request for public law proceedings to be transferred to a county court, Article 9 permits an application to be made to the appropriate county court care centre, requesting that the proceedings be transferred. The district judge may grant this application where, after considering the criteria in Article 7 above, s/he considers a transfer to be in the interests of the child. The procedure for such applications is in rule 4.6 of the Family Proceedings Rules 1991.

Under Article 11 a county court may transfer a public law case back to the magistrates' court, but only if the case has not come to trial and certain conditions exist. These are that the criterion for transfer: (a) does not apply where the criterion was of exceptional gravity, importance or complexity; (b) no longer applies where the criteria was 'consolidation'; or (c) no longer applies in the case of a transfer on the ground of urgency. Amendments to the Family Proceedings Rules[2] provide that before making an order for downward transfer the District judge must seek the views of the justices' clerk concerned. Should s/he, after considering these views, still decide to return the case, s/he must give reasons in writing. A party may appeal against the District Judge's decision to a circuit judge.

Article 10 allows county courts to transfer cases between themselves, where this is in the interests of the child, provided that either the receiving court has, or the presiding judicial officer at that court may exercise, the required jurisdiction.

Article 12 allows a county court to transfer any proceedings to the High Court where it considers that (a) the exceptional nature of the proceedings make them appropriate for determination there;

and (b) that such determination would be in the interests of the child. The same Article allows the High Court to transfer a case to a county court where the proceedings are appropriate for that court and it would be in the interests of the child.

As far as private law applications are concerned these (whether under the Children Act or Adoption Act) must generally be commenced in a county court divorce centre. Where a matrimonial cause is pending, the application must be commenced in the court where that cause is pending. Otherwise, any divorce centre may be used. Articles 15 and 16 deal with the transfer of private law proceedings. Where a private law application is transferred from a magistrates' court to a county court, it can be transferred to any divorce centre. The only exception is where a case is transferred for the purposes of consolidation, in which circumstances the case will go to the court where the other proceedings are pending. Where a contested application for a s.8 order is being heard in a divorce centre, which is not also a family hearing centre, it must be transferred for trial to a family hearing centre. Where a private law application is transferred from the High Court to a county court it may be transferred to any divorce centre, unless it is an application for a s.8 order, in which case it must be transferred to a family hearing centre.

Article 18 provides that where a public application is to be commenced in a county court, or transferred to one, that county court must be a care centre.

Article 19 makes the Principal Registry of the Family Division a divorce centre, family hearing centre and a care centre. It can, accordingly, take all cases under the Order.[3]

Appeals

As a general rule (see s.94(1)) appeals lie to the High Court against the making and refusal to make any order under the Act. There are three significant changes:

- (*i*)   appeals lie to the High Court, not the Crown Court;
- (*ii*) appeals lie against the refusal to make, as well as the making of, a care or supervision order;
- (*iii*) local authorities have full rights of appeal.

The appeal will not be a rehearing.

The exceptions to the general right of appeal are that no appeal lies:

(*i*) against a decision to decline jurisdiction because a case is considered more conveniently dealt with by another court (s.94(2));

(*ii*) against the making or refusal of an interim periodical payments order under Schedule 1 (s.94(3));

(*iii*) against the making or refusal to make an emergency protection order or against any direction given in connection with such an order (s.45(10));

(*iv*) outside the circumstances laid down in the Children (Allocation of Proceedings) Order 1991 (above) for the transfer or proposed transfer of proceedings (s.94(10) and (11)).

Upon an appeal, the High Court may make such incidental or consequential orders as appear to it to be just (s.94(5)). Orders made by the High Court, except orders for rehearing, operate as orders of the original court (s.94(9)). There is provision in the Act (see s.40) for orders pending appeals where an application for a care order is dismissed or a care or supervision order is discharged. This was discussed above. The court may postpone the operation of any s.8 order pending an appeal or make any other interim arrangement (using s.11(7) – the power to impose directions and conditions). In the past stays were not normally granted for more than fourteen days.[4] There is no reason to anticipate this practice will change.

The law on appeals from the County Court and from the High Court is not altered by the Act. Appeals lie, as before, to the Court of Appeal.[5] Leave to appeal is not required where residence, education or welfare of the child is concerned, nor where the applicant has been refused all contact with the child.[6] Leave is not required to appeal against the making or refusal to make a care or supervision order. These matters relate directly to a child's 'welfare'.

Privacy

Under s.97(1), rules have been made enabling magistrates to sit in private when considering whether to exercise any of their powers under the Act. The rules provide that the court shall hear an application in private where it considers it expedient in the interests of the child concerned. As a result care proceedings will be heard in private.

The Act makes no provision regarding the powers of the County Court and High Court to sit in private. The practice of disposing of cases in chambers will continue.[7]

Under s.97(2) it is an offence to publish[8] any material intended, or likely, to identify any child involved in any proceedings before a magistrates' court or that child's address or school. It is a defence for the accused to prove that s/he did not know, and had no reason to suspect, that the published material was intended, or likely, to identify the child (s.97(3)). The court or the Secretary of State may lift the restriction, if satisfied that the child's welfare requires it (s.97(4)). This will be done rarely where it is in the child's best interests for facts to be published rather than have rumour and speculation flourish (Solicitor-General, *Hansard* HC vol. 158, col. 633).

In addition s.97(8) preserves the operation of s.71 of the Magistrates' Courts Act 1980, allowing newspapers and periodicals to publish only the grounds of the application, submission on points of law and the court decision, including any observation made by the court in giving it.

Section 97(2) does not apply to the High Court and County Court. But s.12 of the Administration of Justice Act 1960, as amended by Schedule 13, para. 14 of the Act, prohibits publication of information relating to proceedings before any court in cases where the proceedings relate to the inherent jurisdiction of the High Court with respect to minors, or are brought under the Children Act 1989 or otherwise relate wholly or mainly to the maintenance or upbringing of any minor. However, s.12 does not prevent publication of the names and addresses or photograph of the child or details about the order.[9] The High Court can impose specific restrictions under its inherent jurisdiction.[10]

Evidence of, or relating to, children

It is provided that the unsworn evidence of a child may be heard by a court in civil proceedings, provided that the court is of the opinion that the child understands that it is his or her duty to speak the truth and that s/he has sufficient understanding to justify his or her evidence being heard (s.96(2)). This brings civil proceedings in line with criminal proceedings.[11] The child's evidence may be heard notwithstanding his or her inability to understand the nature of the oath (s.96(1)).[12]

Section 96 also permits the Lord Chancellor by order to make provision for the admissibility of evidence which would otherwise be inadmissible under any rule of law relating to hearsay (s.96(3)).[13] Two orders have been made but, since the second revokes the first,[14] it can be ignored. The Children (Admissibility of Hearsay Evidence) Order 1991[15] states in Article 2: 'In any civil proceedings before the High Court or a county court and in family proceedings in a magistrates' court, evidence given in connection with the upbringing, maintenance or welfare of a child shall be admissible notwithstanding any rule of law relating to hearsay.' Although hearsay evidence is thus admissible, 'this evidence and the use to which it is put has to be handled with the greatest care and in such a way that, unless the interests of the child make it necessary, the rule of natural justice and the rights of the parents are fully and properly observed'.[16]

Self-incrimination

The privilege after self-incrimination in proceedings under parts IV and V of the Act is removed by s.98. No person is to be excused from giving evidence on any matter or answering any question put to him or her in the course of giving evidence on the ground that doing so might incriminate him or her or a spouse[17] of an offence. But any statement or admission made may not then be used against that person or his or her spouse in proceedings for any offence other than perjury. (s.98(2)). As indicated above, this provision means that there is no longer any reason for delaying care proceedings pending the completion of a criminal trial.

Paternity tests

Section 89 amends s.20 of the Family Law Reform Act 1969 which gives the court power to direct tests to determine paternity. Where the person whose paternity is in issue is under 18, the application shall specify who is to carry out the tests. If the court then decides to make the direction, it must specify the person named in the application as the person who is to carry out the tests unless it considers it would be inappropriate to do so. This provision facilitates the choice of options now available (immunological testing and DNA profiling). Applicants may now choose, though the court retains a discretion to refuse the order sought.

Welfare reports

The Act emphasises the importance of welfare reports to a greater extent than did previous legislation. They can now be ordered in relation to any issue under the Act (a wider range of proceedings than previously). The emphasis on the *ascertainable* wishes and feelings of the child (s.1(3)) suggests greater use of welfare reports than in the past. The report can now be prepared by an officer of the local authority (or a person the authority considers appropriate such as a NSPCC officer), as well as by a probation officer. It is, however, unlikely that local authorities will be requested to report as a matter of routine. It is more likely that they will be asked to do so only in those cases where there is an obvious connection. Welfare reports guide, but do not control, the courts.[18] But it is expected that the recommendations in a welfare report will be followed. A court which departs from the recommendations in a report is expected to give reasons for so doing.[19]

Section 7 gives the court power, when considering any question with respect to a child under the Act, to ask a probation officer or a local authority to report to the court 'on such matters relating to the welfare of that child as are required to be dealt with in the report'. This is wider than it appears because a s.8 order can be made in any 'family proceedings' (s.8(4)), so that a welfare report may be ordered in the range of proceedings listed in s.8(3) and (4), as well as in proceedings under this Act (including those under s.4 (parental responsibility orders) and s.5 (guardians) for the first time). The court has a power: it is not under a duty to order a report. It is expected that courts will usually order reports in contested cases and may sometimes find it necessary to order one in an uncontested case (Lord Chancellor, *Hansard*, HL vol. 502, col. 1203). The ordering of a welfare report is likely to delay proceedings. The court should have s.1(2) (above) in mind when considering whether to order a report and possibly also in selecting the reporter.

The report may be made in writing, or orally, as the court requires (s.7(3)). The welfare officer is to file a copy of any written report at or by such time as the justices' clerk or the court directs or, in the absence of a direction, at least five days before a hearing of which s/he is given notice (Family Proceedings Courts (Children Act 1989) Rules 1991 r.13(2)).[20] The report is to be served on the parties (and any guardian ad litem – see below). Any party may question the welfare officer about the report (r.13(1)).

The court's right to consider reports and evidence about matters in reports, regardless of the hearsay rule, is clarified (s.7(4)). The court may do insofar as the statement in the report or the evidence is, in the court's opinion, relevant. Where second-hand evidence is relied upon, the reporter should make this explicit in the report. S/he should also identify the source of the information and his or her reasons (if any) for agreeing with it.[21]

It should be noted that a welfare report may be ordered in care or supervision proceedings. But in most such cases a guardian ad litem will have been appointed (above). The functions of the two are different (the welfare officer reporting about the child's and family's environment: the guardian ad litem representing the child's interests), so that it is possible to have both. But, in the light of scarcity of resources and of expenditure, it is unlikely that appointment of both can be justified, save in the rarest of cases.

Legal aid

The Act makes a number of important changes to the provision of legal aid. Section 99 makes civil legal aid available in care proceedings (though not to a local authority or guardian ad litem).[22] The Legal Aid Act 1988 (Children Act 1989) Order 1991[23] waives the means and merits tests in respect of applications for legal aid by a child, his or her parents and any person with parental responsibility in relation to proceedings under s.31, 43, 44 and 45; waives the means test in relation to an appeal to care proceedings and the merits test in respect of other persons who apply to be or who are joined as parties to the proceedings listed above.

Civil legal aid is also available without either a means or merits test to any child in proceedings under s.25 relating to secure accommodation.

Criminal legal aid is available in proceedings relating to a criminal supervision order under the Children and Young Persons Act 1969 s.15.

Notes

1. See Schedules 1 and 2 of the Children (Allocation of Proceedings) Order 1991, SI No. 1677.
2. Family Proceedings (Amendment) Rules.
3. This is in line with s.42 of the Matrimonial and Family Proceedings Act 1984 (and see also s.92(9) of this Act).
4. *Hereford and Worcester CC* v. *EH* [1985] FLR 975.
5. County Courts Act 1984 s.77 (1); Supreme Court Act 1981, s.16.
6. Where contact is restricted, leave will be required. See *Re H* [1989] 2 FLR 174. Contact by telephone is a restriction: so that leave to appeal against this is required.
7. See RSC Ord. 90, r.7 and Family Proceedings Rules 1991.
8. As to the meaning of which see *Re C No.2* [1990] 1 FLR 263.
9. See *Re L* [1988] 1 All ER 418; *Re W* [1990] 1 FLR 203.
10. See *Re M and N* [1990] 1 FLR 149, and *Re E* [1991] 1 FLR 420, 455. The County Court cannot do this.
11. Children and Young Persons Act 1933 s.38, as amended by the Criminal Justice Act 1988 s.34.
12. See *R* v. *Campbell* [1983] Crim. LR 174.
13. To reverse the effects of *Re H, Re K* [1989] 2 FLR 313 and *Bradford City MBC* v. *K* [1989] 2 FLR 507.
14. SI (1990) No. 143.
15. SI (1991) No. 1115.
16. *Re W* [1990] 1 FLR 203, 227 (Neill L.J.), approved in *R* v. *B County Council ex parte P* [1991] 1 FLR 470, at 478 and 482.
17. But not 'common law' spouse or cohabitant. And see *Rignell* v. *Andrews* [1991] 1 FLR 332.
18. A good illustration in *Re P* [1991] 1 FLR 337 where the judge's assessment of the parties prevailed over the view expressed by the welfare officer.
19. *Stephenson* v. *Stephenson* [1985] FLR 1140; *Cadman* v. *Cadman* (1982) 3 FLR 275; *W* v. *W* [1988] 2 FLR 505.
20. See also Family Proceedings Rules 1991.
21. *Thompson* v. *Thompson* [1986] 1 FLR 212.
22. Civil Legal Aid (General) (Amendment) (No. 2) Regulations 1991, SI No. 2036, r.3.
23. SI (1991) No. 1924.

Index